Praise for *Flagging the Screenager*

'Screenagers is full of the kind of pearls of advice most parents learn the hard way. This book is the ultimate primer to understanding the teenage world; readers will gain the knowledge and skills to enable them to smooth the sometimes rough psychological phases faced by today's teenagers. Innovative and highly recommended!'

—Dr Muiris Houston, *Irish Times*

'As the parent of a "screenager", I am hugely indebted to Harry Barry and Enda Murphy for writing this wonderfully warm, wise and pragmatic book. Showing compassionate and non-judgemental insight, Murphy and Barry provide us with a much-needed roadmap for navigating those sometimes stormy adolescent years. They do so with empathy, intelligence and practical skill. If you are interested in keeping yourself, your teen and your family in good mental health – as, of course, we all are – then this is the book for you. A must-have for every bookshelf, school and library. A must-read for every parent and teen and all those who interact with young people.'

—Carol Hunt, *Sunday Independent*

'Every parent needs this book – beautifully and simply written, it's an informative, comprehensive guide to help bring your teenager and YOU through their adolescence. It's wise, funny, and wry, doesn't talk down to you – the parent – and will help you raise your children in a modern world where the online world has radically changed the goalposts.'

—Cathy Kelly, author and UNICEF ambassador

'It was as if the book was written for the category of individuals we see ourselves belonging to now. But, how do you know us? How do you know that so much of the hard facts relate to us? We are in a special group/fraternity of lost souls in nameless pain. The book is that good believe me. So every daddy, mummy and near relations should read this book – sobering, reflective and relevant in our world of wonderful young adults!'

—Brian and Marcella O' Reilly, who lost their son Carl to suicide in 2012

'We have all likely noticed some of the "screenager" in every young person around us. Surrounded by technology, immersed in virtual communities and sometimes struggling to cope with the "real world", their mental health and emotional wellness can unfortunately become jeopardised.

'*Flagging the Screenager* is a unique resource. Any parent who finds them-selves muddling through the maze of their teen's development from child to adult should read this book. It carefully focuses on young people aged thirteen right up to twenty-five, offering us crucial understanding of the developmental cycles and mental health pitfalls we can all encounter along the way. Parents reading *Flagging the Screenager* will find the information utterly accessible; the superbly supportive, nurturing and empowering tone of its authors is palpable throughout.

'In our work in Console, we know all too well of the powerlessness that par-ents can feel when their young son or daughter is struggling in their develop-ment. In the first instance, even engaging with them can be real challenge. And knowing what to do next or where to turn can feel like negotiating an emo-tional minefield. *Flagging the Screenager* is both an educational and practical guide, bringing fresh and varied perspectives on the mental health of young people as they progress to adulthood with such a demanding world around them. Building a safe, supportive and resilient pathway for our children to adulthood is imperative and, with *Flagging the Screenager*, it is also possible.'

—Paul Kelly, founder and CEO, Console

'Today more than ever, parents feel helpless trying to assist their adolescents into adulthood. For that reason, *Flagging the Screenager* could not come at a better time. It demonstrates in a very practical manner how to become a mentor to your teenager and how to create the optimal environment for them to thrive, regardless of the challenges they face. At its heart, the book is a reminder for all parents to not only cultivate compassion towards their teenagers but also importantly, towards themselves.'

—Barry Mc Donagh, bestselling author of the anxiety treatment program Panic Away

'If you want a top-class practical companion when raising a teen in the twenty-first century then look no further than this book . . . the writing is almost like a conversation and it feels like [the authors] are in the room talking to you with each turn of the page. Backed up with just the right amount of research and science content, the easy-to-read information and guidance in the book is relevant, reliable and real. Jam-packed with examples, stories and suggestions, you will recognise your own screenager and, indeed, yourself in the pages of this book and you will find plenty of nuggets to help navigate this time, which can be a challenging . . . Written by Irish professionals who are hugely experienced in dealing with Irish teens, this truly is a must-read for any parent of a young person growing up in Ireland at this time.'

—Niamh Fitzpatrick, agony aunt for the *Ray D'Arcy Show* and psychologist to the Olympic Council of Ireland

'Simple to pick up, impossible to put down . . . clearly presented and absolutely engaging, expertly written by two outstanding professionals in their fields of expertise . . . a well researched but accessible guide to understanding the neurobiological basis for development in young adolescents. It provides an insight into an invaluable "toolkit" of the essential skill set required by both parents and teenagers to navigate the sometimes turbulent and choppy "developmental" waters . . . during adolescence. It provides a rich source of learning for anyone interested in youth development. Truly outstanding!'

—Maria Carmody, Irish College of Humanities and Applied Sciences

'This is a very accessible read that will help many young people and their families to make sense of the struggles they experience and give them a clear sense of how to cope. I liked this book because it is deeply respectful of the young person whilst also appreciating the pain that parents can feel as they watch their children struggle with the intensity of adolescence.'

—Tony Bates, founder and CEO, Headstrong,
The National Centre for Youth Mental Health

'Having written *Diet SOS*, I totally agree that the food we choose can affect our mood. Reading this book as a mother of two has also made me realise I'm normal – other mums are feeling like I feel. This book is a wonderful journey of discovery!'

—Lisa Fitzpatrick, stylist, media guru
and best-selling author of *Diet SOS*

'I found this book very informative, a great read and thought-provoking. It will be of great interest to any parent of an adolescent child. It is very informative and will educate many a parent on the intricacies of guiding a child into adulthood. Parenting is a challenge with great responsibilities. Every parent today is only too aware of the very high incidence of suicide amongst our youth population – so they need to inform themselves about mental health and also educate themselves on how to promote positive mental health behaviours and lifestyle choices in their own families. This book will greatly assist them in achieving this goal.'

—Dominic Layden, CEO Aware

'This is a superb book, an easy and interesting read, with very relevant background/evidence to the issues covered and real, practical suggestions for parents and all of us to address our own mental health and . . . help others.'

—Eugene Conlon, human resource manager

FLAGGING
THE SCREENAGER

First published in 2014 by
Liberties Press
140 Terenure Road North | Terenure | Dublin 6W
T: +353 (1) 405 5701| www.libertiespress.com | E: info@libertiespress.com

Trade enquiries to Gill & Macmillan Distribution
Hume Avenue | Park West | Dublin 12
T: +353 (1) 500 9534 | F: +353 (1) 500 9595 | E: sales@gillmacmillan.ie

Distributed in the United Kingdom by
Turnaround Publisher Services
Unit 3 | Olympia Trading Estate | Coburg Road | London N22 6TZ
T: +44 (0) 20 8829 3000 | E: orders@turnaround-uk.com

Distributed in the United States by
International Publishers Marketing
22841 Quicksilver Dr | Dulles, VA 20166
T: +1 (703) 661-1586 | F: +1 (703) 661-1547 | E: ipmmail@presswarehouse.com

ISBN: 978-1-909718-26-5
2 4 6 8 10 9 7 5 3 1

A CIP record for this title is available from the British Library.

Cover design by Liberties Press
Internal design by Liberties Press

FLAGGING
THE SCREENAGER

Guiding Your Child Through
Adolescence and Young Adulthood

Dr Harry Barry
Enda Murphy

This book is dedicated to Carl O' Reilly (21 July 1994 to 30 May 2013), a victim of the White Flag, and to his parents, Brian and Marcella, who, along with so many other parents, struggle to find meaning in his passing.

Contents

Acknowledgements

Enda and I would like to start by thanking our editor Seán O'Keeffe of Liberties Press, which is going from strength to strength. We would also like to thank his editorial team – Sam Tranum and Zoe Jellicoe – and their PR team at Gill Hess, particularly Declan Heeney.

We also would like to pay a special tribute to so many people who took the time to review or in other ways support and inform this book, in particular Dr Muiris Houston of the *Irish Times* – we are so lucky to have a medical correspondent of his ilk in Ireland; Cathy Kelly (best-selling author and UNICEF ambassador), who has been so personally supportive for so many years; Carol Hunt of the *Sunday Independent*, a wonderful journalist and a tireless advocate for mental health; Paul Kelly, CEO of that excellent organisation Console; my longstanding friend and colleague Tony Bates, founder of Headstrong, for his insightful comments; Dominic Leyden, CEO of my own group Aware; Maria Carmody and Professor Dennis Ryan of ICHAS, for their assistance and support in so many ways; Niamh Fitzpatrick, agony aunt for the *Ray D'Arcy Show*, for her support; Lisa Fitzpatrick (stylist, media guru and now best-selling author), who has also been so supportive of both of us; esteemed colleague Professor Barbara Sahakian (Professor of Neuropsychology at Cambridge University) for her research insight into the world of depression; psychologist Barry Mc Donagh of Panic Away; Eugene Conlon for his helpful comments; and in particular I would like to specifically thank Brian and Marcella, who in the midst of their overwhelming grief following the death of their son Carl have taken the time to review the book on behalf of parents. We have dedicated the book to Carl. There are also other parents bereaved by suicide that we do not name but who have contributed to this book, and we are profoundly grateful to them.

Enda would like to thank his beautiful wife Mei, who has put up with all the multiple stressors attached to being the partner of a busy therapist, a GP mental health trainer, and now a successful author (who is also involved in so many other projects) – whilst at the same time trying to look after their two wonderful sons Stephen and Sean. He is indeed a lucky man!

I would like to thank my three children: Lara, her husband Hans and my two special grandchildren, Ciaran and Sean; my son Daniel, who has been such a help with all my books; and my son Joseph and his lovely new wife Sue.

I reserve as always my biggest thank-you to my lovely wife Brenda, who is my bedrock and whose love, friendship, support, encouragement and particularly patience have made this book possible. May we continue to grow older and wiser (and in your case more beautiful) together: '*Mo ghra, mo chroi.*'

Introduction

THE TWENTY-FIVE-YEAR CONTRACT

Mr and Mrs Behan sat in front of me (Enda) as they had done at every other meeting over the previous two years. Mr Behan was a senior manager in a big multinational and, in the normal train of events, I suppose, he would have taken a much more active role in proceedings. Not so in this case, however. In all the meetings I had with them as a couple, I never remember him volunteering an opinion of his own about what we discussed.

Not that he was detached, I might add. More that he was a quiet man who would only interject if he felt it was necessary. You see, he was quite comfortable to let the conversation be guided by his wife and myself, and for her to be the reporter of how things were progressing at home with their teenage son, whom I was seeing for therapy.

At the end of our meeting, when I picked up my diary to make another appointment to see them, I realised that it would clash with my wife's first antenatal appointment for our first child, in the Rotunda Hospital that same day. I explained to them that this meant I wouldn't be able to meet them. Mrs Behan was effusive in her congratulations and warmth at our good news. Wishing us the very best of luck, they both stood and headed for the door.

As they left, I noticed Mr Behan looking at me in a very paternalistic way that I had never noticed from him before – a bit like a dad identifying with a soon-to-be dad. I felt particularly warm at this unspoken communication and really felt that I was finally going to become a member of the 'Dads' Club', something I had wanted for many years.

As he passed by me, he placed his arm around my shoulder and, as I sagely waited for him to pass onto me a gem of wisdom, he looked me gently in the eye, smiled and whispered, 'We'll see where your theories get you now, sunshine!'

What's That Noise?

And do you know what? With all the books I've read and all the experience as a therapist that I have gained over the years, nothing has come close to that pearl of incredible insight that Mr Behan gave me that day. Here was a man who was an expert in human resources and managing a huge company with thousands of employees, who had found that nothing that he had learned or experienced had prepared him for being a parent.

And how true this proved to be for me too! Seven months later, as I found myself in the same position, I realised that nothing I had ever learned, done, or experienced had prepared me for that first night at home with my wife and our new baby. I still joke that life was very simple when there was only myself and the dog in it. Then I met my wife and started the long, drawn-out process of realising that the world would never again turn the way I 'knew' it 'should'.

And if that wasn't bad enough, when the children arrived, they too refused to bow and drink from my font of knowledge, deciding that for them, the world would turn as they felt it should and that my philosophies wouldn't be automatically accepted for the pearls of wisdom that I thought they were.

There is a saying that, in theory, there should be no difference between theory and practice, but that, in practice, there most definitely is. Well, nowhere will you find this out more than in parenting. You can read all the self-help books you want, but when you try to put them into practice with your children you will find, like the rest of us, that the theory must have been written for somebody else's family, as it just doesn't get the same result in yours.

There is a coffee shop near where I live that has a wonderful cartoon on its wall. It depicts a mum bending down and fixing a scarf and coat around her son's neck. She looks just like she is doing the universal mum thing, warning him about not getting cold, behaving himself when he's in his friend's house and so on. This cartoon's caption, however, captures beautifully what mums around the world are really trying to say: 'Now remember, to everybody out there, we appear like a normal family'.

We all do it. We try to present an image of what we think a normal family should be like. Something like the Waltons, who had their issues of course, but solved every problem with perseverance and by practising the true family experience, complete with, 'Good night John boy. Good night Mary Ellen.'

And how hard we try to present that image of ourselves to the world, where all is sweetness and light and all problems are dealt with in a truly constructive and educational way. Just like how all the books say it should be.

I remember chatting to a client one time about how nothing prepared me for that first night at home with our first child. Whilst we were laughing at my naivety, the client shared a story about their first child. During the first night home, the baby woke up at about 1 AM crying for a feed and her husband jumped and exclaimed, 'What's that noise!?'

Muddling Through

This 'Waltons' view of parenting is, of course, total rubbish. If you ever want an example of what's commonly referred to in business as 'muddle management', then you need look no further than your own front door. Or mine or Harry's, for that matter. Indeed, go for a walk around your estate and know that behind every door, families are muddling through no more effectively that your family is.

And it's just as well, since in order to be an effective parent, you don't need to be any more than a 'muddle manager'. As somebody once said to me, the secret of parenting is to keep it simple or, as they put it, 'Keep 'em breathing and outa jail for twenty-five years' and 'everything else is a bonus'.

Paul Dalton is a well-respected psychotherapist and business consultant colleague of ours. He says, 'Children are a twenty-five-year full-service contract.' After that, they choose their own way in life, regardless of how they have been reared or what philosophy we have tried to ram down their throats. And thank God for that since, as we will see later on in the book, we can't dictate what our children will do, and neither do we have to. In order to be a successful parent, all we have to do is create an environment in which we can influence the types of people they will turn out to be.

The Parent Trap

So why do it? Why would anybody in their right mind want to saddle themselves with all the crap that goes with trying to raise a family? How is it in our long-term interest to put ourselves in a situation where we live in constant anxiety? Where no matter what we do, we will always believe that we're doing it wrong. Where we live in a constant world of guilt and hurt with just the briefest glint of satisfaction, which is all too fleeting and elusive.

Well, do you know what? Hard and all as this is going to be to accept, having children is a vital ingredient in our emotional development and in maintaining good mental health.

One of the most common misquotes in the world is attributed to Charles Darwin: life is all about survival of the fittest. Darwin never said that. What he actually said was that the survival of a species was not determined by their strength or intelligence, but by their ability to adapt. He correctly identified adaptation to our world as the one quality that determined survivability. Overcoming obstacles, he argued, was not about changing situations to suit us, but about developing our ability to adapt, so situations we can't change won't destroy us.

Somewhere over the last 150 years since Darwin introduced his theory of evolution, this message has been lost. We believe that we must learn always to conquer and control our environment. Therefore, we believe that we must drive and teach our children to beat their world into submission, overcoming all obstacles by determination, motivation and endurance. We are not advised – and we do not teach our kids – how to adapt to events. Adaptation, that most vital ingredient in survival, is lost in the race for success and perceived happiness, the obsessive pursuit of which results in defeat, depression, anxiety and unhappiness.

So where and how are we supposed to learn how to adapt? When it is in our very nature to avoid situations that force us to adapt, where are we to learn this most vital skill? Well, Mother Nature has the most wonderful way of providing us with the opportunity to learn it. She makes us instinctively want to have children. When our kids arrive, we find that the irresistible force (us) has suddenly met the immovable object (the baby). And from the start, the baby makes all the rules. Suddenly we go from being the masters of our own destinies to having our world dictated to us by a three-kilogram being that is all demanding at one end and has no sense of responsibility at the other.

And it doesn't get better. As you probably have already found out, when your kids enter their teenage years, the demands at the 'head end' get greater and greater and the irresponsibility at the other end doesn't improve much either. Navigating your children through their teens and into adulthood is as much about learning to identify and develop your own adaptation skills as it is about trying to teach your kids these skills. After all, how can you teach what you don't know? So this book is as much about *your* mental health journey as it is about your teenager's.

A number of years ago, I developed an approach to therapy where I saw teenagers with their parents present. However, instead of focusing on the teenagers' difficulties, I got the parents to give honest accounts of their teenage experiences, like when they had their hearts broken for the first time, and how difficult they found it to cope. I then taught the teenagers how to listen to their parents. This resulted in them identifying more and more with their parents' experiences and gradually opening up about issues in their lives.

You wouldn't believe the effect this has had on both the teenagers and their parents. Love, acceptance and bonding become the scaffolding of their relationship instead of tension, silence and arguments. Parents gradually become more like mentors to their children, instead of supervisors. And the most effective way to teach your kids the skills is to let them see you fumble your way through.

As we shall see, learning how to adapt to life with our children is as important for our mental health as adapting to our development is for teenagers. Life is a constant evolution toward wholeness that we all share by learning how to live. It is only when we have mastered these skills ourselves that we can mentor our children in exploring and learning how to live their lives.

Think of how a lioness teaches her cubs to hunt. She doesn't just show them the successful kills. She shares the whole experience of the hunt with them. This includes letting them see her failures and mistakes. As the cubs grow, they learn as much by seeing her get it wrong as they do by seeing her get it right.

So how are Harry and I going to demonstrate this? What are we going to show that hasn't already been shown in the many excellent books on teenagers out there? Well, we believe that the secret of this book will be in its ability to give you the flavours of both your experience and your teenager's experience, instead of just giving you a list of ingredients and expecting you to put them all together yourself.

Probably the first thing you will notice that makes this book different from others is that we are describing adolescents as being between thirteen and twenty-five years old. There is a common fallacy that when we reach eighteen we are in some way 'grown up'. As we shall see, the most vulnerable years in our lives are from eighteen to twenty-five. Yet when we finish school we leave a structured, uniform world and are let loose with few of the skills we need to cope.

A vital function of this book will be to describe the journey we go through to develop from children into adults. We will explore how the adolescent brain develops, and how different and vulnerable it is from the adult brain. We will also look at how teens develop feelings and emotions, and how they view and interact with their worlds as they see them. Most importantly though, we will look at how to create the optimal environment in which they can develop their mental and physical health and prepare themselves for all the challenges they will experience as adults.

WHY HAVE WE WRITTEN THIS BOOK TOGETHER?

Harry and I would seem to be a most unlikely pair. To realise this, all you have to do is look at the two of us together. Harry's wife Brenda sometimes likens us to the two Ronnies. For starters, we have completely different personalities and have travelled very different paths throughout our lives.

Harry is a real academic, complete with leather-elbowed tweed jacket, who likes nothing more than to study – in great depth – any topic he takes a fancy to. Having worked as a GP all his life, he likes to take a subject and analyse it to death in order to understand its structure and how it works.

In contrast, I was unable to sit still for longer than ten minutes as a child, so my mum used to say I was like a person with briars in his pants. Even now, as I get older and hopefully more mature, my concentration span rarely exceeds forty minutes. And I'm not just like this in Ireland. In China, where I also work, my Chinese nickname can be translated into 'little bee'.

Neither do I come from an academic background. Before I was ever a therapist, I was a community mental health nurse, and it was in that particular crucible – in which I spent each working day teaching people in one of the most deprived areas of Dublin emotional survival skills – that I had most of my professional education.

So how did two very different personalities end up working so closely together over so many years without killing each other? And what do they have in common that makes this possible? Well, for starters, whilst we may have very different personalities, we have both worked at the coalface of mental health delivery. I first got to know Harry when we shared a car journey from a conference we had attended in Galway.

As we travelled back to County Louth, we talked about how frustrated we both were with society's lack of understanding of mental health and illness. In discussing this frustration, Harry and I realised that we had a total meeting of minds and a shared desire to teach people what mental health really is – and its importance in our lives.

Do you know that every week in Ireland at least ten people take their own lives? (As horrendous as that sounds, we think we are massively underestimating that figure.) Think about that for a moment. As you read this, several people in Ireland are making preparations to deliberately end their lives.

A significant number of these are young men between the ages of fifteen and thirty. Today, as you read this and go about your daily life, the chances are high that several young Irish men are living in such horrific worlds in their heads, feeling so isolated and tortured, that they can't see any solution except to kill themselves.

Why is this happening? Why is it so difficult for them to reach out? And in cases where they do reach out, why is it that the help offered is not only ineffective but often actually drives them further and further into their isolated worlds?

Some time ago, I was asked to give a talk to some teenagers who were preparing for their Leaving Certs in my local secondary school, Scoil Uí Mhuirí, in Dunleer, County Louth. The school asked me to talk to them about stress management. I said I was more than willing to do that but if they wanted to make the session much more effective it might be more useful if I could also speak to the parents.

You see, no matter how good a talk I gave, there is only so much you can do in forty minutes. If I could also speak to the parents, though, I could teach them how to understand what was going on in their teens' heads and how to support them. Since they are in daily contact with their children, teaching parents how to teach their teenagers would be a much more effective way of getting the message across.

So the school organised two talks: one for students and one for parents. At the students' talk I described the kind of thinking that goes on in our heads when we are feeling anxious as teenagers. How our minds can become very critical of ourselves, constantly telling us that we are not as good as other people, and never will be. That everybody else is normal except us and that we are so useless that we'll always be among life's losers. Not only that, but how this internal voice can also tell us that we are the only ones like this. That we had better hide it from everyone, because if we do tell anyone we will only get into bigger trouble and end up in an even worse hole than the one we are in now.

You could have heard a pin drop in the classroom. You see, I knew that when I described this 'pathological critic' to them, at least 50 percent of them would identify with it. I knew that by telling them that these kinds of thoughts and voices are incredibly common in teenagers, I was telling them that they were not as unique as they thought they were.

I ended the talk by telling them that if anything I said made any sense, they should tell their mum or dad or a teacher they trusted. In case they felt they couldn't talk to anybody they knew, I left my phone number and email address on the whiteboard so they could contact me. I also told them I was not asking them to make contact so that we could give out to them but so we could teach them how to switch off the voices in their heads. Within twenty-four hours, I had twelve contacts from students who had been at the talk. Each had the same story: that I had described them exactly and that they couldn't believe that other teenagers felt like them.

I then talked to their parents. Believe it or not, over one hundred twenty parents attended that night, which illustrated to me how much parents are crying out for guidance on how to protect their children. I still think of that night. The information I was giving them was no more than the basics of mental health, basics that should be familiar to parents, that they should view as no more mysterious than the importance of healthy diet in preventing heart attacks.

But the information wasn't familiar to them. As with every other group I talk to, when I asked the parents where they thought emotions came from, not one of them could tell me. What a damming indictment of us as health professionals whose job it is to teach this. We spend our whole lives living with – and dealing with the fallout from – emotions, but they are so poorly understood that not one person could tell me where they come from or why some people feel one thing and others feel something else.

At the talk we looked at this. We looked at how our brains process emotions. We examined where and why emotions occur as they do, and how our thinking and experience can determine them. We looked at the effects alcohol and drugs have on them and the most common difficulties that I see people having when their emotions end up turning on them.

The feedback after my talk was so positive that the vice principal, Ray

21

Donagh, and I decided to run a six-week programme for parents to look deeper into these issues and to learn how to promote the emotional well-being of their kids. To be able to show their kids why mental health is so important and what they need to do to get it.

We also looked at what parents could do to promote their own mental health and how they could become people their kids could confide in. We covered topics including: how to be an effective parent or at least avoid doing too much damage to our kids, how to evolve from a parent to a mentor as our kids grow older, and how to coach our kids on becoming mentally healthy adults.

The programme was a great success, so much so that I spoke to our local parish priest, Father Murtagh, and the chairperson of Dunleer community council, Eugene Conlon, about running a similar programme for leaders of community groups in the area. Once again, the response was incredible. In a town of only about three thousand people, over forty leaders representing more than twenty-five community groups attended, giving up one night a week so they could learn how to promote the emotional well-being of their charges. And this experience in Dunleer is only a microcosm of what is happening in Ireland. Because, in Ireland today, parents have a colossal desire to understand mental health so they can help and protect their children.

There is a wonderful expression, 'If we only knew what it is that we already know', which is very apt when we look at mental health. Over the last ten years or so, there has been an explosion of discussion on mental health, which has led to a great deal of information being put out into the public arena. Unfortunately, even though there is so much talk about mental health in the media, there has been little or no reduction in the number of people who take their lives every year.

In fact, during the Celtic Tiger, you would have been forgiven for thinking that, with so much prosperity, the suicide rate and incidence of depression would have fallen. Not so. During that era, the suicide rate did not significantly alter even as the economy boomed, which should have rung alarm bells for people who believed that the secret of happiness is having what you want financially or materially in life.

As we shall see later in the book, our understanding of mental health is so poor that we still see mental health as a euphemism for mental illness. This is like telling someone that unless they have a physical illness such as a heart attack they can't possibly have a problem with their physical health. Furthermore, if we don't differentiate between health and illness, we can't possibly understand things like the importance of diet in health and teach our poor heart-attack sufferer that he needs to change his diet, lose some weight, and get some exercise if he wants to avoid another heart attack. Similarly, with mental health, there is no understanding of how to avoid depression and anxiety, and there isn't much out there that will teach me how to overcome it or what I can do to prevent it reoccurring.

The problem isn't that we don't have the information or understanding required to promote mental health. The problem is that there are very few people out there who can put it all together into one package that will simplify our understanding of mental health and how and why we need to get it. That was why Harry and I were so completely on the same page.

Both of us could see all the theories, therapies and medicines that were out there. Both of us could see how all the theories were showing us various aspects of mental health, which were all correct. What was frustrating was that each group not only had its own theory, but most had the arrogance to believe that every other theory was wrong and shouldn't even be let into the debate, let alone be accepted as valid. Neither would they talk to each other. Sitting in their own little ivory towers, they stuck their noses in the air and disparaged anybody who had a different theory about mental health.

And that was what was most infuriating for us. You see, because both of us worked on the frontlines of mental health and illness, we couldn't cherry-pick clients that fitted into our philosophy and dismiss everyone else. We knew that different clients with different problems required different solutions. We knew that what was useful for one person might not necessarily help another. We knew that, to be of help in the real world, with its real-world problems, we had to gain skills and insights from nearly every theory. So we didn't have the luxury of practising only one way of doing things. Anyway, we saw that most of the theories were really saying the same things and coming to the same conclusions.

We could also see that each theory was like a different piece of the jigsaw. However, health professionals couldn't understand what it was they already knew. They couldn't put the pieces of the jigsaw together into one unified theory that would explain how all the factors that were involved in mental health fitted in with each other.

So during that conversation, on that journey back from Galway, on that fine Sunday afternoon, Harry and I agreed to work together to improve people's understandings of how all the theories fitted together. We also wanted to show that once we understood how all these theories fitted together, then problems could be much more easily identified, leading to very straightforward solutions in most cases.

Both Harry and I have devoted our careers to furthering this understanding. Over the years we have both concluded that mental health is not just something that we lick off a stone sometime in our twenties or thirties. It is an insight and skill that needs to be understood and practised from the day we are born until the day we die – hence this book. Adolescence and early adulthood are when most mental-health growth takes place, but they are also the periods during which the developing adult has the least support, and is sent out into the world with no idea of the fundamentals of mental health.

Look at any popular psychology section in any bookshop and you will find plenty of books on how to turn out the perfect adolescent. This book is not an attempt to reword or repackage all the excellent information out there. All those books have the ingredients for what to do and say. The purpose of this book is to provide you with the flavour of what it's all about, rather than just giving you another list of ingredients.

Hopefully, by reading this book and grasping what mental health is and how it develops, all the self-help books will now make a whole lot more sense to you. It's a bit like tasting a dish and then reading the ingredients. You can now understand how the oregano fuses with the sauce to give the dish its distinctive flavour.

So let's get on with the story. Harry is going to explain what we mean by the term 'screenager', and why we chose it. He will also share his experiences with a Leaving Cert class that unveiled what adolescents really want to know about their journey into adulthood.

SO WHAT IS A SCREENAGER?

The term 'screenagers', which combines the words 'screen' and 'teenagers', was created in 1997 by Douglas Rushkoff in his book *Playing the Future*. It is a term that is now used to describe teenagers – and those in their early twenties – who are technologically savvy in their usage of computers and the Internet. As far back as 1997, Rushkoff saw a chasm opening between members of this age group and their parents, who were struggling to keep up with all the new technology.

It is almost two decades since the term was first used and, in many ways, the chasm has increased. Many parents are now feeling completely helpless as they struggle to assist their adolescents on the difficult road to emerging adulthood. Many of their teenage and young-adult children are equally adrift, and lack the skills necessary to survive in a fast-moving technological world.

We chose the term 'screenager' because it so perfectly describes our kids' age group. Our teenagers and young adults are so immersed in the world of technology that many of them are struggling to separate their online worlds from real life. To ignore the impacts of technology and social media on how our adolescents are developing would be very foolish.

We were going to make this book an exploration of the world of the teenager and how parents should approach this phase in their children's development. There seems to be a belief that the journey into adulthood finishes at eighteen but, in practice, as any parent will tell you, this is not the case. The reality – as most family doctors, therapists and parents know – is that the most vulnerable years are between eighteen and twenty-five, the period during which the emerging adult has the greatest freedom and least support. The vast majority of significant mental illness – 75 percent – actually appears for the first time when people are between the ages of thirteen and twenty-five. As we will see later, there are many reasons for this but the key ones probably relate to brain development and significant life stressors experienced during this critical period.

It is also worth noting that the excellent 'My World Survey' national study of youth mental health in Ireland (see bibliography) carried out by Tony Bates's Headstrong group found that adolescence is increasingly seen as including young people aged twelve to twenty-five, which very much fits in with our own opinions. In Section 2:1, the study said:

> Adolescence refers to the period of life during which an individual makes the transition from childhood to adulthood. In keeping with World Health Organisation (WHO, 2005) policy, and also that of countries such as Australia and New Zealand, which have been the pioneers in youth mental health, the age range denoted by the adolescent period in this report covers the age span from 12–25 years. The terms 'young people' and 'youth' are also commonly used to describe those aged 12–25.

There is a misconception that by the time our adolescents have reached seventeen or eighteen, have done their Leaving Cert examination, and are ready to move on to third-level education, they have learnt enough skills from both their parents and school for the journey ahead. In reality, many are extremely apprehensive about the future and know they are not really fully prepared.

To illustrate this point, I would like to share with parents a recent meeting I had with about one hundred fifty Leaving Cert students at a wonderful local secondary school for girls: Our Lady's College in Greenhills, Drogheda. I had been asked to talk to them for two hours as they were preparing for their Leaving Cert. The meeting was part of a mental health week. In preparation, I asked the teachers to encourage the girls to draw up a list of significant issues which were causing them concern. It was a most revealing list, including concerns such as how to deal with:

- Anxiety in relation to exams, and panic attacks

- Pressure they felt from their parents to do well in exams

- Disappointment in relation to exam results

- Failure in life

- Body-image problems

- Fear of the future and the unknown

- Feelings of depression and low self-esteem

- Stress, and concerns about how to achieve happiness in life

- Relationship difficulties with the opposite sex

- Stress in terms of 'coming out'

- Making the right choices in college and in life

On reviewing this list, I felt the main issues could be summarised as follows:

- Change

- Emotions

- Anxiety

- Depression

- Conforming – peer group pressure

- Performing up to the expectations of parents and self

- How they viewed themselves

- How others viewed them

I then decided to give the girls a short talk, and try to offer them some simple information on some of the above issues. I broke them up into ten groups of fifteen students. What I was really doing was getting them to tap into their own natural reserves to try and 'problem-solve' the issues they had presented to me. I did so by asking each group one of the following ten questions:

- **Group One:** What should they do when they found themselves getting very anxious in the lead-up to the Leaving Cert?

- **Group Two:** What should they do if either they or somebody close to them was feeling very down?

- **Group Three:** Why do we all fear failure so much, and how can we challenge such fears?

- **Group Four:** Why is it important to learn that life is not fair and that we don't always get what we want when we want?

- **Group Five:** What are the main challenges they would face on leaving school and moving on to college or a new job?

- **Group Six:** How much time did they spend on phones/social media and so on, and was multi-tasking with media when studying going to harm their results?'

- **Group Seven:** What are the difficulties involved in somebody 'coming out' in terms of their sexuality, and how should the whole group assist?

- **Group Eight:** What does the group feel are the main issues in relationships with the opposite sex, and what are their solutions?

- **Group Nine:** Why do so many students end up doing the wrong course in college, and what does the group feel we can do to deal with this issue?

- **Group Ten:** Why do so many students feel under pressure from their parents to perform in the Leaving Cert, and what do members of the group feel they can do to deal with this?

What emerged from the groups and the follow-up discussions that ensued as each group leader presented their group's findings was really quite extraordinary. These wonderful young people opened up honestly about their fears and concerns. The list of worries one group gave in relation to their fears about going to college for example was very revealing, as was their reaction to my question about how much time they spent on their phones and on social media. They felt it was at least three and a half hours a day. I shared with them some research findings on this and its effects on their grades and opened their eyes as to how much sleep they needed – which we will be reviewing later.

I also opened up about my own fears and anxieties when going to college at their age and shared with them some experiences from my own life. This had quite a powerful effect, as I was showing vulnerability. This is one of the key messages of this book. As parents, it is extremely powerful to share one's own vulnerabilities and experiences of life as a teenager and as a young adult with our children, when they are going through these phases.

I hope those wonderful young people remember the two hours we spent together for the rest of their lives. We ended up discussing many of the research findings and key concepts in this book. They left having learned that:

- Life is not fair.

- We don't always get what we want.

- We have to learn to accept discomfort as part of life.

- We can't control life.

- We may fail at some things in life but are never in ourselves 'failures'.

- It is normal to be anxious.

- The physical symptoms of anxiety are uncomfortable but not dangerous.

They also learned:

- The importance of recognising the signs of major depression and approaching somebody for help if we are in trouble.

- The importance of empathising with peers who are in difficulty with depression and assisting them.

- How to stop rating ourselves and learn to accept ourselves without conditions by becoming members of the Raggy Doll Club, which we will discuss later in this book.

- Key lessons on how to study properly for exams.

- How to do a 'three-minute breathing space' as part of their preparation for exams and to do this during an actual exam, if they 'freeze'.

- The difference between the 'real world' and the 'virtual world'.

- The importance of examining their interactions with the world of technology, and how it was influencing their lives.

- Some key advice on relationships, and the importance of respecting each other, whether gay or straight.

- That we will get out of life what we put into it: 'perspiration is more important than inspiration'.

There is so much that we – both adults and young people – can all take from the above insights. If all of us were to absorb these messages, we would have a better chance of being happier and more fulfilled in our lives. And if you think about it, isn't this what mental health is all about?

These students were able to recognise not only that the journey toward adulthood did not end at eighteen but that they would continue to face a significant number of hurdles on the road. In many ways, they confirmed the decision to expand this book to assist the parents of young adults in their early and middle twenties, in addition to the parents of adolescent teenagers.

It is worth noting that Headstrong's 'My World Survey', which I mentioned earlier, found:

- An increase in young people's levels of depression, anxiety and stress across the developmental period of twelve to twenty-five years of age.

- A steady increase in levels of alcohol consumption, frequency and volume of drinking, number of alcoholic drinks typically consumed, and binge drinking across the twelve-to-twenty-five age group. Young people move outside the normal range for drinking at eighteen and remain there until they are twenty-four or twenty-five.

- The use of avoidant coping, a negative coping strategy, peaks at twenty or twenty-one years of age, then declines toward twenty-four.

- At eighteen to nineteen years of age, young people report high levels of substance use, which continue until they are twenty-four or twenty-five.

- Levels of both self-esteem and optimism generally decrease from twelve to eighteen years of age, reaching their lowest points at eighteen or nineteen. Levels increase gradually from about nineteen onwards.

- The use of a positive coping strategy (problem-focused coping) is lowest at fourteen to fifteen years of age and gradually increases until twenty-four or twenty-five.

- Levels of seeking social support are highest at twelve or thirteen years of age, drop at eighteen to nineteen and remain low until twenty-five.

All of this information from our adolescents shows that this is a particularly stressful period for them. But whilst the young person is on this journey out of adolescence and into early and mature adulthood, we as parents are on a parallel journey of discovery and learning. Until they reach the age of eighteen, we need to act as parents to our children. From then on, we need to act as mentors to them. In order for us to be effective in these roles, we have to examine the skills we would like our young people to learn, and see if we need to find these in ourselves.

To follow on from Enda's comments about 'muddling through' as parents, I am at the other end of the parenting cycle from Enda, having three adult children and two grandchildren. My wife and I have muddled through the task of guiding our children into adulthood. It has not been easy and we – like all the parents reading this book – will have regularly struggled with the many challenges of being a parent and then a mentor. But somehow we managed it and our children are finding their own paths in life. They have taught us a lot and, hopefully, in return, we have been able to pass on some key life skills to them.

The really important message in this book is that parenting adolescents is a normal process which brings significant challenges but also many rewards. There is no 'perfect' way to parent or mentor and there is, thankfully, no such thing as a 'perfect parent' – just, as Enda will describe later, Raggy Doll Parents. I am very happy to include myself in the latter category and hope that by the end of this book you will have joined us in the club.

Both adolescents and parents will go through significant changes on the journey into adulthood and, as we have already noted, change is always challenging. Hopefully, this book will go some distance toward helping you as parents survive and grow during the process.

NOTE FOR READERS

When Enda and I came to put this book together there was an immediate recognition that we both had different areas of knowledge and experience. Not only that, we wrote with very different styles.

Enda sees people from all age groups but has developed particular experience in dealing with teenagers between the ages of thirteen and eighteen. He does this by helping parents develop the skills they need to understand their teenagers and help their teenagers deal with difficulties. His expertise includes using cognitive behaviour therapy (CBT) to manage depression, anxiety and substance abuse. He has been supported by another Raggy Doll – Professor Denis Ryan of the Irish College of Humanities and Applied Science – in trying to more accurately define what mental health actually is.

Enda has started to use his insights to develop new ways of helping peoople to recover from conditions like anorexia nervosa and is at present developing his own model of how to help families overcome this condition, which may be the theme of a future book.

I, on the other hand, have found myself honing my skills with young people between the ages of seventeen and twenty-five or thirty, assisting them and their parents in overcoming conditions like depression, panic attacks, general anxiety and social anxiety. I would like to think that I have developed an increasing body of experience in identifying depression and teaching people how to manage it holistically. I am currently a member of an international group examining the role of cognitive difficulties in this illness.

I have found myself becoming more and more fascinated by how the brain actually works – particularly the developing brain – and what affects it. Having all too frequently had to watch the devastation that it causes, I have also become passionate about trying to reduce the appalling suicide rate in Ireland, and especially about how to reduce deaths in the screenager group. I believe that we must do everything in our power to increase our understanding of what 'lies beneath' suicide if we are ever to be able to develop effective approaches to dealing with this epidemic.

My brother-in-arms Enda and I may be chalk and cheese but, by combining our skills and experience, we believe we have put together a book that will help you understand your screenager in a way that you may not have been able to before. Out of this understanding, you will be able to utilise your own resources in supporting and guiding your teenagers and young adults on their journeys to adulthood.

To avoid killing each other, we decided that each of us should remain free to write in the style he felt most comfortable with. We also felt it was best to assign different topics to one or the other of us, depending on which of us we felt had the most relevant message. The consequence is that, using a rugby analogy, 'we pass the ball on a regular basis'.

We feel that this approach will give the reader more unique insights into the workings of the adolescent mind, from many different perspectives, and that it will also, hopefully, widen and deepen the insights and skill sets of parents.

SECTION ONE

The Stages of the Adolescent's Development

CHAPTER ONE
The Brain's Development and Your Adolescent Screenager

One could ask what brain development has to do with the journey from adolescence to adulthood. Is development not more to do with their social development, hormones, and physical changes and how they deal with relationships and their peers? Whilst all of these are important and will be dealt with in subsequent chapters, the story of how the brain develops between the ages of thirteen and thirty is a crucial piece of the jigsaw. Many of the difficulties that young people – particularly teenagers – and their parents experience have their origins in how the brain matures and develops during this phase.

As a parent have you ever wondered about the following?

- Why are my child's emotional state and behaviour so different between the ages of thirteen and seventeen than they were at ten?

- Why does my daughter seem much more advanced for her age in so many areas than my son of a similar age?

- Why is it impossible to get my teenager out of bed in the morning and into bed at night?

- Where do the major mood swings and outbursts of anger come from in the teenage phase?

- Why do young men in emotional difficulty remain silent whilst young girls communicate with each other?

- Why do teenagers take risks, and why are they behaviourally more impulsive than young people in their twenties?

- Why are teenagers and young emerging adults more likely to become involved in risk-taking when they are together than when they are on their own or with their families?

- What are the effects of bullying, severe stress and abuse on the developing brain of the teenager or young emerging adult?

- What are the effects of alcohol, nicotine and substance misuse on the developing brains of our teenagers?

- Why are diet and exercise – and particularly obesity – now seen as critically important in how our teenagers and young emerging adults grow and develop not only physically but mentally?

- Why are some teenagers and young emerging adults more resilient when it comes to stress?

- Is technology, in all its forms, harmful or helpful to the developing brains of our children?

To answer these questions, we must enter into the world of the developing brain and explore how it influences so much of what happens to our young adolescent screenagers. We begin our journey by looking at the normal adult brain, with a particular emphasis on the parts of the brain involved in our logical and emotional behaviours. It is not essential to read this section, and some may want to skip it altogether, but it will assist those parents who are interested in understanding themselves before exploring the world of their teenagers and emerging young adults. We will then examine the three ages of the brain, with special emphasis on the developing brain, which is so critical for the journey toward adulthood.

THE ADULT BRAIN

Aptly described as the 'boss organ' of the body, the brain, encased within our bony skulls, is analogous to the central processor of a computer. It receives, compiles and evaluates information from within the body and from the external environment, makes the necessary decisions, and issues instructions to every other organ structure in the body. It is composed of around 10 billion cells. These cells are of two basic types: neurons and glial cells.

Neurons are the decision makers. Neurons are basically individual cells that receive, process, and pass on information. They, like all other cells in the body, are fluid-filled units surrounded by fine cell membranes, which help them to remain distinct from one another. In their centres lie the chromosomes that harbour our genes. Each neuron is connected to thousands of others to form pathways. Each section of the brain is connected by these pathways.

Neurons constitute only 10 percent of adult brain cells. The average neuron is like a little factory, with a central body shape, lots of little spike-like projections at one end and a single tail at the other! The central body contains both our genes and the molecular machinery required to run the factory. The spikes, which are called dendrites, receive all the information being sent down the line from other neurons. The tail, which is called the axon, passes the relevant information on to the next cell. The real product of the factory is information.

Each dendrite is receiving information from the axon of another neuron, and each neuron has thousands of dendrites, so information pours into each neuron. The so called plasticity of the brain (the capacity of the brain to change our thoughts, emotions and behaviour) is based on the number of dendrite connections each neuron chooses to have. Increase the numbers and the pathways get stronger; decrease them and the pathways get weaker.

Glial cells support, protect and nourish neurons. If neurons make up only 10 percent of adult brain cells, glial cells make up the remaining 90 percent. Many researchers now feel that glial cells may play a much greater role in brain function than previously thought. Just like a large company, the brain assigns different functions and responsibilities to each department. This mainly involves the neurons; the glial cells are the support staff servicing all neurons, regardless of department.

Within an organisational structure as large as the brain, good communication is a prerequisite for efficient operation. Adjacent neurons must be able to communicate unimpeded. Departments must also be able to easily exchange important information. To address this concern, as a company would, the brain has an excellent telephone system installed, with cables connecting units within a particular department and also linking one department to another. The brain has an ingenious means of passing information from one neuron to another. Each cell has the ability to activate itself electrically and pass this charge on to the next cell, causing it to activate also. As each neuron is an isolated cell, the brain has developed a practical way of sending information from one to another.

Between neurons in the brain are hundreds of small gaps or meeting points, which are known as synapses. The neuron which is passing on information produces chemical messengers which it releases in a small bubble into each of these gaps. These chemicals cross the gap, attaching to receptors on the surface of the neighbouring neuron. They release their information and return to their cell of origin to await further instructions. These chemical messengers are called neurotransmitters. As soon as the information has been communicated from the first cell to the second, the second may decide to fire based on the information it has received, repeating the process and activating a third. A pathway is formed.

A brain has over 100 trillion synapses, which form a huge web of pathways – a little like the World Wide Web. In order to be more efficient, the brain has a 'use it or lose it' approach. So if we are learning a new skill, pathways are formed and strengthened. If we stop using it, they will start to weaken. As we will see later, this is important in how the developing brain works.

The brain is composed of two parts or hemispheres connected by a thick band of nerves we will call the 'brain bridge' (the corpus callosum). In some senses we have 'two brains', each side having a different approach to the world as we see it. Without the bridge between them, life could become very confused indeed! The left side controls the right side of the body. It is the logical part of our brain. It assists us in being practical, analytical, organised, factual, better at mathematics, and capable of zoning in on matters. It is also important in processing/comprehending, written/spoken language and positive thoughts/emotions. The left brain seeks to provide rational explanations for our experiences (even if incorrect), often in response to information from the right brain, thus keeping everything orderly.

The right side of the brain controls the left side of the body. It is the creative part of the brain. It helps us to store visual information and comprehend the emotional significance of language. It helps us to be imaginative, artistic, spatially aware, intuitive and able to examine the bigger holistic picture. It processes negative thoughts and emotions. It gives us the context for situations; when we access memories, it provides us with a fuller picture than the left brain. Crucially, attention/awareness is a function of our right brain, so it struggles to compete with the practical left brain in our everyday lives. When we are anxious and imagining the worst, the right brain is in overdrive!

The two sides of the brain are in continuous communication, particularly the two frontal lobes. This allows us the best of both worlds, as we can fuse them together to form a rich tapestry where creativity and practicality, the small print and the bigger canvas, exist side by side.

The Male Brain versus the Female Brain

There has been much research done (and fun had) assessing the differences between male and female brains, which are clearly 'hard-wired' differently. Sex hormones play an important role in this wiring process, mainly in the womb. The male brain is slightly bigger, with more neurons; women score with more connections among all the parts of the brain. Men focus on individual issues, women on the bigger picture. The bridge between the two hemispheres of the female brain has more connections, with one study suggesting up to 30 percent more. This explains why many women are multitaskers, with the uncanny ability to carry out a number of jobs simultaneously. The hippocampus is larger in women and the amygdala or 'stress box' is larger in men.

The speech area in men is almost completely situated in the left hemisphere while, in women, it involves both. There are also more neurons in parts of the female brain associated with language processing and comprehension. So women are naturally more talkative than men. This is important in emotional distress, particularly depression and suicide. Women tend to verbalise difficulties openly – often to each other – whereas men often have these conversations within themselves, which is riskier. This may explain why we struggle with young adult males and mental illness. Nature has set the stage!

The main male emotional centres are in the right side of the brain. In women they are more evenly distributed between the two sides, explaining why women are inclined to be emotional in situations where men would be more logical. As the right brain is the main source of negative emotions/thoughts and the left side is the main source of positive ones, the male in emotional distress finds it harder to cope. A reduction in the number of connections between the two hemispheres in the male brain makes intervention by the left side more difficult, explaining the difficulties men have in dealing with such distress. Later, we will examine the role of the developing brain in the process of dealing with emotional distress.

The Logical Brain versus the Emotional Brain

We have an emotional brain and a logical brain. This is key to what we will be dealing with throughout this book.

The Logical Brain

The logical part of the brain – the prefrontal cortex or 'frontal mood department' – is situated at the front. It takes up 29 percent of the total grey matter of the brain and is of great importance in our lives. It is the thought-producing, decision-making part of our brain. Its functions, partly related to mood but mostly related to behaviour, are as follows:

1. Analysing situations – particularly new ones – and making judgments and decisions based on information received. This includes future planning.

2. Managing short-term memory.

3. Preventing impulsive and destructive behaviour, including self-injurious behaviour and aggressive acts toward others.

4. Helping to produce and maintain a normal mood, and to produce

positive thinking. The logical brain is probably the source of self-consciousness.

Of primary interest when it comes to mental illness is the left prefrontal cortex, which mediates positive thoughts and impulsive behaviour, is often called the 'executive decision-maker' and is very influential in both depression and suicide.

The Emotional Brain

The emotional part of the brain – the limbic system or 'limbic mood department' – lies in its centre. Composed of different sections with corresponding functions, the limbic system is responsible for:

1. Response to stress

2. Preservation of normal mood

3. Feelings of joy and pleasure

4. Processing memory

5. Appetite for food and sex.

Within the limbic mood system, there are several sections – which we will call 'boxes' – each of which is involved with its own functions:

1. Memory Box/Hippocampus: This is where memory is manufactured, filtered and organised before being sent to other parts of the brain for storage. It is also involved in the retrieval of memories, and it plays key roles in putting recalled memories into context and in our spatial memory. This box becomes very active when we are sleeping, particularly when we are dreaming. It's likely that memories are consolidated at these times.

2. Stress Box/Amygdala: This unit controls the response to perceived threats from both within the body and the external environment. Most experts also feel that it is the main processor of the primary emotions of fear, hate, love and anger. It is integral to stress and

anxiety, and it plays a large role in how the brain stores emotions related to unpleasant memories that may or may not be consciously accessible. The negative thinking prevalent in depression probably originates here (or, more accurately, the emotions associated with the thoughts). This box is larger in males than in females.

3. Pleasure Box/Nucleus Accumbens: This section is activated when we are participating in rewarding activities like eating, drinking alcohol and having sex. In the biological illness of addiction, this box is affected by abuse.

The logical and emotional brains are in constant communication. When this communication breaks down – or when communication between sections of a mood department is disrupted – the brain descends into chaos, and illness is a likely consequence.

There is a greater flow of information from the emotional brain to the logical brain than vice versa, probably for evolutionary survival reasons. This may explain why our emotions (fear, for example) frequently overpower our thoughts and direct our behaviours and yet we often have difficulty in persuading our thoughts to overpower our emotions and direct our behaviours! As we will see later, this is key to how teenagers and young emerging adults get into difficulties.

The prefrontal cortex (the logical brain) and the limbic system (the emotional brain) – and their individual sections – are in constant communication with all the other parts of the brain. But, in particular, they are constantly receiving, assimilating and passing on information through a variety of neural pathways to each other.

The primary channels of communication between the two mood departments (and their individual sections) are a series of three long collections of neurons which we will refer to as 'mood cables'. Each cable will be named after the predominant chemical messenger used by its neurons. Because they are so important to the normal health of the mood system, we will be dealing with these cables regularly throughout this book.

Because the information carried by each neuron in these cables has to travel a distance from its source, the brain uses its glial support cells to manufacture an insulation-type material called myelin and surround the cables with it, much as the electrical wires in our homes are covered with insulation. This speeds up the passage of information along the cables. This whole process of myelination, as we will see later, is critical in how the brain of the young person develops and matures.

The three main mood cables and their corresponding control boxes are:

1. The Dopamine Mood Cable: Situated below the limbic mood department at the base of the brain is the dopamine control box. The dopamine cable travels from this box and continues through the limbic mood department, before moving on to the prefrontal cortex and other structures. It uses the neurotransmitter dopamine, which is produced and mediated by the dopamine control box. Of the brain's 1 billion neurons, a modest forty thousand make up this cable, but the well-being of the entire mood system depends on this small structure. It is important in our reward pathways because we learn more quickly when deriving pleasure from doing so. This is essential to how children and young adults learn. This cable produces feelings of joy and pleasure, and its malfunction is linked to depression, addiction and schizophrenia. Underactivity in this cable is now thought to be the source of most of the symptoms of children with hyperactivity disorders, as well as the lack of enjoyment of life found in depression and chronic stress. Overactivity can lead to addiction and the elevated moods found in bipolar disorder.

2. The Serotonin Mood Cable: Also situated at the base of the brain is the serotonin control box. The serotonin cable runs from this box through all the sections of the limbic mood department, connects with the frontal mood department and then moves on to pass

information to almost every part of the brain. Its links with the memory and behaviour boxes are of particular importance. This cable uses the neurotransmitter serotonin to communicate, which is produced and mediated by the serotonin control box. Similar to the dopamine cable, the serotonin cable is composed of a relatively small number of neurons. What it lacks in size, however, it makes up in significance by virtue of the massive number of connections it makes with all the sections of the mood system and, indeed, with the rest of the brain. This is the primary mood cable, which regulates mood, sleep, concentration, memory, appetite, sexual drive, stress and destructive behaviour. It is also 50 percent less active in women, which may partially explain their increased incidence of anxiety/depression. There is a lot of interest in the concept that the serotonin system can be 'reset' at crucial stages in our development as children. If we grow up in an environment that is hostile because of poverty, abuse and so on, our serotonin cable may be underactive when we come under stress as adults. It is also felt to play a key role in how our brain actually develops. There is evidence that certain genetic predispositions to malfunctions in this system make us more vulnerable to stress and depression. Underactivity in this cable is associated with impulsivity, aggression, depression, borderline and anti-social personality disorders, and suicide.

3. The Noradrenaline Mood Cable: The source of this cable also lies in the brainstem, i.e. the noradrenaline control box. From there, it travels up through the limbic and frontal mood departments before dispersing throughout the brain. It has a strong connection with the stress box. The main chemical messenger used by this cable is noradrenaline, the production of which is mediated by the noradrenaline control box. This cable, like the other two, is composed of a relatively small number of neurons: around twenty-five

thousand. It keeps us alert, vigilant, driven and sleeping normally. It also helps us to manage stress. It does not operate properly in patients suffering from depression and anxiety.

Our Stress System

Before we leave the adult brain let us briefly mention our stress system, which is so critical in keeping us alive and well. Stress is a universal phenomenon. Everyone experiences periods of acute stress (exam pressure, for example) and chronic stress (financial pressure or job difficulties). The body also has to deal with the internal stress of infection and illness. Stress is now felt to be pivotal in the creation and maintenance of certain mental illnesses such as depression and anxiety.

The coordinator of the body's stress response is the stress box, which is situated in the limbic department of the emotional brain. When under attack from internal or external stress, the logical brain activates the stress box. The stress box then releases CRH, a 'peptide messenger', which activates two areas in the brain – the hormone control box and the brainstem – which send information to the adrenal stress glands through the blood stream and spinal cord, respectively.

The brainstem instructs the adrenal glands to release adrenaline and noradrenaline into the bloodstream. This response to stress lasts for seconds or minutes. These hormones prepare the body for combat with the immediate threat. The heart rate increases, the blood pressure rises, the mind is vigilant and alert, the mouth becomes dry and the stomach starts to churn. The body is diverting resources away from non-essential organs toward those which will be used in combat, in order to maximise the person's chances of survival. This is known informally as a 'fight-or-flight' reaction.

The hormone control box also has a role to play here. Composed of two structures – the hypothalamus and the pituitary gland – it controls all the major glands in the body and is in charge of our internal biological clocks/rhythms. The hormone control box also receives instructions from the stress box and sends a message via the bloodstream to the adrenal stress glands, instructing them to release glucocortisol. This is a longer process, which can last from minutes to hours. Glucocortisol is a critical hormone, and is involved in making glucose available to all the cells in the body. Every cell in the body has receptors for this hormone, and the neurons in the brain are no exception. Glucocortisol also helps to break down fats to release more energy.

Glucocortisol, adrenaline and noradrenaline feed back to the brain. In other words, if their levels in the blood are high, the brain starts to reduce the drive to produce more – particularly when the stressor is gone. All then goes back to normal.

A useful way of combining all this information to form a unified concept is to take the first letters of the frontal mood department ('f'), the limbic mood department ('l') the adrenal stress gland ('a') and the stress hormone glucocortisol ('g') to form the word 'FLAG'. Flags have universal significance in our lives. A green flag suggests all is well, red flags warn of danger, and yellow, purple and white flags can be taken to mean fear, debauchery and surrender, respectively. Based on these concepts, the green flag will represent normal mental health, the red flag depression, the yellow flag anxiety, the purple flag addiction, and the white flag suicide. We will examine later in the book how some of these conditions have an impact on the road to adulthood.

This then is the brain, which controls so much of what happens in our emotional and rational worlds, in its adult stage. But, as we will now explore, the story of the brain throughout our lives is one of constant change.

THE THREE AGES OF THE BRAIN

The brain passes through three major ages during the average lifespan:

1. Developing: From zero to thirty. We will examine this age in more detail in a moment.

2. Mature: Between thirty and sixty-five, the brain is incredibly efficient at processing information, assessing complex situations in our emotional and rational worlds, and making decisions in our busy

lives. This is because it has set up many strong pathways (between our emotional and logical brains, in particular), which help us get to the essence of situations faster than when we were in our teens and twenties. We could call this the age of the 'wise brain'. Most of us reading this book will be doing so using our mature brains and will pick up the essence of its messages quite quickly. This is because of our experience and the maturity of the pathways in our brains. In many ways, having a mature brain can make it more difficult to cope with the very immature teenage brain and associated teenage behaviours, as they do not seem logical to us. Clashes between teenagers and their adult parents, as we will see later, are often created by the significant difference between the developing brains of the former and the mature brains of the latter: more on that later.

3. Ageing: From sixty-five to the ends of our lives, the number of neurons and connections in the brain begin gradually to decline due to vascular changes and natural attrition. The brain retains many of the features of its mature age but becomes less efficient.

The Developing Brain

For the purposes of this discussion, let's look in more detail at the developing brain. Although we will be concentrating mainly on the key changes that occur between the ages of thirteen and thirty, it is important to start at the beginning. We will divide this first age of the brain into three stages:

1. Stage One: 0–12

2. Stage Two: 13–19

3. Stage Three: 20–30

The Developing Brain: Stage One

The brain begins it lengthy journey around day eighteen in the womb. Within three months, hundreds of billions of neurons are formed and organised rapidly into the different sections that will make up the future adult brain.

By the sixth month of pregnancy, the foetal brain has actually developed too many neurons, so it carries out a selective pruning. It is a case of survival of the fittest: developing cells must start communicating or die; those that are unable to form synapses are destroyed. This is a very important stage in the brain's development.

In the last few months in the womb, during this massive pruning process, the prefrontal cortex seems to become particularly vulnerable to damage. If certain genetic vulnerabilities/intrauterine environmental influences are present, a susceptibility to illnesses like schizophrenia, autism and bipolar depression may become established at this stage, even though it will not reveal its presence until later. Brain development in the womb can be particularly affected by viral illnesses, nicotine, alcohol, stress or untreated depression in the mother.

Our genes are the chief architects of brain development in the womb. Sex hormones exert a major influence on our brains' development and whether our brains are hard-wired in a predominantly male or predominantly female pattern. Although male or female sex organs are decided in the womb by the presence of either testosterone or oestrogen between the sixth and twelfth weeks of pregnancy, it is not until the second half of pregnancy that the same hormones decide whether the future emerging brain will be male or female in type.

At birth, most of the neurons we need for life are already present but the brain is only 10 percent formed vis-à-vis the adult brain.

From birth, empathy pathways in the brain swing into action, and anything affecting the mother has instant effects on the baby's developing brain. In the first two years, interactions between the infant/toddler and his or her parents/family, together with the general environment the child encounters, will have a major impact on the child's future developing brain.

Conscious memory pathways only emerge from three onwards, whilst unconscious emotional memories are laid down from birth. The memory box matures from the age of three onwards, which explains why, although we are strongly influenced emotionally and socially by events and interactions in those first few years of life, we have little conscious recall of them.

Between the ages of six and twelve, the brain experiences a massive growth in the number of connections among its individual neurons. This process reaches its peak just before puberty, between the ages of ten and twelve. Once again, a large pruning process has to occur or efficiency suffers.

It was accepted in the past by the scientific and medical communities that, by age twelve, the brain was fully formed and that no new neurons could be formed. It is now known that that is not true and that the development of the brain is a dynamic and ongoing process.

The Developing Brain: Stage Two

Between the ages of thirteen and nineteen, a huge reorganisation of the neurons and their synapses begins. This is probably activated by a combination of our genes working together and a massive release of sex hormones.

Although some neurons may be lost during this stage, it is mainly the connections between them that are selectively destroyed. The result is a reduction in the number of synapses but an increase in overall efficiency. This stage starts with a pruning of parts of the brain responsible for vision, hearing and coordination, before moving on to the emotional brain. It also begins the process of pruning the logical brain but this, as we will see, is only completed in earnest by age twenty-five or thirty.

By the end of this stage, the brain will have lost 15 percent of its tissue (much of it from the prefrontal cortex), but what remains will be working effectively. As we will see, though, the development process is not over yet. Pruning is important during this phase of brain development as it is very much influenced by environmental experiences and makes the teenage brain more versatile and adaptable to deal with the demands placed on it.

If we want to come to terms with the significant emotional and behavioural changes that our teenagers exhibit between thirteen and nineteen, we must understand the importance of the above process. As the limbic system is responsible for how we feel, it's inevitable that feelings will run riot during this period. If we feel down or have relationship difficulties for example, the pain will be more intense; the same applies to positive emotions. As the prefrontal cortex can only execute weak control over the limbic system at this stage, emotions will influence thoughts and actions more than common sense will.

This explains the excessive behaviour of many teenagers, their exuberance on the one hand and their total disregard for consequences on the other. Without an effectual prefrontal cortex influence, impulsive and often reckless behaviour like binge drinking, unprotected sex and joyriding becomes common in this group. This is why the teenage years are so turbulent for those going through them and so impossible for those who have to deal with teenagers (i.e. parents). We will examine the neurobiological underpinnings of risk-taking and impulsivity later.

This phased development of the mood system of the teenager/young adult has huge implications for how messages relating to smoking, alcohol and drug misuse should be communicated to young people. These are an issue because our pleasure box, dopamine cable and limbic system are much more active during this phase of development, due to the immature prefrontal cortex's inability to exert control. The pleasure that such activities bring outweigh their inevitable negative consequences in the mind of the teenager. In spite of this fact, parents, teachers and health professionals attempt to reach young people on an intellectual level. The only effective mode of communication is one which evokes an emotional response.

As a result of our increased understanding of the biological development of the adolescent brain, experts are beginning at last to understand the reasons why previous attempts to reach young people have failed and have now come up with new and exciting ways of circumventing the dangers of the dreaded teens. These involve encouraging intuitive or instinctive reasoning rather than logical thinking in potentially risky situations. Such an approach could help many young people to avoid tragedy.

Mainly due to hormonal differences, there is a delay in the speed of the development of the male brain compared to the female brain, which is most obvious in early adolescence. This means that female adolescents seem to have an edge, academically, until the late teens. There are also clear differences in how the sexes learn, due to the organisation and functioning of their brains.

There are several parts of the emotional brain that grow at different rates in adolescent females and males. The hippocampus or memory box, important to long-term memory, is more sensitive to oestrogen and grows faster and larger in young women, which may contribute to their stronger social skills and explain why they often outperform young men in exams up to the late teens. In general, young women are more comfortable in social situations, as they are able to deal better with emotions and relationships. The amygdala or stress box is more responsive to testosterone and grows larger in young men. This may explain why young male teenagers may prefer contact sports, may have a stronger sex drive and are often more assertive than their female counterparts.

In general, though, the amygdala becomes more active during this period in both male and female adolescents. The importance of this is that, during this phase both sexes – but particularly the boys – are more likely to misinterpret facial-emotional expressions in adults. This can lead to many misunderstandings as they are often misreading the signs that parents or teachers are sending out. At the heart of this difficulty is the poorly developed prefrontal cortex in the early part of this second stage of brain development. Its role in assessing adult facial responses is weakened, and the task is taken over more by the emotional brain's stress box, which is the one misreading the signs. This only begins to right itself at the end of this second stage of development.

So a clear picture is developing here in our discussion of this stage of brain development. If the amygdala is, for example, making the teenager more emotional and this teenager is constantly misreading the emotional facial cues coming from parents and teachers, then trouble is inevitable. Add to this the immature prefrontal cortex and we can understand the turbulent world of the adolescent and, by extension, of their sometimes despairing parents. This is so for both males and females, but especially the former.

Dick Swab, a world-famous Dutch neuroscientist, in his recent book *We*

Are Our Brains: From the Womb to Alzheimer's, makes the perceptive (and in some ways, humorous) observation that during this teenage stage of brain development the role of parents is to act temporarily as their adolescent child's prefrontal cortex. This is because the prefrontal cortex is still very immature during this phase and so Swab feels that, in the teenager, its normal role of planning, organisation, providing a moral framework and setting limits is significantly challenged. This would point to the importance, as we will examine later, of 'parents being parents' during this phase.

It is not that the prefrontal cortex is not active when carrying out many everyday tasks during this period, but rather that it is not as efficient in this stage of brain development as it will become later, so it has to work harder to get such tasks done. This is why teenagers tire quickly when asked to do novel tasks: their brains have to work harder.

The Developing Brain: Stage Three

By the end of the second or adolescent/teenager stage of brain development, the architecture of the future, fully mature adult brain is in place. But a lot of further pruning still has to take place before the fully developed brain appears, particularly increased myelination of the tracts leading from the prefrontal cortex back to the limbic system. This mainly happens between the ages of nineteen and twenty-five, but some further layers of myelination reaching up into the prefrontal cortex continue until we are thirty.

We have already discussed myelin, which is analogous to the white sheaths we often see on electric wires. Its job is to speed up communication between different brain regions. In our case, we are interested mostly in its role strengthening links between our logical and emotional brain areas. This gradual upgrading of connections explains why young emerging adults seem to become gradually more mature in relation to emotional control and behaviour as they enter their early and mid twenties. They begin to problem-solve better and deal with emotional situations more effectively as they reach their mid-twenties and then thirty.

From nineteen onwards, in fact, the prefrontal cortex is slowly taking control of matters. By the time the developing brain has passed twenty-five years of age, it has almost evolved into the mature brain. So, from twenty onwards, the parent's role increasingly becomes to act as mentor, rather than parent.

While this chapter has all been about the physical development of the young adolescent brain, in the next chapter, Enda will illustrate how this process influences the actual development of the unique people we all come to be.

CHAPTER TWO:
How We All Become Who We Are

Sigmund Freud was a very complex man. He is widely regarded as the father of psychotherapy, so I suppose no book on how our minds work would be complete without a reference to him. He is said, however, to have remarked once that anybody could be helped to understand themselves through psycho-analysis – except the Irish. So considering that this book will use the experiences of Irish families in describing the world of the teenager, we will unfortunately have to leave Freud out of the rest of our story.

So why mention him at all? Well, one reason he is vital to our story is that he had a sidekick called Erik Erikson. And it is the bold Erik that is a crucial ingredient in understanding why we are the way we are. Erikson was a student of Freudian theory. He took a lot of what Freud said and put it into a frame-work which made understanding why we become who we are much easier to grasp.

He observed that, as we grow through life, we all pass through eight dis-tinct stages of development. There probably isn't a psychologist or therapist out there who hasn't heard of Erik Erikson and his theory of psychosocial development, as his theories form the basis of most psychology theory. Funnily enough though, outside of the psychotherapeutic community, he is virtually unknown.

Erikson argued that, as we live through each of the eight stages, we are con-fronted by challenges and questions about what we are that we need to resolve. He also identified what happens when we are not able to overcome the chal-lenges posed by each stage, and it is this aspect that makes Erikson's theory vital to our understanding of adolescence and why some kids find adolescence so difficult to cope with.

So let's take some time to look at each stage and examine how each stage affects us.

STAGE ONE: TRUST VERSUS MISTRUST (0–1)

In this first stage, Erikson argued, our view of our world is almost completely centred on having our basic needs met. In our first year, we are totally dependent on our parents and any other primary caregivers that are introduced into our lives: crèche workers, babysitters and other family members, for example. Our understanding of the world will depend on our interaction with these people and whether they fulfil our basic needs.

If our caregivers are reliable in providing us with food, warmth and affection, then we will view the world as trustworthy and feel we can depend on others to protect us. If, however, caregivers are negligent or fail to provide for our basic needs on a consistent basis, then our view of the world will be one of mistrust, and we will feel the world is a dangerous, unpredictable place and that others are not to be trusted.

Erikson argued that successful completion of each stage is dependent on the successful completion of the stage before it. So if a child has learned how to trust others, they can then proceed healthily to the next stage. If, however, the child has learned to mistrust others, this can create havoc when they try to leave their parents' nest to explore their world. This mistrust can continue into adulthood, creating problems which can haunt us until we die, unless we learn how to resolve it.

STAGE TWO: AUTONOMY VERSUS SHAME AND DOUBT (2–3)

This period covers the toddler years. During this stage, we start to learn how to walk and talk. With the development of these skills, a whole new world of opportunity opens up. We venture out to explore our horizons. We also start to exert our will over others, which is why they're called the 'terrible twos'. We are still very dependent on our parents to provide us with security but, as any parent will tell you, the girls start to wreck your head and the boys start to wreck your house!

As we progress, we start to become more competent in areas like dressing and feeding ourselves. Of course, this can lead to all kinds of trouble, as the toddler's idea of his capabilities is usually at odds with his parents'.

If our caregivers encourage us to try new things, like using the bathroom or tending to our own hygiene needs, and show patience when we hit everywhere with the food except our mouth, then we start to learn how to be autonomous, self-sufficient and confident in attempting new tasks. If, however, caregivers are very restrictive, refuse to allow us to perform tasks we are capable of, or tease us over our early attempts at self-sufficiency, we will develop a sense of shame and doubt about our abilities and may become very reluctant to try new challenges.

Parents have to strike a balance between allowing the toddler autonomy and asserting their will, in order to protect him, the house, other children and, indeed, their own sanity.

STAGE THREE: INITIATIVE VERSUS GUILT (4–6)

Having become confident and autonomous in Stage Two, we now are able to practise showing initiative in attempting new challenges. We do this by charging into any task that takes our fancy. It would appear that our initiative and activities have specific purposes, even if, to adults, these seem to be simply to be on the move and to dismantle everything around us to see how it works.

During this period, we start to learn how things work. Mum gets upset at this and not that. Dad gets grumpy at that and not this. If I throw the toy at the window, it makes a very loud smashing sound and mammy puts a very funny face on. Similarly, if I pull the cat's tail, he runs off.

Whilst all these activities can create mayhem around us, they are crucial in the development of our courage and independence, even if many of them will bring us into conflict with parents and teachers. We may start taking risks –

like wanting to cross the road unaided – or even become aggressive by hitting others or throwing things. Believe it or not, studies have shown that over 30 percent of actions by children in this age group involve aggressive behaviour. Sometimes we become incredibly frustrated if we don't get the desired result from our activity.

If our parents and teachers provide us with encouragement and guidance in how to make realistic choices, we develop confidence in taking on tasks and activities. We also learn how to cope with the distress when things don't turn out as we had planned. If, however, our parents or teachers see our attempts as annoying and bothersome, or dismiss the relevance we attach to them, we develop a sense of guilt about our needs and ideas.

STAGE FOUR: INDUSTRY VERSUS INFERIORITY (7–11)

Having successfully got this far, we now enter the world of learning to put work before pleasure and understanding that, if we want to achieve a long-term goal like passing an exam, then we must put up with taking actions which don't give us immediate gratification, like completing homework. As we grow, we start to want to complete tasks instead of just superficially playing and changing activities every five minutes. We may start building Lego or develop interests that require understanding more technical concepts, like computers and games.

We also become more aware of ourselves as individuals. Erikson believed that this stage was crucial to the development of our self-confidence. If we are encouraged to persevere at tasks and praised for our efforts and achievements, we become industrious in completing tasks and putting work before pleasure. Life at this stage provides us with more and more opportunities to get the recognition of teachers, fellow pupils and relatives. These may take the form of producing things, doing things for others and completing our homework well. As we achieve this recognition, we start to become more industrious and diligent, showing more and more willingness to take on more and more difficult tasks.

Unfortunately for our parents, we also start to test where we fit in on the pecking order and may start to get aggressive and argumentative with them, our siblings or others. Once again, we require grown-ups to be patient and encouraging, sometimes acting as referees and sometimes judges, juries and executioners!

If, though, we are teased over our efforts, or bullied or regularly criticised for not achieving the 'expected' results, we will feel we can't meet our parents' and teachers' expectations. We will develop a sense of inferiority about our abilities and where we fit in with our peers and the world.

STAGE FIVE: IDENTITY VERSUS ROLE CONFUSION (12–19)

We now enter the period that is the junction between what we are and what we will become, the bridge between childhood and adulthood. We start to think about the roles we will play in society when we grow up.

Erikson argued that, at this stage, we develop an identity crisis. At each previous stage, we identified ourselves in various ways. We thought of ourselves as firemen, princesses, soldiers and fairies. In adolescence, however, we develop the need for a new identity that cannot be achieved in any of the ways we identified ourselves with before. In other words, who still wants to be a fairy at sixteen? In trying to establish who we are, we may experiment with a variety of activities. We may take up music and form a band, or identify ourselves with various political movements.

How we view ourselves is shaped by how we appear to others. Whilst we want to be treated as individuals, we feel compelled to fit in with our peers. This outer sameness conflicts with our inner uniqueness, so we enter a period of role confusion. The effect of this role confusion shouldn't be underestimated, as navigating it involves balancing conflicting messages about how we view ourselves, what we see ourselves becoming and what society expects us to become.

As adolescents, we are faced with the need to re-establish boundaries for ourselves, and to do this in the face of an often hostile world. This role confusion is compounded by commitments having been sought by parents, teachers and others before our identity roles have been formed. An example of this is insisting that fifteen-year-old Junior Cert pupils choose subjects to study for the Leaving Cert, effectively making them choose their future careers when they are hardly able to load the dishwasher.

Adolescence can be the very best of times at 10 AM and the very worst of times by 11 AM. The huge changes in our bodies are matched by huge changes in our abilities to understand the world, our own intentions and the intentions of others. Adolescents need space to explore their world and the people they meet in it. They need space, support and guidance to develop an understanding of who they are. At this stage, no matter how they have been reared, adolescents will choose their own ideologies.

Erikson believed that if, as adolescents, we are given enough space and time to explore our world safely, we will develop a deep understanding of who we are and great confidence in taking on the world in the next stage. What will emerge is a balance between the perspectives of 'this is what I've got' and 'this is what I'm going to do with it'. Once we have achieved this, we have established our identities. If, however, parents, teachers and society are too insistent about the direction we take as adolescents, we will give in to their wishes, forgoing experimentation and true self-discovery. This can result in a reluctance to commit, which can affect our lives and relationships in later life.

STAGE SIX: INTIMACY VERSUS ISOLATION (20–34)

Integrating into society our definitions of who we are is the central task of emerging adulthood. It is when our theories about ourselves are tested in the crucible of the real world. As we emerge into the adult world, we still retain a lot of characteristics of our adolescence. As Harry and I show throughout this book, this period, especially between twenty and twenty-five, is one of the most vulnerable in our mental health development, and yet it is the period during which we have the least control of our own behaviour.

In all the previous periods, our parents, school and society exerted huge influences over our choices and freedoms, but these influences seem to disappear once we reach eighteen and leave school. We are suddenly expected to be able to practise self-restraint and make decisions that require maturity that developmentally we haven't acquired yet. Parental authority has vanished. We are now free to make our own way in the world.

At the start of this stage, we still want to blend our identities with those of our peers. We want to fit in, but risk rejection if our attempts at relationships fail. This can lead to isolation, as our egos are still very fragile and we can find the rejection too painful to risk. If, however, we have a good concept of our own identities, we become capable of establishing and forming long-term commitments to others and are now ready to form intimate relationships. As we mature, we develop the ability to make the inevitable sacrifices and compromises that mature relationships require.

This is the period where parents gradually relinquish their central parenting role in our lives and develop the mentoring role that is vital for the emerging adult to successfully navigate this period.

There are two more stages in Erikson's theory, covering middle age and old age, but they are outside the scope of this book. I'll hand you back to Harry now, who will explain how our adolescent brains develop.

SECTION TWO

Key Factors Influencing the Adolescent's Development

CHAPTER THREE
Understanding Your Adolescent's Developing Brain

In Chapter One, we discussed the three ages of brain development, with particular emphasis on Stage Two (ages thirteen to nineteen), which is so important to understanding why our adolescents behave the way they do. In this chapter, we will examine key factors that influence the brain development of your adolescent screenager:

- Impulsivity, risk-taking and pleasure-seeking

- Substance misuse/abuse

- Sleep

- Severe abuse and bullying

- Stress

- Lifestyle

- Technology.

IMPULSIVITY, PLEASURE-SEEKING AND RISK-TAKING

As adults, all of us, in varying degrees, are:

- Impulsive: we will sometimes do things on the spur of the moment without really thinking through the potential consequences.

- Pleasure-seekers: we will seek out pleasurable feelings and activities, particularly in the short term. This is often called short-term hedonism.

- Risk-takers: we will take a chance even though we know that there may be significant negative consequences if things go wrong.

Classical examples of the above behaviours might involve impulse buying, weekend binges or reckless driving. Many assume that being impulsive is the same as taking risks. In reality, these are two quite distinct behaviours.

Whilst all three of these behavioural characteristics are part of the adult world, they are also relevant in any discussion of the world of the teenager and emerging young adult. We know from research and from our experiences of this age group that all three behaviours are magnified. To understand why this should be the case, we have to relate them back to our discussion of the developing brain.

Risk-Taking and Pleasure-Seeking

We know that pleasure-seeking and risk-taking go hand in hand not only in the teenage phase but also in the early twenties. The human brain has evolved to give us a real surge of dopamine anytime we learn or try something new, take risks or enjoy food or sex. This is because, as human beings, we will all have to constantly take risks, and we will also have to eat and have sex to survive and procreate. The brain rewards us by triggering our pleasure systems to release dopamine, which gives us a buzz or sense of pleasure.

But why do teenagers seem to have an exaggerated tendency to both seek out pleasure and take risks? Well, we know from our earlier discussion that the emotional limbic brain is much more active from thirteen to eighteen and that the controlling prefrontal cortex is less developed during this stage. The teenage brain experiences regular 'dopamine surges' during this phase of development. These have their origins in the emotional brain. They feed into the prefrontal cortex, which, unfortunately, has weak control pathways feeding back to the emotional brain at this stage of brain development. There is also a suggestion that the pleasure system in this age group is actually less active at baseline than in adults, so to get a pleasure hit or buzz requires more risk-taking or pleasurable activity.

Obviously teenagers, like adults, will vary enormously, so some will be programmed to seek out riskier behaviours and more pleasure than others. Much of this relates to genes (particularly key dopamine genes) and the environment they were exposed to at an early age. It is interesting to note that the early and middle stages of adolescence are where the logical brain's ability to temper such risk-taking is at its weakest. Increased risk-taking at this time is likely to be due to a particular stage of brain development that favours behaviours driven by emotion and rewards them over more rational decision-making.

It used to be thought that adolescents were just poor decision-makers due to this lack of logical control but, as discussed in an excellent 2012 article in *The Lancet* by Sawyer et al, some data now suggests that they will sometimes make risky decisions despite understanding the risks. This may be because they are more influenced by stressful or emotionally exciting situations when making such decisions – especially in the presence of their peers. Other research suggests that adolescents tend to take part in risky behaviour more when they get some reward for it, than if this is not the case.

All this suggests that, particularly in the early teens and mid-teens the logical prefrontal cortex simply gets overruled by the willingness to take risks in order to experience the dopamine hit of a new experience or sensation. It also suggests that risk-taking in the presence of one's peers is significantly magnified.

It is also of interest that although children under the age of ten do need dopamine activity to encourage them to do certain things (to learn, for example), it is only in the teenage stage of brain development that these risk- and pleasure-related dopamine surges occur. It is also interesting to note that by the age of eighteen these surges finally seem to be tempered by increasing control pathways emanating from the logical prefrontal cortex. Young emerging adults in their early twenties, and particularly males, are still inclined to take risks and engage in pleasure-seeking behaviour, but are more likely to do so under the influence of alcohol or substances, when the logical prefrontal cortex gets knocked out, allowing such behaviours to run riot.

Parents reading this section may wonder about the relevance of this information. It explains many of the behaviours that our young adolescents exhibit, especially with peers. These include unprotected sex under the age of sixteen, binge drinking, experimenting with glue sniffing and drugs, reckless driving and the tragedy of 'neck nominations'. We need to understand that, even when our young teenagers are aware of the risks associated with these things, they may be sucked into these behaviours to achieve the dopamine pleasure surge we have discussed.

One can also justifiably ask, has this drive for pleasure and risk-taking not always been with us? Did we not all survive it and just get on with it? In practice, although the age at which puberty arrives is getting lower, the process is just the same now as fifty years ago. But in the past, society, for all its faults, did exert much stricter limits during this crucial developmental stage, so there were not as many potential pitfalls, such as easy access to alcohol and substances. Before social media, the influence of the peer group may also have been more diluted. But we will be dealing with some of those issues later.

Impulsive Behaviour

Many people mix up impulsivity with risk-taking. In practice, they are quite different, particularly among adolescents. While the dopamine surge is critical to our understanding of risky behaviour and pleasure-seeking, the manner in which the brain controls our impulsive behaviour is different. The process of gradually gaining control of our impulsive behaviour is a slow, linear one that occurs between the ages of thirteen and thirty. It is of great importance because the pathways of control come more from our logical prefrontal cortex back to our emotional brain than the reverse. One of the main pathways of control involves our serotonin cable, which is gradually maturing during this phase.

This is of great importance, as self-harm and suicide attempts can involve impulsivity, and the younger the teenage brain, the more likely this is to be the case. This can sometimes explain tragic deaths by suicide of young teens, in whom the ability of the logical brain to check the impulse to self-harm is more limited than in later stages of development, when different influences may be present. Many professionals will have dealt with near-misses, when the act was impulsive in nature. One can also look at situations in which young teenagers have dived into rivers or lakes on impulse and it has ended in tragedy. So understanding the graded nature of impulse control is relevant.

Impulsivity is also important, as we will see later, in situations where a young adolescent is depressed. Self-harm may be more of a risk for younger adolescents. It is important to note that if we drink alcohol or use substances at any age – but particularly in our early or mid-teens – we may switch off the impulse-control pathway from our logical brain and leave ourselves exposed to tragic consequences.

THE POTENTIAL EFFECTS OF SUBSTANCE MISUSE/ABUSE

Over the last decade, there has been an increasing amount of evidence of the potentially deleterious effects of alcohol and some commonly used illegal drugs on the developing brain between the ages of thirteen and nineteen. Of greater concern is the increasing evidence of longer-term effects on the future adult brain. This is not surprising since, as we have already discussed, the brain of the adolescent is going through a critical period of structural and functional restructuring and is at its most vulnerable to the effects of these substances on its immature neurons and synapses. This can give rise later to longer-term structural and functional changes that can predispose the young emerging adult to significant depression, panic attacks, general anxiety, cognitive difficulties and addiction – and even potentially trigger episodes of schizophrenia.

To illustrate these difficulties, let's examine the effects of some common substances that are misused and sometimes abused, particularly between the ages of thirteen and nineteen: alcohol, nicotine and cannabis. There are many other possible examples, but what makes these three stand out is that their use is totally accepted by this age group and by many in society as being 'normal' and 'relatively safe'.

We can misuse or abuse any substance or activity. Misusing a substance is much more common. We see it every weekend in the form of binge drinking.

Here, we are not addicted to the substance but simply misuse it to get drunk, deal with stress or anxiety, or simply to fit in with our peer groups. A significant number of us, however, may become addicted to the substance; we call this 'substance abuse'.

It is worth examining what research tells us about the effects of these key substances on the developing brain and what messages you as a parent can draw from this.

Alcohol

There is a growing and worrying body of research building up about the effects of drinking significant amounts of alcohol on brain development between the ages of thirteen and nineteen – and particularly when such drinking starts before the age of fifteen. It is not surprising that alcohol misuse should occur regularly in this age group, given the dopamine surge and the lack of prefrontal cortex impulse control.

The major concern is that the effects of significant alcohol usage during this phase will lead to structural changes in the developing brain that will spill over later into cognitive and behavioural problems. A number of studies have, for example, demonstrated that adolescent drinking can lead to brain structure abnormalities, memory difficulties and poorer cognitive and academic performance.

Two important areas illustrating such structural abnormalities are the memory box (the hippocampus) and the prefrontal cortex. A significant number of imaging studies have demonstrated altered brain structure and function in alcohol-dependent and alcohol-abusing adolescents and young adults, compared with healthy individuals. Of major concern is that some studies have reported smaller prefrontal and hippocampal volumes, along with other changes. This is almost certainly the reason for the poorer cognitive ability and the memory difficulties already mentioned.

It has also been shown that, in some cases in which significant alcohol consumption under fifteen was involved, the hippocampus was smaller than in cases in which alcohol consumption had begun at a later stage. Clearly the age of onset of significant alcohol consumption is extremely significant for the future adult brain and the young adult. Of some concern here is that females who start drinking alcohol earlier seem to exhibit greater deficits than males, for example in changes within their prefrontal cortexes.

We know that early alcohol exposure (before the age of fifteen) can start to remodel the dopamine pleasure system in the brain, which we have already examined. The changes here may even change gene expression to make the young teenager much more likely to move further into the world of addiction. In other words, it may 'reset' the brain's pleasure system, making it much more likely that the future adult will develop alcohol or other addictions. Some research has found a 40 percent chance of lifetime alcohol dependence when teenagers started drinking at fourteen or younger, versus a 10 percent chance if they started drinking at twenty-one. Obviously other factors will influence our chances of developing alcohol addiction (particularly our genes and our family and social histories), but clearly the earlier the developing brain is exposed to alcohol, the greater the risk.

The damage early drinking may do to the memory box and the prefrontal cortex is significant, and can explain memory and cognitive difficulties that will not only cause learning difficulties during the teenage and school phases, but may continue into adult life. We also face a significantly increased risk of developing major depression if we start drinking significantly before the age of fifteen, and this may have its basis in these structural and functional changes.

We also know that, due to the above effects on the developing brain, those who start drinking under fifteen are up to seven times more likely to be involved in road traffic accidents. This makes sense, as alcohol removes the normal control of the prefrontal cortex. Those who start drinking under fifteen are also more exposed to unprotected sex, unplanned pregnancies, sexually transmitted diseases, sexual assaults, accidents leading to significant head injuries, increased aggression leading to fights and increased risks of violence and suicide.

Nicotine

As almost one-third of the Irish population still smokes, despite all the health warnings, it is of major concern that the vast majority were exposed to nicotine for the first time between the ages of ten and twenty. So it is well worth examining what this substance does to the brain during this phase of development.

There is now significant evidence that regular exposure to nicotine during this phase particularly targets the limbic emotional brain, and especially the dopamine pleasure system, in such a way as to reset it to face a lifetime of addiction to the substance. There is also evidence that it interfaces with the serotonin system so it may predispose the future addict to mood problems. Nicotine has also been found in this age group to trigger the stress box in such a way as to reduce normal anxiety levels. Because it is also feeding the dopamine system, the need for food can also be reduced. Meanwhile, the logical prefrontal cortex is too immature to counteract this process. Research has also shown that, unfortunately, the adolescent is also less likely to suffer unpleasant adverse effects from using nicotine, which puts them more at risk.

It is easy to see why we have a continuous stream of new nicotine addicts emerging from the adolescent female group, in particular. The combination of the pleasure-system buzz, the reduction in anxiety, and the built-in weight-control mechanism makes nicotine very desirable for adolescent females between the ages of twelve and eighteen. The tragedy is that they are being exposed to a drug which is capable of resetting their brains to crave the drug for life. All of this explains why tobacco companies are more than happy to see their products consumed by this age group.

One final note of concern is that, if adolescents' brains are exposed to nicotine regularly, the resetting of their pleasure systems has been shown to make them more prone to developing addictions to other drugs and substances during their lifetimes.

Cannabis

Cannabis, also known as marijuana or hash, is probably, after alcohol and nicotine, the most common substance misused or abused in Ireland. Its active ingredient is tetrahydrocannabinol (THC). It is commonly smoked along with nicotine. Here we are only going to focus on its effects on the developing brain.

Like alcohol and nicotine, there is increasing concern that chronic misuse of this drug during the key thirteen-to-nineteen stage of brain development may create long-term difficulties for the user. Research has shown, for example, that regular usage, particularly in the early teen phase, can damage critical connections being set up between key brain regions, resulting in structural and functional changes in the brain. These abnormalities were in interconnecting areas of the brain important in working memory, attention, decision-making, language and executive-functioning skills. Some of these structural and functional deficits may persist even if the user stops in his or her early twenties. It seems as if cannabis may in part be doing this by interfering with myelination, which is so critical in the brain's development. In one study, memory-related structures in the brains of such users were noted to have shrunk, possibly reflecting a decrease in actual neurons.

The final result is significant difficulties with memory, academic performance and everyday activities. As with alcohol and nicotine, the earlier the person uses the drug, the more likely they are to reset their dopamine pleasure system, predisposing them to long-term addiction not only to cannabis, but to other substances.

There is also a significant concern that regular daily use, particularly when it begins in the mid-teens, may predispose the young person to 'demotivational syndrome'. This is where the dopamine system becomes reset in such a way that the young person may end up lacking all motivation to become actively involved in real life. This can happen to them either in their teens or, as often noted by both authors, in their mid-twenties and onwards. We have seen this particularly in young males, and it is a condition that causes significant distress to parents and families, who often have to deal with the fallout.

Because of the effects on the developing brain, particularly on its dopamine system and on its connections between key regions, there is a strong link between cannabis use and early psychosis. There is much debate on whether the psychotic changes in schizophrenia are already present and simply triggered by the usage of cannabis. Whilst this is seen as the most likely scenario, there is increasing interest in whether significant usage may actually alter the developing brain, making schizophrenia more likely to appear. Whatever the mechanism, there is little doubt that cannabis use can trigger psychosis in those who are vulnerable.

There is also a lot of debate as to whether the usage of cannabis between the ages of twelve and nineteen triggers depression. Because of the changes seen in those using this drug regularly during this phase, it is of no surprise that, clinically, they are often seen concomitantly. For the present, there is probably not enough proof to say that cannabis definitely causes depression. But if the latter is present, it is crucial that managing cannabis usage be seen as a key part of managing the depression.

Finally, it should come as no surprise that, due to links between the pleasure box and the stress box in the emotional brain, it is quite common for the stress box to trigger panic attacks in the teenager and emerging young adult.

Headstrong's 'My World Survey' noted that: '49 percent of 20–21 year-olds, 55 percent of 22–23 year-olds and 58 percent of 24–25 year-olds state that they have smoked cannabis'. Whilst much of this may have been experimental rather than persistent use, it is a worrying statistic.

Think of cannabis if:

- You see round scorch marks or holes in the clothes of a young person (possibly due to ash falling from a joint)
- You notice a sudden increase in lack of motivation or apathy
- You notice a significant drop-off in memory or academic performance
- There is a sudden appearance of increased anxiety or panic attacks
- Mood seems to be dropping, but quite intermittently.

THE SLEEP TIME BOMB

We spend one-third of our lives asleep and yet many fail to understand just how critical to our brain sleep is. So let's first examine the role of sleep for the brain in general.

Sleep is essential for normal brain function because it allows our brains to heal/repair themselves and to reorganise/strengthen our memories. It involves two phases, which alternate: NREM (deep) sleep deals with healing and repair and REM (dream) sleep, with memories. In the former, the brain is quiet; in the latter, it bursts into activity – particularly in the second half of the sleep cycle.

These bursts of REM sleep last about twenty minutes, and they are when we dream. REM stands for 'rapid eye movement'; during this phase, our eyes oscillate back and forth. Dreams are created by the memory box in the brain passing information to parts of the brain where previous memories are stored, explaining their 'jumbled nature'.

During sleep, the brain secretes melatonin, making us drowsy, and generally switches off its serotonin and noradrenalin systems. On waking, melatonin levels fall, and the serotonin and noradrenalin systems switch on, making us alert.

The average sleep cycle is eight hours, but we now know that adolescents and emerging young adults require up to nine and a half hours of sleep to function normally. This compares to twelve hours for a newborn baby and eight hours for the normal ten-year-old or mature adult. We know through very recent studies that the brain is actively 'remodelling itself' even when asleep during the key thirteen-to-twenty-two period of brain development, which may explain the need for extra sleep during this period. We also know through research that the internal clock that controls sleep patterns works differently in adolescents and emerging adults than it does in adults. All parents can relate to this difference. Since time immemorial, parents have struggled to get their adolescents and young adults in their early twenties out of bed in the morning and to bed at a reasonable time at night.

Whilst there is a humorous side to this daily household conflict, there is also an underlying time bomb ticking away in our modern lives, which is leading to a lot of sometimes unrecognised difficulties.

Mother Nature, probably for evolutionary reasons, has designated that although teenagers and young adults require more sleep, their brains still release melatonin much later in the day than adults. Starting around puberty, melatonin, which we now know is important in inducing sleep, is released two hours later at night and persists later into the morning. Consequently, teens do not feel tired until later at night and have a hard time waking up early. Their higher morning melatonin levels make it more difficult for them to actually come to in the morning, as melatonin keeps them groggy and sluggish.

We can immediately see the difficulties. If the average rising time for getting ready for school is, for example, 7.30 to 8 AM, and the young person has not gone to bed until midnight or later, then he or she suffers from a daily shortage of one and a half to two hours of sleep. This can build up into a significant weekly level of sleep deprivation, which can have very serious consequences for the developing brain, which we will examine in a moment. In one study of high school students in the USA, it was noted that the majority of teenagers were sleep-deprived, with up to 20 percent falling asleep in class (Carskadon, 2002).

Another issue is that, as we have already noted, most of our REM dream sleep occurs in the second half of our sleep cycle – especially just before we are due to wake. If adolescents and those in their early twenties are woken out of that cycle too early, they miss out on some REM sleep which is so crucial for the developing brain.

'But what about the weekend?' one might ask. Well, there are some experts who feel that the pattern of teenagers going to bed much later at the weekend and getting up much later is creating its own problems. It makes it difficult for the teenagers to make up for the sleep they lost during the week, and suddenly changing their schedule at the weekend means they experience something like jet lag for a few days after the weekend. You may know what it is like to experience six-hour jet lag: welcome to the world of the teenager.

Add in some other significant factors present in the lives of modern teenagers and young adults – bedroom TVs and computers, smartphones that stay on all night so they can keep in contact minute by minute with friends, and excessive alcohol consumption at weekends – and you have a potent mixture to cause significant sleep deprivation in this age group.

Why should we be concerned about this issue at all? Well, increasing amounts of research are revealing just how important it is to try and counteract this sleep shortage.

We know that the brains of teenagers who lack sleep have higher glucocortisol levels. We also know that chronic sleep deprivation in this group can lead to increased risks of depression, accidents (including road traffic accidents), anxiety and aggression, and also to poorer academic performance, sleepiness during the daytime and greater difficulties with emotional regulation and memory. I would refer those who would like to know more about this to Richard Millman's excellent article on the subject (see bibliography).

Before I leave this section, here are a few more tips for parents:

- There is ample evidence that your adolescent between the ages of thirteen and twenty-two needs at least nine hours of sleep per night.

- There is a lot to be said for a decision to strongly promote a bedtime of 11 PM at the latest, particularly during school times.

- There is also a lot to be said for insisting that smartphones be left in the living room and that Internet access is cut off after 11 PM at night. This will greatly increase the chance of the young person getting sufficient sleep, while also greatly reducing the risk of night-time cyberbullying and the resultant suicide risk (more on this later).

- Be aware of – and even discuss with your teenager – the weekend jet-lag effect. Try to get them to go to bed at a reasonable time on at least one weekend day and to wake up before midday. At least ensure that a Sunday night-time schedule is enforced.

- If your child is doing major exams, then it is better for them to try to go to bed at a normal time rather than cram. It will be more beneficial, cognitively, for them to have sufficient sleep.

- There is evidence that a bedtime goal of 11 PM will reduce significantly the risk of your child developing major depression in adolescence.

- Remember, as we have already discussed, that until your child is eighteen, you are essentially acting as their prefrontal cortex, so you may have to take a firm line on some of the above issues.

- Unlike school, college lectures are not structured, so adolescent screenagers have to set their own boundaries. It becomes the norm for them to have lots of (often alcohol-fuelled) social late nights. Their sleep cycles become disturbed and the weekend jet-lag effect is really common. This can lead to a host of secondary issues, such as missing lectures, falling behind in studies, experiencing increasing anxiety and, in those vulnerable to it, having an increasing risk of depression. It is worth discussing all this with your screenager before he or she gets to college, even detailing your own experiences if they are relevant.

- When we are waking up, it is the emotional brain which comes to first, before the logical brain. This is why so many adults and adolescents notice symptoms of anxiety first thing in the morning – even before their logical brain has had a chance to review what is coming up that day. This may in some cases relate to anxiety-provoking dreams they have just before waking up. Many adolescents may begin to 'abnormalise' themselves for getting these normal feelings of anxiety. Enda will be dealing more with this subject later in the book.

THE POTENTIAL EFFECTS OF ABUSE AND BULLYING

It is well worth examining briefly the negative effects of some of these key environmental influences on the developing brain. In general, bullying and abuse can significantly influence the delicate pathways and structures in the brain of the adolescent and emerging young adult. We will be dealing with some of these issues in their own right later, but here we will just examine the neurobiological risks.

Of all of the possible stressors experienced by our developing screenagers, abuse and bullying are the most likely to cause difficulties and are associated with much higher levels of depression, anxiety – and, indeed, self-harm and suicide. But what effects do they have on the developing brain of the adolescent and emerging young adult? Well, some recent evidence should give rise to concern.

Take, for example, the study that investigated the effects on 848 young adults aged eighteen to twenty-five of significant verbal bullying by members of their peer groups in late childhood and early adolescence (ages eleven to fourteen). Neuroimaging showed that in some of the subjects, there was an abnormality in a part of the brain known as the corpus callosum, a thick bundle of fibres that connects the right and left hemispheres of the developing brain (the 'brain bridge' we mentioned in Chapter One). The average reduction in the size of the corpus callosum was 40 percent. Of major interest was that the neurons involved showed a reduction in myelination, which is critically important, as we have discussed, in making brain connectivity more efficient. They also showed that substantial peer bullying of this type was associated with twice the risk of significant depression and three times the risk of significant anxiety (Teicher et al, 2010). This research followed up on previous research tracking a group of adults between the ages of eighteen and twenty-five who had experienced significant parental verbal abuse between the ages of three and thirteen, which also noted changes involving key connections within the brain (Choi et al, 2009).

Other research on similar bullying showed that affected boys had experienced a 'resetting' of their stress systems, with much higher levels of glucocortisol. As we know that this can lead to damage in the hippocampus or memory box, this may explain why teenagers who are being bullied are at higher risk of memory problems and depression. This information on bullying and the adolescent brain can be equated with similar previous evidence that sexual or severe physical abuse can lead to higher glucocortisol levels, a smaller hippocampus when the adolescents become adults, and a higher rate of depression in the future.

Consider, for example, research carried out on one hundred ninety-three volunteers who had experienced childhood verbal, physical or sexual abuse, physical or emotional neglect, bereavement, parental separation or parental discord (Teicher et al, 2013). Three sub-regions of the hippocampus or memory box were between 5.8 percent and 6.5 percent smaller in such volunteers than in those who reported no maltreatment. Once again, the assumed cause was high glucocortisol damaging the hippocampus due to the stress system being reset to a higher level as a result of the abuse.

We must be much more aware of any form of severe stress created – in particular, by the forms of abuse investigated by Teicher – on the developing brain. Are verbal and other forms of bullying that gay and lesbian teenagers experience reshaping their brains, making them more prone to depression and more at risk of self-harm and suicide? Is this similarly affecting some young males who may not be gay but are still targeted and labelled as being gay? The wounds this may be leaving on their adolescent developing brain may be considerable!

It is also worth mentioning another common cause of stress: the pressure on young teenagers to have sex. From a developmental point of view, as we have already discussed, young teenage males are more interested in sex for pleasure and less for intimacy. Young female teenagers are more interested in intimacy and friendship, and less driven toward sex. But both groups come under great pressure from their peers to be seen to be sexually active. I recall one female class explaining to me that if a couple was going out for three months, this would be seen as a 'serious relationship' and sex would be expected.

The difficulty with this is that many young girls are feeling pressurised to have sex earlier than they are really comfortable with. It is interesting that, as we will see later in the book, research has shown this to be one of the common reasons for self-harm. On the other side, young men are, unfortunately, less inclined to think about the consequences of unprotected sex, as their dopamine surges quickly overrule such concerns. But they feel real pressure if they are not seen by their peers to be 'scoring'; they can become increasingly anxious about this. The real risks appear when they are described as being 'gay' if they are not having sex with girls – even if they are heterosexual. This form of bullying is extremely damaging, as we have noted.

These are areas for possible future neuroscientific research, as we may be losing some teenagers and young emerging adults to suicide because of these often subtle forms of bullying, due to changes in their vulnerable developing brains.

In summary, we need to become much more aware that bullying – even of the simple verbal type – during the crucial adolescent phase, in particular, can leave long-term scars on the developing brain. If we don't, we will continue to see the consequences of depression, anxiety, addiction and suicide in the adolescent, emerging-adult and future-adult populations.

STRESS, RESILIENCE AND THE DEVELOPING BRAIN

There is increasing evidence that, from birth to thirty, the developing brain is highly susceptible to overactivity of our stress systems. This can occur, as we have already seen, due to any number of external environmental experiences, such as bullying or physical, verbal, emotional or sexual abuse. The common denominator seems to relate to higher levels of glucocorticol, which have the capacity to reshape the structure and functioning of the developing brain. This is increasingly seen as one of the real risk factors for the development of depression in the adolescent and the young adult.

We have already noted how the hippocampus or memory box is particularly sensitive to bullying and abuse, but we are all unique – we all have varying levels of resilience, which affect how well our stress systems can cope with what life throws at us. Forty to sixty percent of how we cope with stress, and the resulting potential for adolescents to develop anxiety/depression as adults, is probably genetically set up at birth. The rest is down to how our environment affects such genes – a process we call epigenetics.

One of the genes involved in predisposing us to anxiety and depression is responsible for the manufacture and general levels in the brain of a key protein called the 'serotonin transporter' (the SERT molecule). This little protein has been under observation for the past decade as a potential culprit for anxiety/depression. The gene which controls the levels of this protein is passed on through generations. All of us have either short or long copies. It has been known for some time that those with two long copies are much more 'resilient' to stress than those with either one long and one short copy or particularly two short copies. The latter two are much more likely to suffer from anxiety and, to a lesser extent, depression. They produce fewer SERT proteins, so more serotonin builds up in synapses within the mood cable serotonin serves. Their serotonin system is 'over-hyped'. Although this had been known for some time, it did not explain why this triggered anxiety/depression in some people and not others.

The key seems to lie in the stress box and, to a lesser extent, some parts of the prefrontal cortex. It now seems as if those with two short versions of this gene have stress boxes that are constantly hyper-vigilant, even when they are not directly attacked by stress. Those with two long versions do not demonstrate this vulnerability. It seems as if the short version also affects our prefrontal cortex and memory boxes, reducing the normal ability of the brain to control this tendency. Over time, people with the short gene have more difficulties coping with stress, anxiety, depression and suicidal potential – all potentially triggered by successive/significant bouts of stress.

If we grow up in an environment which encourages the stress box to be constantly overactive – such as a very anxious, perfectionist, deprived or abusive house – we will develop pathways by adulthood which predispose us to anxiety. When real-life pressures come, as they inevitably will, those of us with short versions of the gene will have hypersensitive stress boxes that are easily sent into 'overdrive'. This causes a huge outpouring of glucocortisol, which can lead to an increased risk of developing anxiety/depression. Those of us with the long versions are less at risk. They seem also to ruminate less about the potential negative possibilities major stress might bring about. Many feel that this is the main difference between the two groups.

There is a growing feeling that this mix of short-version genes and epigenetic environmental stress is a classical model explaining why some are more vulnerable to stress anxiety and, to a lesser extent, depression. In some children, the short versions intermingle with early childhood stressors like separation and neglect to set up anxiety pathways. As we grow older and stress increases, these pathways become more consolidated. If children grow up in calm, supportive homes that encourage them to gradually learn to handle stress, they are less likely to develop such paths.

This 'resilience' gene is part of a wider pool of genes predisposing people to anxiety. Although a constant 'background' factor predisposing us to cope (or not cope) with stress, expression of this gene is completely dependent on how stress activates it. How much does our family environment affect the expression of our genes? We now know that a complex dynamic is involved. It was initially thought that the overall atmosphere in a particular home would be the only factor relevant. It now seems that the position of the child, their individual personality and the way they relate to their parents and siblings all contribute to the 'melting pot', with the final result intermingling with their genes to determine how susceptible to problems particular brain pathways are.

This helps to explain why one child might be more prone than another to anxiety, depression and addiction, despite being reared in a similar environment. Love is the most positive environmental influence. Next is resilience, our learned ability to cope positively with the stresses of life. Stresses such as rejection, the absence of love and abuse are the most damaging.

For parents who may wonder how all this information is of any practical use, a recent seminal research project demonstrates its importance. The project was carried out by a large research team including a colleague, Barbara Sahakian, professor of Clinical Neuropsychology at the University of Cambridge's Department of Psychiatry and Behavioural and Clinical Neurosciences Institute. They examined morning salivary levels of glucocorti-

sol in a cohort of adolescents and co-related these with any history of depressive symptoms. In the study, they measured levels of glucocortisol in saliva
from two separate large groups of teenagers. The first group of 660 provided
samples on four school mornings within one week and then again twelve
months later. A second group of 1,198 teenagers gave samples over three
school mornings.

The researchers then divided the teenagers into four sub-groups. These
varied from Group 1, which consisted of teenagers with normal levels of glucocortisol and less severe symptoms of depression, to Group 4, which included
teenagers with higher levels of glucocortisol and more severe symptoms of
depression. Tracking the teenagers for three years, the team found that those
in Group 4 were, on average, seven times more likely than those in Group 1 to
develop clinical depression, and two to three times more likely than those in
the other two groups. Further analysis showed that boys in Group 4 were fourteen times more likely to develop clinical depression than those in Group 1,
and two to four times more likely to develop it than boys in either of the other
two groups. Girls with similarly elevated glucocortisol levels were only up to
four times more likely to develop the condition.

There was much to ponder in this research. Firstly, it highlighted the critical connection between our stress system and our vulnerability to future illnesses such as depression. Secondly, it highlighted a potential biomarker
(salivary glucocortisol) which might help us to distinguish which boys with
depressive symptoms were more likely to go on to develop significant depression. Thirdly, it noted that girls seem to have higher basal levels of glucocortisol than boys, but that boys with higher-than-usual basal levels seem to have
more significant long-term mental health difficulties.

There is little doubt, then, that the critical time to intervene to try and
reduce long-term problems with depression – and most likely anxiety and
other mental health difficulties – is when your child is a teenager or young
emerging adult. We will be examining later what we can do to improve
resilience and to learn how to deal with emotional distress. As parents and,
later, mentors, we can play important roles in assisting in this process.

THE IMPORTANCE OF LIFESTYLE

We have already dealt with some key lifestyle issues, such as sleep and sub-stance misuse, but it is important before leaving this section to examine the importance to the developing brain of exercise and diet.

Exercise

Simple exercise is one of the most powerful tools at our disposal in the battle to stay physically and mentally well throughout our lives. A rapidly increasing volume of evidence strongly supports this statement. Regular exercise posi-tively regulates cognitive functions, mood, motivation and the ability to cope with stress, and strengthens the immune system. It improves memory and the ability to plan and problem-solve. It helps lift depression, reduces feelings of helplessness and alleviates anxiety. It also improves interest and drive, allevi-ates the negative effects of chronic stress, and increases bodily defences against infections and cancers.

Exercise has many positive effects in the brain. It increases levels of a crucial brain enzyme called BDNF and also connections in the neurons of key mood structures – particularly the prefrontal cortex and hippocampus – and pathways. This is important at all times, but particularly in depression, as we will see later. It increases activity in the serotonin and noradrenalin mood cables and improves motivation by increasing activity in the dopamine mood cable. It also increases levels of endorphin 'feel-good' messengers in the brain, encourages the produc-tion of new cells in the hippocampus or memory box, and reduces levels of the stress hormone glucocortisol. All this combines to improve mood, general brain function and memory, to reduce stress and to keep us mentally well.

But what evidence do we have as to its effects on the developing brain? A recent analysis of multiple trials carried out around the world examining the links between exercise and academic performance of children and teenagers between the ages of six and eighteen showed a significant positive relationship. The mechanisms of action seemed to involve all of the above, but particularly the increase in brain-growth factors like BDNF, which are critical in forming healthy new connections in the developing brain. (For more on this, see Singh et al, 2012, in the bibliography.)

This came on top of other research which had already shown that active children as young as ten already had bigger hippocampuses or memory boxes than their unfit peers. This is a staggering piece of research in that it shows just how our lifestyles can have significant effects on the actual structures of our developing brains, not to mention their functioning. The same children, not surprisingly, did better on memory tests. (For more on this, see Chaddock et al, 2010, in the bibliography.)

Other research is showing that adolescent and adult brains do, however, respond differently to exercise. The positive message here is that the adolescent brain, through changes like increasing BDNF, seems to get longer-lasting responses to exercise than the adult brain. This was seen to improve cognition, memory and mood.

In terms of the emerging young adult between twenty and thirty, there is a risk that exercise can fall by the way. Since this is often the time that significant mental health difficulties arise, it is particularly important that the message is conveyed to adolescents and young adults that staying fit and exercising is often the shortcut to staying mentally well, apart from all its other physical benefits. It is also well worth pointing out the benefits to young college students, for example, of increased cognitive and memory performance due to an exercise regime: there are really multiple benefits.

The message here for parents is to try to involve your children in any form of sport or exercise from as early an age as possible. We should be leading by example. It is hard, if we are couch potatoes ourselves, to be advising our young adolescents to exercise more. There are also great advantages to involving children and young teenagers in team sports, as much as possible, as there is also a social dimension to them.

Thirty minutes of brisk exercise three to five times a week is ideal. Any form of exercise is acceptable – walking, jogging, weightlifting, swimming, football, hurling – and all are equally effective. The preference, though, would always be for aerobic exercise and, if possible, team sports.

Diet

It has been well documented by the Department of Health, the media and many health experts that too many of our children and adolescents are either overweight or obese. This is part of a national obesity problem, which is leading to significant health risks such as Type 2 diabetes and heart disease. In 2007, 19 percent of boys and 17 percent of girls between the ages of thirteen and seventeen were overweight or obese. That year, 38 percent of the population was overweight and 23 percent was obese, according to the Health Service Executive's 'HSE Framework for Action on Obesity 2008–2012'.

We know from the same report that overweight or obese children and adolescents seemed to continue to be overweight or obese into adulthood. The report noted that boys who are obese at thirteen or older are twice as likely to be obese as adults, and that two out of every three girls who are obese at the same age will also be obese as adults. In a 2014 *Lancet* global review of overweight and obesity worldwide, 25 percent of Irish boys under twenty were overweight or obese (almost 7 percent of these were obese) and statistics for girls in this age group were similar. Even more alarming, almost two-thirds of our male population over the age of twenty were overweight or obese, and almost half of our females fell into the same category.

This is clearly an alarming situation for the physical health of our adult population and also our screenagers. But what are the consequences for our developing brain during the adolescent and young-adult phases?

Some research done in the USA, where there is an even greater problem than in Ireland, is extremely worrying. More than 50 percent of American teens are overweight or obese and thirty to 40 percent of those who are obese show signs of 'metabolic syndrome'. This syndrome is characterised by high blood pressure, low levels of 'good' HDL cholesterol, high triglycerides (body fats), a large waistline and insulin resistance; it is seen as a real risk factor for future heart attacks and full-blown diabetes.

What's important for our discussion, though, is that researchers have been able to show key structural changes in the brains of teenagers diagnosed with obesity and metabolic syndrome. The hippocampus or memory box was actually found to be smaller in those scanned, and there were also worrying findings of disruptions of key connections between the two sides of the brain, and between the prefrontal cortex and the limbic emotional brain. These adolescents were also noted to have significantly reduced cognitive functional capacity, lower overall IQs, memory, concentration and attention problems, and poorer academic performance (Yau et al, 2012).

Although such data is clearly related to significant obesity, it throws up concerns that the diets of our children and adolescents may pose risks beyond simple physical risks to their health. If poor diet leading to obesity is already affecting at least one-fifth of our adolescent population, then we may begin to find the developing brains of our teenagers and emerging young adults actually being reshaped by the food they are imbibing, with long-term consequences for their future.

From the mental health point of view, poor diet will lead to an increased risk of clinical depression, particularly if it leads to overweight or obesity. We know that abdominal obesity leads to an increased release of inflammatory markers into the blood, which can travel to the brain and increase the risk of clinical depression.

Obesity can, and unfortunately often does, lead to a significant risk of bullying by peers, as we will discuss later. We have already dealt with the potential brain-structuring changes related to such verbal bullying. One of the other potentially serious consequences of this type of bullying may be a major drop in self-esteem, leading to clinical depression, self-harm and suicide.

The message here is similar to that regarding exercise and the developing brain. As parents, we need to understand that the developing brain is extremely sensitive to diet. What is needed is a return by the whole family to a simple balanced diet within the budget limits of the household. Sweet drinks, including all diet minerals, should disappear completely. The pattern for teenager obesity is usually set earlier on by the family diet, so, as parents, we have a real responsibility to start introducing our children to a healthy diet as early as possible. If we wait until our child becomes an obese teenager and young emerging adult, we may have already lost the battle.

Here are a few simple tips for parents to keep in mind when it comes to their own diets, as well as those of their adolescent screenagers:

- Include a sensible mix of fresh fish (particularly oily types like salmon, mackerel and tuna), eggs (especially free-range), meat, vegetables, cereals, nuts, flax seeds/oils, grains and fruit.

- Prepare your own food, and avoid fast food and highly processed packaged food.

- Reduce all portion sizes across the board and across all age groups. This is absolutely critical.

- Instead of focusing on any one adolescent who may be obese, it is much better to concentrate on making the diet of the whole house much healthier.

- Avoid high-stimulant drinks like coffee and Coke, which many with depression and anxiety use in abundance.

- Avoid high-sugar 'hits', as bouncing blood-sugar levels are not helpful to brain functioning.

- Try to completely avoid all minerals and fruit juices, which are often very high in sugar.

- Avoid 'extreme diets' sometimes recommended by alternative 'experts', which often exclude key nutrients/supplements.

- The main supplements accepted as useful for our developing and mature brains are omega-3 fish oils, and the key B vitamins folic acid, B6 and B12.

- Instead of focusing on diets, it is better to focus on when, how much, what and – most of all – why we are eating.

- It is better to examine the whole area of diet as a long-term lifestyle issue, rather than focusing on short-term quick-fix measures that are usually bound to fail.

TECHNOLOGY AND THE DEVELOPING BRAIN

The capacity of technology to influence the developing brain is well worth examining in detail. This includes TV, videos, mobile phones with instant text messaging, smartphones, computers, tablets and so on – all of which are becoming faster and more efficient. The Internet has literally changed how we view the world. Many feel it has the power to negatively change our developing brains, but others challenge this view.

Many parents have a reasonable grasp of modern technology but are still miles behind their teenagers and emerging young adults in terms of usage. Usually, by the time parents have come to terms with one thing, our children have already moved on to the next. For example, our teenagers are fed up with their parents wanting to be friends with them on Facebook to keep an eye on their antics, so they are beginning to move en masse to applications like WhatsApp, where they can have unmonitored communications. They are also moving away from more traditional sites to avoid being caught out by future employers examining, for example, their Facebook posts.

In this section, though, we will focus on research examining whether or not this new world of information technology and instant communications is actually damaging the brain at a particularly sensitive stage of development. There is little doubt that, whether we like it or not, the lives of our young teenagers and emerging adults are totally dominated by this new phenomenon, something that is increasingly being seen as a worldwide issue. There has been some excellent research done in the past few years highlighting the extent of the problem.

In 2010, a Kaiser Family Foundation survey that looked at the usage of technology by young people between the ages of eight and eighteen unveiled the following staggering statistics:

- Those surveyed spent an average of seven and a half hours on a typical day on non-school-based entertainment media technology.

- Many were multitasking, watching TV, looking at a computer and texting all at the same time. In such cases, if the time they spent on each task was added up separately, the time they spent on technology would actually have worked out at around ten hours a day.

- Such technology multitasking was done at the expense of many other non-technology activities, such as exercise, chores, spending time with friends and completing school work.

- The average breakdown of time spent with each form of media was: four and a half hours watching TV, two and a half hours on computers, one and a quarter hours on video games, and fifteen minutes watching movies.

- A quarter of those surveyed accessed social media sites more than ten times a day, and half accessed them at least once a day.

- More than 75 percent of teenagers had a mobile phone, and texting was their main form of mobile communication. Girls sent an average of eighty texts a day and boys sent an average of thirty. Of those teenagers who were able to drive, 50 percent admitted to texting while driving.

- Thirty-one percent multitasked with technology while doing homework, and 25 percent admitted to doing it up to a quarter of the time.

- Heavy technology users' grades were noted to have suffered significantly in more than 40 percent of cases, compared to just 23 percent of light users'.

If we accept that this survey was done in the States more than four years ago, and that young people in Ireland have embraced the world of digital technology and smartphones with gusto, then it seems likely that the above data would equally apply here in Ireland, with increasing technology dependence in the intervening period. Recent research we, which will discuss later, supports this assumption.

The fact that our teenagers and young emerging adults are becoming extremely dependent on digital technology, and particularly on their mobile/smartphones and social media sites, has been highlighted by further research at a worldwide level. Once again, this research is extremely revealing as to the extent of the problem.

In 2010, Susan Moeller, a journalism professor at the University of Maryland in the USA, studied two hundred students aged eighteen to twenty-one who had been asked to 'unplug' from all forms of media for twenty-four hours, particularly digital social media. Her findings attracted worldwide interest, so her research was extended eventually to include one thousand students from five continents, in what became known as 'The World Unplugged' or the '24 Hours Without Media' project. The students were asked to detail their experiences of being unplugged. She summarised her findings, many of which were quite worrying, in an excellent 2012 article (see bibliography).

- The first key finding was that many of the participants used the terms 'addiction' or 'dependence' after their experiences of being 'unplugged' for twenty-four hours.

- Some noted that they felt sad or depressed when unplugged.

- Some noted how removal of their mobile phones, for example, unveiled significant loneliness in their real lives.

- Some commented on how bored they were, which exposed just how difficult it was for them to fill the time – in a creative manner – that they normally spent plugged in.

- A significant number failed to make it through the twenty-four hours unplugged. They reconnected with their digital worlds.

- Many noted that they were constantly texting and on Facebook, and that they could live without TV and newspapers, but 'couldn't survive' without smartphones, iPads, iPods and similar devices.

- Some described the removal of their links to the Internet as like being 'turned off life support', whilst others felt that their mobile phones were almost an extension of themselves.

- Some noted how much their face-to-face social interactions with their parents or friends were enhanced by the removal of technology for the day.

- Many were surprised by just how much social networking had been distracting them from real life, in terms of both time spent and potential other activities.

- Many students commented on the benefits of being unplugged, including a sense of liberation or freedom, more contentment, and time to do things they had planned to do. Despite this, very few planned to repeat the exercise.

But what do we know about the use of technology in Ireland, amongst our own adolescents? Well, the 2014 report 'Net Children Go Mobile: Initial Findings from Ireland', based on an EU/DIT research project, revealed the following:

- Smartphones stand out as the most-used device for Internet access on a daily basis by nine to sixteen-year-olds in all contexts. Thirty-five percent used smartphones, while 29 percent used laptops and 27 percent used tablets.

- Most Internet use is, in fact still at home. Sixty-three percent of children report using the Internet several times a day or at least once a day at home.

- Forty-six percent of children access the Internet from their own bedrooms on a daily basis, and 22 percent say they do so several times per day.

- Forty-four percent of nine-to-sixteen-year-olds own a game console, 40 percent a smartphone, 28 percent a tablet, and 27 percent a mobile phone that is not a smartphone.

- Entertainment, such as listening to music and watching video clips, continues to be the most popular online activity for all age groups.

- The next most popular use of the Internet is visiting social networking sites, especially for teenagers, for whom this is – with listening to music – the most-reported online activity.

- Instant messaging applications such as Skype and WhatsApp are used daily by more than a third of thirteen-to-sixteen-year-olds.

- Ninety percent of all fifteen- and sixteen-year-olds have a profile on a social networking site. Notably, almost 40 percent of eleven- and twelve-year-olds also have social-networking profiles, despite the age limit of thirteen for most social networking services.

- Eighty percent of children who use social networking primarily use Facebook.

- Ten percent of fifteen- and sixteen-year-olds say they use Twitter as their primary social-networking platform.

- Thirty-six percent of children between the ages of nine and sixteen have profiles on a media-sharing platform.

- Instagram is the most popular media-sharing platform. Forty-two percent of children between the ages of nine and sixteen say it's the one they use most often. Thirty-four percent say they use YouTube most often.

- Twenty percent of children in Ireland say they have been bothered by something on the Internet in the past year, a doubling of the figure reported by the research network EU Kids Online in 2011.

- Twenty-five percent of thirteen- and fourteen-year-olds and 37 percent of fifteen- and sixteen-year-olds say they have experienced something that bothered them or that they wished they hadn't seen.

- Twenty-two percent of children have experienced a form of bullying, online or offline. Thirteen percent of thirteen- and fourteen-year-olds say they have been bullied on a social-networking site.

Girls are more likely to experience bullying than boys, and are more likely to say they were upset by it.

- One of the risks that young people most often encounter is seeing potentially harmful user-generated content. Thirty-five percent of girls aged thirteen to sixteen have encountered some form of harmful content. Fifteen percent encountered hate messages, 14 percent anorexic or bulimic content, 9 percent self-harm sites, 8 percent sites discussing suicide, 7 percent sites discussing experiences with drugs.

- Forty-seven percent of older teenagers have seen sexual images in the past twelve months, compared to 11 percent of younger children.

- About half of older teenagers who had seen sexual images said they were upset by the experience.

- Ten percent of thirteen- and fourteen-year-olds and 22 percent of fifteen- and sixteen-year-olds report having received sexual messages online. Four percent said they were 'very' or 'a little' upset.

- Twenty-two percent have had contact online with people they have never met face-to-face.

Based on these major pieces of research, it is easy to understand why there is increasing concern about the long-term effects of this 'technological cultural revolution', which is influencing the lives of our children and young adults so much. There is little doubt that many adults are also caught up in this world, but at least their brains are mature. The key question is whether the effects of digital technology and social media are altering the young developing brain in a negative manner, with possible long-term consequences for our screenagers.

Part of the difficulty in answering this question is that there is little real neuroscientific evidence to support or deny this possibility. This is in contrast to the effects of diet, exercise, abuse and substance misuse, for which clear structural and functional data has emerged. Most of the evidence to date has come from more classical behavioural studies. One concern is that the developing brain is laying down key pathways and connections during this phase, and that negative consequences of technology use will end up leaving long-term emotional and cognitive difficulties when the young person becomes an adult. Choudhury and McKinney, in an excellent review of this issue, argue that there is little solid neuroscientific evidence at this moment in time that digital technology is leaving long-term scars on the developing brains of our adolescents (see bibliography).

One of the difficulties in this debate is that through the process of neuro-plasticity, the capacity of the brain to change in response to environmental factors is being seen on the one hand as very flexible and adaptable and on the other as leading to fixed long-term defects in the developing brain. So what is the truth? I feel that we can make the following conclusions:

- There is nothing wrong, per se, with modern technology, and it is here to stay whether we like it or not.

- As with everything, whether it is being used in a healthy manner or being misused or abused determines how big an impact it has on our lives.

- It will have both positive and negative effects on the emotional, social and cognitive development of the brain and young person.

- We need to examine the emotional effects in relation to empathy and concerns that young people are becoming more narcissistic ('it's all about me').

- As parents, we need to be aware of both and try to mitigate the more negative effects.

- All the changes that happen as a result of technology use must be affecting the normal plasticity of the developing brain but, so far, we are not seeing any evidence in scans of the kinds of fixed changes that result from other activities.

- It would seem that the brains of screenagers are not developing harmful fixed pathways, just different pathways to their parents when they were young. Only time will tell whether these changes are better or not.

- There may be secondary issues in relation to spending too much time on technology, physical effects such as obesity, lack of sleep and lack of physical exercise. As we have already seen, if severe, these may end up affecting the developing brain functionally and structurally.

- One final note of concern is TV and movie violence. There is evidence that repeated exposure may reduce grey-matter tissue in the left side of a key part of the prefrontal cortex called the orbitofrontal cortex in healthy male adolescents. This is an important part of the logical brain. It controls the tendency toward aggressive behaviour and is also important in empathy. Only time and further research will reveal whether this will lead to significant difficulties when these adolescents become adults, in relation to violence and a lack of empathy.

Later we will examine how parents should approach the practical issues of dealing with technology in relation to their teenagers. But it would be helpful for many parents, before we leave this section, to have a more in-depth overview of just what are seen as the main concerns. I found Jim Taylor's 2012 book *Raising Generation Tech* to be extremely helpful in drawing up this summary up and I would strongly advise parents rearing children and young emerging adults of all ages to read this book if they would like to get a balanced picture of the effects of technology.

It is important to grasp that many of the issues we are going to discuss are ones that affect the teenage and young emerging adult brain even in the absence of technology. The real debate is whether, in some cases, technology is adding to difficulties that would naturally be present during this phase. I would also advise parents to try to apply some of the information below to themselves, as this will make it more relevant to them.

We can group the main issues into three categories: cognitive effects, emotional and social effects, and lifestyle and general health effects.

Cognitive Effects

Here we are interested mainly in what negative and positive effects technology and multitasking can have on key cognitive or thinking domains such as attention, memory and decision-making.

- One of the main concerns about the shift to digital technology is that the brain is no longer allowed sufficient time to concentrate on any given piece of information or task. This is unlike in the past when, while reading a book or an article in the paper, there was more time to digest the material. The key here is distraction: there is no doubt that it is much harder to get a more in-depth grasp of a subject when this is present.

- One of the objections to this new world is that the brain may be being retrained to look at data more superficially and may therefore fail to understand it in depth.

- Because memory retention is based on the brain's ability to focus attention on something, it seems inevitable that those who use technology a lot at this age will struggle to retain information. This has a lot of implications for education, as we noted in relation to previous research, which showed that grades were often affected.

- Since the developing brain is being bombarded with information, much of which is of little use, information overload is a significant issue. The question has to be asked, is the developing brain losing its ability to think its way through this mound of data and come up with suitable plans and solutions? Does this make our young people less creative, less adaptable and less adept at finding solutions? Are young people falling into the trap of assuming that information is the solution to problems, rather than what one does with the information?

- One could ask whether the increasing epidemic of self-harm and suicide is an expression of the resulting reduction in problem solving ability.

- Among the key issues noted in the research detailed above were the problems created by media and other multitasking. We know that multitasking can affect the quality of the tasks performed. This is clearly illustrated by the examples of texting when driving, and using social media/texting and watching TV when studying. There also has to be a concern about the stress the developing brain is under when trying to multitask with different forms of media for up to ten hours a day.

- We know that technology can also contribute to major deficits in young people's decision-making. As we have already detailed, the prefrontal cortex of the developing brain is quite immature, so it is really no surprise that teenagers in particular, but also early emerging young adults, make many decisions which are clearly wrong. But it does seem as if technology not only makes this easier to do but also potentially more destructive. For a clear example of this, one only has to look at the whole area of cyberbullying, with suicide as a potential consequence. Other areas include 'sexting' or sending pictures of a sexual nature by phone, and putting up on Facebook examples of stupid or even dangerous behaviour which may have long-term consequences for employment.

- The biggest problem with technology and decision-making is that it is 'instant' in nature, so there is little time for proper deliberation on issues. In the past, they may have ended up making the same decision, but chances are that they would have at least thought about it and possibly engaged with their peers or family before-hand. So in many ways technology is aggravating the developing brain's difficulties with impulsivity and risk-taking.

- The biggest advantage of the early introduction of technology to our children, teenagers and young emerging adults is that they learn the cognitive skills necessary to succeed in a world where technology will lie at the heart of future progress for both them and for society in general.

- It has also been shown that our visual and spatial skills and reaction times are significantly enhanced by the use of technologies such as video games.

- We are moving into a new world where there will be so much information coming at young people – far more than their parents had to deal with – that there is a body of opinion which believes that knowing how to retrieve information may be more important than simply remembering it.

Emotional and Social Effects

This is where some of the greatest concern has been in relation to this new world of technology and the developing brain. Many have become concerned about issues relating to empathy-loss and narcissism, the dangers of confusing virtual reality with reality itself, the seemingly overpowering nature of social media, and how all of these will impact on the developing brain. But there are, as we noted above, many positive effects which we must also consider.

- In the past, young people learnt their value systems and senses of self through their families, friends and peers. This is how they formed their senses of identity.

- A significant concern is the increasing tendency of young people to see themselves and judge their worth through social media. Nowadays, young people see themselves more and more through the eyes of others in social media sites like Facebook. In many ways, this allows them to form a virtual-reality sense of self which has nothing to do with the real them and more to do with the number of Facebook 'friends' they have. It is almost as if they are creating a hologram of themselves in a different dimension.

- The problem with this is that they may begin to see themselves more as virtual people than as real people and make assessments and judgments accordingly. So if I am unable to reach the dizzying heights of some of my peers in terms of numbers of Facebook friends and quality of data on my site, then I see myself as a failure. We now have the phenomon of 'Facebook depression', where young people actually become quite low in mood when this happens.

- One of the obvious casualties of this can be real-life friendships and relationships with family members and loved ones. These can be seen as of secondary importance to the virtual-reality world. As a result, much of the wisdom and advice on real life that can be gained through them can be overlooked, as can the emotional support of these encounters. There is also some evidence that heavy technology users may value their parents less and actually, on occasions, feel more alienated from them.

- There has been significant concern amongst many experts, therapists and psychologists that one of the major casualties of living in this virtual world is empathy. This is our ability to sense where a person is at emotionally and is one of the most important human skills for adolescents and young emerging adults to learn. It is felt that this is best done face-to-face. This is because our emotional brain learns to pick up on all the small facial and bodily reactions that form parts of our everyday social interactions. So common sense would suggest that the more interactions we have in the real world, the better we will be at picking such signs up in key relationships later in our adult lives.

- There have, however, been mixed findings from efforts to assess virtual versus real-life empathy. Some findings have even suggested that a body of adolescents may improve their empathy skills by spending time on social media. Other research is more critical and points more toward a gradual reduction in empathy amongst this age group in the past thirty years and a rise in narcissism – a culture of self-promotion and a total disregard for others.

- There is increasing concern about the potential for violent videos and computer games to desensitise the developing brain and further reduce empathy.

- One would worry about the consequences of cyberbullying, which may result from such a loss of empathy. Whilst bullying always has been (and always will be) a factor in the life of the teenager and young emerging adult, there is little doubt that the problem can be particularly insidious and potentially lethal when it is going on day and night through digital technology and social media.

- Another significant issue is Internet addiction, which could be the subject of a separate book. The most obvious Internet addictions are to pornography, chat rooms and online gambling. There is also the issue of video-gaming addiction. All of these have, at their heart, a dopamine pleasure-surge. There has to be a concern that such addictive behaviours would end up as long-term issues due to their effects on the developing brain.

- There is some evidence that, for some young people who are socially anxious, social media can be extremely helpful, allowing them to interact with their peers in a safe manner, and that this can help them subsequently in real-life socialising.

- There can be little doubt that modern technology is incredibly useful for sharing all kinds of information among young people. It is particularly helpful when our children are far away on holidays or gap years, or working abroad. It allows them to stay in touch with loved ones and friends.

Lifestyle Effects

It is fairly obvious that spending a large amount of time on the various forms of digital technology and social media may significantly affect lifestyle.

- The most obvious casualty is sleep, and we have already detailed the significant risks that a lack of sleep poses for the developing brain. If one is spending a lot of time late at night on social media, then the quantity and quality of sleep we get is inevitably affected – particularly if the user feels very anxious or even down over negative information being aired about them online.

- This is why I feel that parents may have to seriously examine the whole role of technology in all its forms after a certain time of night. This may involve, as we discussed earlier, leaving phones in a central area of the house at a certain time, turning off computers and the Internet and shutting down video games. The ideal, of course, would be to declare all bedrooms technology-free zones but, in many houses, this would be seen as unworkable. So it is best to come to an agreement with teenagers, particularly those who are most vulnerable to a lack of sleep, to abide by certain rules and regulations – but more of that later.

- How much does the reduction in grades noted in the research above have to do with heavy technology usage causing lack of sleep? It is quite likely to be a key player.

- Another casualty of such heavy usage is a lack of exercise, and we have noted the significant consequences of this to the adolescent and developing brain.

- Heavy usage can also generate issues in relation to nutrition. The user is exposed to subliminal marketing of both unhealthy foods and alcohol, which can lead to excess consumption of both. We have already examined the effects on the developing brain of being overweight or obese.

- There are some other areas that can also impinge on a healthy lifestyle. There is a lot of concern that exposure to sexually explicit videos, TV programmes and online pornography may increase the likelihood of teenagers having sex at an early age when they may not be emotionally ready for it.

- Of even greater concern is the possibility that regular exposure through the above mediums to extreme violence may increase aggression, sexual violence and even bullying in all its forms.

- One of the hidden negative consequences of heavy technology use in relation to everyday life relates to a concept beloved of Albert Ellis, the father of CBT: low frustration tolerance. At its simplest, this means we are extremely intolerant of not getting what we want when we want it. Modern digital technology and media are the antitheses of patience and delayed gratification. Because so much happens instantly through them, there is an expectation that real life should behave accordingly. As all of us who are older and hopefully a little bit wiser know, real life is just not like that.

- The results of this can often be seen in our teenagers and young emerging adults, who sometimes feel that life should change so that it mirrors the virtual reality of the social and cyber world they inhabit. A real problem then occurs when they start to rate themselves as failures when that doesn't happen.

- The two potential mental health problems that can emerge from this are depression and addiction. The question to be asked here is whether new pathways are being set up in the developing brain as a result. It is likely that they are. But they may not necessarily show up as structural changes which may have long-term consequences. They may instead demonstrate themselves as functional changes in terms of negative emotions and behaviours.

★

Before leaving this section on brain development, I would like readers – and particularly parents – to once again examine the questions we posed at the beginning of Chapter One and see if you can now answer them:

- Why are my child's emotional state and behaviour so different between the ages of thirteen and seventeen than they were at ten?

- Why does my daughter seem much more advanced for her age in so many areas than my son of a similar age?

- Why is it impossible to get my teenager out of bed in the morning and into bed at night?

- Where do the major mood swings and outbursts of anger come from in the teenage phase?

- Why do young men in emotional difficulty remain silent whilst young girls communicate with each other?

- Why do teenagers take risks, and why are they behaviourally more impulsive than young people in their twenties?

- Why are teenagers and young emerging adults more likely to become involved in risk-taking when they are together than when they are on their own or with their families?

- What are the effects of bullying, severe stress and abuse on the developing brain of the teenager or young emerging adult?

- What are the effects of alcohol, nicotine and substance misuse on the developing brains of our teenagers?

- Why are diet and exercise – and particularly obesity – now seen as critically important in how our teenagers and young emerging adults grow and develop not only physically but mentally?

- Why are some teenagers and young emerging adults more resilient when it comes to stress?

- Is technology, in all its forms, harmful or helpful to the developing brains of our children?

How well did you do?

I'll now hand you back to Enda, who is going to explain how the environment we grow up in is vital to our emotional well-being. He will also introduce us to the 'invalidating environment', which can have such a significant impact on how our adolescents grow and develop.

CHAPTER FOUR
The Invalidating Environment

Some years ago I was asked by a school in Dublin to give a talk to a group of students who were due to finish school that year. The principal of the school had told me that the teachers had experienced a lot of problems with this particular class and that the school was concerned that, because of various incidents during the year, the class would leave with a 'bad taste in their mouths' about education, which might deter them from pursuing further opportunities. The principal was hopeful that I might be able to help them change this view.

As the group hadn't met me before and were unsure of who I was, their initial reaction was one of quiet sullenness. They had a kind of defensive attitude toward what they perceived as another 'do-gooder' who, like every other adult who had been sent to them, was going to try to motivate them into trying harder to succeed at their exams.

Unfortunately, they also knew that, whatever kind of approach I proposed, it was unlikely that they would be able to succeed at their exams. As a result, they would more than likely fail again. Of course, this would reinforce their view of themselves as a group who were at the bottom of the academic pile.

Indeed, the attitude that I saw with this group can be found in most every school in the country. For various reasons, many adolescents find it difficult to learn in the traditional school format and, unfortunately, the traditional educational system is too rigid to adapt itself to these students' needs. It's as if when Plan A fails, the educational system resorts to . . . Plan A.

Alas, the result is that every year we send our most vulnerable children out into the adult world without having given them some of the most basic life skills. So where in God's name are we going wrong that we do this every year and can never figure out what to do to solve this problem?

ZONING OUT

As I started to talk, I could see most of the group starting to switch off. It's very easy to spot teenagers when they start to zone out like this. If you look closely at them you can see a blankness start to appear in their eyes. They may be looking at you, but they are gone off to some other universe where they hide until it's safe to come out again.

And that's what teenagers do. When they feel threatened or afraid, adolescents will zone out and hide until it's safe to come back to the world again. But, hang on – this is school, not prison. How could school be such a threat to children and adolescents that they have to develop the survival skill of zoning out to protect themselves?

What was it they were trying to protect themselves from? The school in question was one I regarded as among the best. At the very least, it was as good as any other school in the country. The staff and managers were of the highest quality, committed not only to the academic curriculum, but also to the physical, mental and social development of their charges.

So why then, with everybody in the school trying to help them, would they see teachers and health professionals like me as a threat? That is what I could see happening right in front of me. Teenagers trying to survive in what they had learned to regard as a hostile environment. As I saw that I was losing them, I decided to go on to Plan B, which entailed me just stopping talking and sitting in silence. As the silence got longer, I could see the group starting to become uneasy about what I was doing. (Well it isn't called the 'pregnant pause' for nothing, you know.) The ones who had zoned out started to zone back in to see what was happening. When I saw that I had most of them back, I decided to ask them a very simple question.

I asked them who they thought had the most committed attitude toward school, their own class or the 'A' class where all the top students were. Now I started to get their attention! After a few seconds the first answer was volunteered by one of the lads at the back of the class. He argued that since they would do the best in their exams, the 'A' class were the most committed. I then asked if any of the rest of the class agreed with this. They all answered, 'Yes.'

Next I asked them to think about their answer, because it was my opinion that the reverse was true. From what I was able to see, they had the stronger commitment to education. Now, at this stage, I have to admit that whilst the students in this class were not the most academically minded class I'd ever seen, they were no eejits. They may have agreed to meet with me, but there was no way that they were going to let me stand there and patronise them. I could see some of them getting ready to zone out again so, before they could, I asked them if they would like me to prove it to them.

I assured them that I was not in the business of patronising anybody, purely for the reason that it doesn't work, especially with teenagers. However, if they wanted me to prove it, they would have to listen to what I said. And do you know what? For the rest of the time I had them listening intently to everything I said, arguing points with me and generally getting totally involved in the discussion.

I didn't once have to ask them to stop interrupting me. I didn't need too. In fact, it was even better than that. When one of the students made a smart comment, it was his classmates who told him to shut up.

So how was I able to do that? How was I able to get a group of fourteen adolescents who collectively had the attention span of a goldfish to listen to me and engage with a topic that, five minutes previously, they had been totally unaware of?

MOTIVATION

One of the most misunderstood concepts in our understanding of what life is all about has got to be how we understand the theory of motivation and how we try to teach ourselves to get it. You see, motivation is a very easy thing to achieve when we want to do something or can see the reward we will get if we do it.

Real motivation, however, is doing what is right even though every fibre of our being rebels against us doing it. In other words, doing the right thing and enduring all the discomfort that this will bring in the short term so as to achieve a goal that we cannot see or understand.

All the 'A' class had the 'easy' motivation. They understood how school worked and how to get what they wanted out of it. They knew how to study and do well in exams. They also knew that if they followed the path they were on, they would attain a result that they could see and that they wanted.

My class, however, had the 'hard' motivation. They couldn't see the benefit of education or how what they were learning could be of use to them. Neither had they ever been able to figure out how to use the school system to get a result that they wanted. To illustrate this I asked them how they felt about studying, which prompted a collective groan. I feigned surprise at this and asked them how many hours a day they studied. Of course, I got the answer I was expecting: none of them studied very much, if at all.

I then decided to drop my first hand grenade into their laps. I asked them if anybody had ever taught them how to study. Once again, I was met with a collective blank stare. Pushing the boat out a bit further, I asked them how they felt having to face school every morning. Collective groan again. They described to me how much they hated it.

Putting two and two together, I asked them why – if they hated it so much – they continued doing it. Why did they get up and go into school every morning? Now I had them really bamboozled. None of them quite knew why they were doing it, they just did it. Next I asked them how hard they thought the 'A' class found going into school. Of course, because they were going to get so much out of school, they would find going much easier.

So going into school for the 'A' class didn't require much motivation, did it? Not like my class of misfits. Every morning, all of my class had to drag themselves out of bed to do something that they hated. My argument was that since my class of misfits had to put a thousand times more effort into going to school, they were more motivated. I asked them if they had ever thought of this and they all answered, 'No.'

I then explained that one of the greatest skills they would get out of school would be to be able to consistently do something that they found hard and didn't like. Not only had they learned to do this, they had learned how to do it consistently, which has got to be one of the most important things we need to learn as we grow. This is called resilience, and this class had it in spades.

LEARNING THE FUNDAMENTALS

It never ceases to amaze me how we dictate to our children what we expect of them without ever thinking that we need to teach them how to deliver it. We think that if we just get them to behave in a certain way, they will magically learn the skills they need. I asked the class at what point in their school lives they had realised that they were never going to be able to deliver what was expected of them. Immediately, one of the boys looked at me and said, 'The first day.'

This young man had spent six years attending school, without one person realising that if they wanted him to achieve what they wanted him to achieve, they would have to teach him how to do it. Not only that, but in trying to help him in the only way they knew how, his environment challenged him at every turn to deliver.

If they could take one thing away from what I was saying, I told the class, try to realise that in facing school and the hurt it caused them, they had achieved something that most of the rest of the school hadn't, and probably wouldn't until they came upon their own adversity.

No matter where life took them in the future, they would have the emotional resilience to overcome it. And that was what they had learned from their school experience – how to survive. If they could understand this, they could hold their heads up high and say, 'I stood and I survived.'

CHARACTERISTICS OF AN INVALIDATING ENVIRONMENT

Over the years, I've often heard it said that teenagers will never listen to their parents. I've never been able to learn precisely where this piece of 'wisdom' hailed from. Even though it is often regarded as a fact, I regard it as one of the most inaccurate 'facts' swirling around the popular-psychology world. I regularly see teens and kids for help and have never had one that didn't open up under the right conditions.

Learning how to communicate with kids and adolescents is not all that difficult when you understand the principles of how to do it. It is easier to implement these skills whilst in therapist mode, though. Trying to implement them as a parent is more complicated and difficult. I would love to be as effective when I'm in my parent role as I have learned to be when I am wearing my therapist hat. Oh, that life would be so simple. Getting a kid or adolescent to engage 'positively' is much easier when I'm wearing my therapist hat.

You see, when I'm seeing youngsters as a therapist, the dynamics of the relationship are far simpler than when it's a parent/child relationship. As a therapist, I can focus on fixing a particular problem and be balanced and friendly, without having to worry about whether they ate their greens and so on, which I would have to worry about if I was in parent mode.

However, whilst it may be more complicated in parent mode, the fundamentals are the same. The basic philosophy in interacting with children and adolescents is to remember that our role is to teach them how to live in *their* world, not in ours. Giving them the tools and teaching them how to use them has got to be our focus. The world that your children experience in the school playground will be the same as what they will experience in the work environment as adults.

There is, however, a pitfall that all of us parents fall into: creating an invalidating environment. This happens when, instead of teaching children how to understand and handle their world, we create a vague atmosphere that reinforces the belief that because they are feeling what they are, there must be something wrong with them. Let's take some time out to look at how this happens and why it is so destructive.

INVALIDATION

In order to understand what I'm talking about, I want you to imagine that your youngster comes in after playing in the garden and complains that he is hungry. As you are hassled because you're up to your ears trying to finish something, you snap back that you can't understand how he could be hungry as he just had his lunch an hour ago. Sounds like a comment that any parent could make, doesn't it? Indeed, hands up any parent who hasn't snapped at your kids over something like that, hinting at them to get out of your hair and stop annoying you?

There is, however, another way to look at the above situation. This time, I want to look at each part of this simple situation and examine the learning to be had for your youngster.

Some years ago, a therapist called Marsha Linehan described a type of environment in which kids were prevented from learning and, instead, were taught that they must be abnormal because they were not feeling or reacting in the 'correct' way. Linehan argued that, in this type of environment, the child's emotional expressions were either ignored or – if acknowledged by their parents, school or health service – were not regarded as an accurate interpretation of what they had experienced.

To make things worse, this environment places a huge emphasis on self-control and self-reliance. Any difficulties that the child might experience in trying to understand the situation are ignored and problem-solving is seen as always possible, given the proper motivation. Any failure on the part of the child to perform to the expected standard, therefore, is attributed to a lack of motivation or some other negative aspect of their character.

Linehan argued that if a child is exposed to this kind of environment, the child will experience particular difficulties.

1. The child will not have the opportunity to label or understand their emotions.

2. The child will not be able to respond to events, since any difficulties they might experience will not be acknowledged.

3. While the relevance of any difficulties they face in learning how to cope with the world will be ignored, the child will be chastised for not knowing what to do.

Since the child is never taught how to deal with situations, they will become more and more dependent on the environment for indications of how they 'should' be feeling and to solve their problems for them. In essence, therefore, the environment gives the child no option but to become dependent on it, but then rejects the child for doing so.

It's like the Irish mammy doing everything for her son, to the extent that he never learns how to take care of himself. She then moans to anyone who'll listen how frustrated she feels that he won't get up off his arse and do things for himself. The reality is that he has neither been taught to do things nor been let do things for himself at any time.

DINNER TIME

Now let's look at how the invalidating environment fits into our little one complaining of being hungry. What the child has done is describe a feeling that they have concluded is hunger. By telling the child that they couldn't be hungry as they had their dinner an hour earlier, the parent is teaching the child one of two things:

1. That whatever the child is experiencing could not be hunger, as it's not possible to be hungry an hour after a meal.

2. That if the feeling of hunger is real the child must be abnormal, since feeling hungry after a meal is abnormal.

So the learning to be had by the child after this small event is that they are mistaken in what they think they feel or there must be something wrong with them. If you imagine that the child experiences this type of invalidation in all their interactions with their 'life teachers', then you might just see how the picture develops. Whilst this kind of thing does occur to some extent in all families (including mine), it's not just in the home that you will find it. If you look around, you will notice that it occurs in many other places.

It also occurs in crèches, schools and other places children spend time. All these environments run in a way where about 60 percent of kids will fit in without any significant difficulty. If, however, your child is one of the 40 percent that doesn't fit snugly into this type of structure unaided, then they will encounter the invalidating environment in all its glory. Indeed, I read a while ago that if we count in those kids who experience difficulty learning the skills but just 'withdraw into themselves', therefore not becoming a management problem for the school, then the percentage who do not fit snugly into these structures can be as high as 60 percent.

Institutions, however, have a very clever way of handling their 'management problems'. In very subtle ways, they intimate that if your child is not fitting in there must be a problem with the child – and, by inference, a problem with your parenting abilities.

Hands up any parent who has ever heard an institution admit that it is their rigid structure that's at fault and, instead of tailoring their solution to respond to the problem, they go back to front and insist that you twist the problem to fit their solution.

Oh, and if you correctly realise that this is putting the cart before the horse, then you are automatically invalidated and dismissed as a 'problem parent' and, as we all know, one of those parents who is a big part of the problem.

EMOTIONAL SKIN

Along with the consequences listed above which occur as a result of invalidating environments, there is one more that we need to understand before we move on to another topic. This is the concept of emotional regulation or, as we call it, 'emotional skin'.

Look at your foot and notice the layer of skin around your heel. This thick layer of skin is designed to protect your foot from injury. Now rub an emery board and notice that, even though you rub vigorously, you don't feel any pain. Now I want you to imagine that the skin has been removed from your heel.

Now imagine rubbing the same emery board over it. This time, instead of not hurting, it's going to have you hitting the roof with the pain.

Linehan argued that, as we mature, we grow an 'emotional skin' over our emotions. This skin helps to protect us from the emotional effects of what we encounter. If, however, as we grow, we encounter invalidating environments like those I've discussed above, instead of growing emotional skin that helps us to protect ourselves, we end up with bare emotional nerve endings. The net result of this is that little things hurt us a lot.

Not only that but, when we get hurt, it takes so long for us to soothe our emotions that, before we can do so, something else occurs that hurts us again. Over time, our emotions remain in such a state of heightened stimulation that the structures of our brains actually start to change.

We are going to meet the invalidating environment throughout this book. It sticks its nose into nearly all our daily interactions with our kids. As parents, we all have a tendency when giving out to our kids to focus on what we want them to do. We see our teens' attempts to express themselves as answering back. So we demand of them to be where we want them to be without ever realising that we need to show them how to do it.

The invalidating environment, however, doesn't reside exclusively in our parental attitudes. As we will see in subsequent chapters, it can occur in nearly every place we send our teenagers to learn. It can be found in schools and clubs. It can even be found in the expert health services where we bring our teenagers when they run into difficulties.

Harry is now going to take us briefly through the physical and sexual development of the screenager.

CHAPTER FIVE
Physical and Sexual Development

At the same time as teenagers and young emerging adults are going through significant developmental changes in brain structure and function, they also have to cope with major changes in their physical and sexual development. It is not necessary to delve into these in any great detail, so below is a brief summary of the main changes. We will also examine their relevance to parents.

PHYSICAL DEVELOPMENT

Whilst the major changes in brain development start from age thirteen, physical changes in girls can start at around ten. We call this phase puberty. For boys, these changes are delayed until twelve or thirteen. There are some commonalities at puberty between boys and girls, but many differences. It is the sex hormones, along with some other key hormones, that drive these changes. Let's examine the main ones:

- Both boys and girls will start to grow taller and gain weight.

- Boys will continue this right up into their early twenties, whilst girls are normally fully grown by eighteen.

- Many boys (if they are not obese) worry during the early and middle parts of the adolescent phase that they seem to be too 'skinny' and feel they should be 'working out' to counteract this. In practice, it is usually only in the early twenties that many males begin to fill out, as their muscles naturally strengthen.

- Both boys and girls, as we will discuss later, can develop body-image problems at this phase, and the effects of these can be carried into their twenties.

- Both will develop pubic and axillary hair, with boys also developing additional facial hair.

- Both will start to produce sebum on the face and trunk and may be prone to acne, particularly from the mid-teens onwards. I would counsel parents to be very sensitive to acne, particularly in boys, as many will develop secondary emotional difficulties if it is not taken seriously and managed properly.

- Both will start to sweat more, with secondary body odour.

- Girls will start to develop breast tissue and menstruate. As they move into mid-adolescence and beyond, the risk of pregnancy due to unprotected sex will keep many of their parents awake at night.

- Many girls will develop quite painful periods or dysmenorrhea. This is most often present just before the period begins and for twenty-four hours afterwards. This can be quite distressing for some girls.

- Boys will begin to have an increase in penis and testes size and will also notice their voices change in timbre, usually becoming deeper. They may also start to have erections and some ejaculation, particularly when in bed at night, about which they may feel embarrassed.

- As both male and female adolescents enter their twenties, these physical changes will have consolidated, and by twenty-five, the fully mature, physically filled-out emerging young adult has arrived.

- It is important to mention the risks of obesity during this phase of physical development, as it can lead to many physical and emotional difficulties. We have already dealt with the significant structural and functional consequences of obesity on the developing brain, but it is also important to note the significant risks of bullying that may accompany obesity.

- One practical comment to mothers. Many female adolescents between the ages of sixteen and twenty-five who are sexually active end up on depot progesterone contraceptives. Whilst these achieve the objective of providing contraceptive cover without the need to take a pill daily, they are inclined to significantly add weight. This may be one of the hidden reasons for the increasing obesity issues in girls of this age – along with poor dietary habits, a lack of exercise and alcohol consumption. If your screenager is already overweight, then you might want to discuss other options with her.

It is important for parents to be fully aware of the sensitive nature of the above physical developmental changes. This is because many young teenagers struggle to deal with them and, on occasion, abnormalise themselves, leading to emotional difficulties. It is essential that, from the beginning, they should have frank, open discussions about these changes. Most parents are quite happy to do so but some may find the subject too embarrassing.

I would strongly counsel all to not only make themselves more aware of the above changes but to try and empathise with young adolescents as they go through this difficult phase. It is well worth sharing with the young person your own difficulties and fears whilst at that stage. This will help to normalise the period of time for them and make them more likely to open up to you regarding any difficulties.

SEXUAL DEVELOPMENT

Not only are adolescents and emerging young adults trying to cope with the above physical changes to their bodies and brains, they are also trying to deal with their sexual development. This relates to how they view the physical changes to their sex organs detailed above, their attractiveness to others and the search for their sexual identity. Let's examine some of their main issues:

- One of the biggest issues for both boys and girls, from mid-adolescence onwards, is confusion and uncertainty in relation to sexual identity. This can be significantly influenced by the opinions and actions of their peers.

- Many will have a reasonable idea as to their sexual orientation by fifteen or seventeen, although some may take longer. As it is considered 'normal' by their peer group to be heterosexual, this can be a difficult period for those who are more attracted to their own sex.

- Because those around them are in the main heterosexual, this may end up with the adolescent feeling that it is 'abnormal' to be gay. It may also lead to risks of depression and self-harm if they start to rate themselves as failures.

- These risks are significantly increased if sexual bullying (either face-to-face or online) becomes an issue for the young person involved.

- For some who are heterosexual but do not conform to what is perceived to be 'normal' in terms of interactions with the opposite sex, suggestions that they may be homosexual can be extremely damaging and can lead to self-harm.

- For those who are heterosexual, there can be different issues in relation to whether they are physically attractive to the opposite sex. This can lead to significant anxiety from the mid-teens onwards.

- There are also concerns and pressures as to whether one should be sexually active and at what age. Once again, peer group pressures can create a lot of anxiety for those not in relationships and, indeed, for those who are. This is a very significant issue for many girls and is one of the risk factors, as we will see later, for self-harm.

Once again it is very important for parents to be fully aware of these concerns and, as suggested above, to try to set up clear lines of communication in relation to this area from the beginning. Also, as before, try to share stories about your own anxiety during this phase of life. If you feel there are signs that one of your children is gay or a lesbian, then try and open up a conversation on this if the opportunity appears. Many young people are anxious about how their parents might view this information and may be getting very emotionally distressed about 'coming out' to both their parents and their peers. It is better to have this conversation before a self-harm episode rather than afterwards. How you react to the information may also go a long way toward them accepting themselves as normal, rather than ending up with feelings of self-loathing and hurt.

In relation to heterosexual relationships, it is important to remember that emotions are exaggerated between the ages of thirteen and nineteen. So relationship difficulties and breakups can be very upsetting and stressful during this phase. It is useful to share your own experiences about what happened to you at this stage of life. It is also important to get across the message that life is composed of discomfort and pain as well as joy, and that just because a relationship breaks up does not mean that you are 'worthless' as a person. If handled well, such life occurrences can be learning opportunities. We will be examining such concepts in more detail later.

These difficulties with sexual identity and relationships are also present between the ages of twenty and thirty. Young men between the ages of sixteen and twenty-five, in particular, can have major difficulties with jealousy, anxiety, low self-esteem and depression. This can occur whether they are coming to terms with being gay or going through the breakup of a significant relationship. Adolescent and emerging adult males can often struggle to come to terms with these realities. Both of these issues have for some time been noted as major factors in some screenager suicides. Clearly, there is much work to be done on assisting them in learning to deal with the emotional fallout of these difficulties.

Up to the age of nineteen, parents can play quite active roles in helping them to deal with such issues. From then on they must become mentors. This means, as we will discuss later, allowing them to make the running in relation to how they handle such situations whilst being there for them with advice if requested. This can be a delicate balance!

In the next section, Enda will illustrate just what is going on in the minds of screenagers and discuss the key skills they need to learn.

SECTION THREE

What's Going On in the Minds of Screenagers, the Skills They Need and How They Learn Them

CHAPTER SIX
Where Do We Want Them to Be?

In *Five Steps to Happiness*, I remarked that whilst I would have loved to have been able to claim that the insights I described were my own, I couldn't. Most of them came from some of the most wonderful people I could ever have met. One of these was a woman who was responsible for starting me on my journey to becoming a psychotherapist. Her name is Maria McCarron, and she is a fellow therapist. If I am to be honest, I have to attribute about 50 percent of what I know to her.

Maria became my clinical supervisor when I was training, and I still have vivid memories of sitting in the 'chair' talking about cases and despairing that I would never be able to achieve the insight into human emotions that she had. In direct line of sight from the 'chair' was a cheap photocopy stuck to the wall with a quotation that has since become ingrained into my emotional brain. It simply said: 'Unless we know to what port we wish to sail, then no wind is favourable.'

And how true this is, especially when applied to how we try to raise our kids. If you ask parents what they want for their kids, most will answer that, first and foremost, they want their sons or daughters to be happy. If, however, you ask them what they are doing to achieve this, you'll be met with blank stares. At most, you'll come away with some extremely vague strategy that sounds good but neither explains where the 'port' is nor provides a compass with which to find it.

If you find this confusing, then try this one on for size: define happiness. And when you do come up with a definition, try to figure out a way to achieve it.

HAPPINESS

Don't look at Harry or me for an answer either, as we are no more qualified than your good self to answer the question. However, now that we have dispelled any notion you may have had as to our expertise in the area, there are certain things that we both have learned over the years that might illuminate the whole area of happiness and how *not* to try getting it.

Wherever I look and whenever I hear people discussing the subject, I never fail to come away with the idea that, in human philosophy, we believe that happiness is a place that is always one step in front of where we are at the moment and that if we only manage to tick certain boxes in our lives, we will get there. This leads us to develop personal philosophies that usually involve participating in self-centred actions that we believe will make us happy, but only succeed in making us miserable.

Happy people have learned that 'Life is a journey, not a destination.' The same can be said about recovery from depression and other mental illnesses, as the components that make up recovery are exactly the same as those required to live happily. In my own thirty-one years of trying to help people who are unhappy, the only conclusion I have come to is that happiness is a natural state that we revert to when we stop doing things that are making us unhappy.

Maybe instead of looking for boxes to tick in order to be happy, we need to look at what we do as humans that makes us unhappy. It is only by doing this that we can understand what kind of learning environment we need to create in our homes so that our children can grow into these philosophies and learn these skills.

From my own personal and professional experience, I believe that in order for both our adolescents – and indeed ourselves – to achieve happiness, we need to develop certain qualities. In order to do this we need to learn certain skills, which can be broken up into six categories:

- Physical health
- Mindfulness

- Meaning
- Activities of living
- Mental health
- Education

Harry is going to take us briefly through the first two categories. After that, I will take over again and go through the remaining four categories.

Category One: Physical Health

I explained in Chapter Three the importance of physical health in terms of the brain development of the healthy screenager. But physical health is important for all of us, not just for the screenager. It is an integral part of our search for happiness – and yet one that is regularly ignored.

Physical health involves exercise, proper nutrition, the avoidance of obesity and the sensible use of alcohol. It also involves making sure we are not overrun by modern technology and are getting sufficient sleep. I have already laid out the best steps to take to achieve these goals in Chapter Three.

What is critical here is that we have to be honest with ourselves and question just how physically healthy we are as adult parents. Our children learn at the feet of the masters – namely us – so if we wish them to become physically healthy as part of their journey toward happiness, we must start with ourselves. The motto should be, 'A healthy body is integral to a healthy mind.'

Category Two: Mindfulness

In the introduction I recalled my encounter with the Greenhills Leaving Cert students, and how I mentioned to them that one of the skills that would be very useful around exam time was creating a 'three-minute breathing space'. This very simple, powerful exercise is a form of mindfulness. We will demonstrate it later, but first let's examine just what mindfulness is all about and why it is being researched increasingly to try and decide if it would be worth introducing at both primary and secondary level.

Mindfulness is the awareness which develops when we pay attention to events experienced in the present moment within the framework of our minds/bodies in a non-judgmental and accepting manner. This is being increasingly recognised as a useful tool in assisting those so distressed by negative emotions that they struggle to come to terms with the negative thoughts lying underneath.

Practising mindfulness involves some form of meditation, which can be defined as a mental technique that involves focusing the mind on an object, a sound, a prayer, breathing or conscious thoughts, in order to increase awareness of the present moment, helping a person to relax, reduce levels of stress or enhance spiritual or personal growth.

- Mindfulness helps us to notice what is happening in our experience, especially when engaging in compulsive patterns of thought such as rumination, which can prompt destructive or addictive behaviour.

- It offers a way for people to stay with experiences, including whatever may be unpleasant or difficult, rather than pushing them away.

- This produces a change in perspective on those thoughts or experiences, enabling people to see that their thoughts are just thoughts, not facts or reality, and they need not be driven by them.

- This new perspective allows choice. Rather than being driven by compulsive reactions to experiences, mindfulness creates a mental space that enables people to respond differently.

- It helps us move from the world of doing to the world of being.

The three-minute breathing space is a wonderful mindfulness exercise that I believe all of us would benefit from practising. It can be done at any time of the day, and it is particularly useful at times of stress. It involves finding a quiet space and, if possible, a comfortable posture, closing your eyes, and doing the following:

- Minute One: Focus your mind on your inner experiences, whether these are your thoughts, emotions or physical sensations. Do not try to change or challenge them, just become 'aware' of them.

- Minute Two: Focus on the simple physical sensation of breathing, and particularly on your abdomen rising and falling with each breath, again not trying to control it in any way. This will help you to 'centre' yourself.

- Minute Three: Increase your focus or awareness to your body as a whole, including your posture, facial expression and sensations, with acceptance and without judgment.

This is often called a 'mini meditation' and, if performed two or three times a day, the benefits are enormous. It is an exercise we, as parents, could begin to build into our lives and one that I feel we should share with our screenagers. Perhaps we should do it with them a few times. It would give us a wonderful opportunity to talk about how stressed and anxious we get over all the slings and arrows of life, and how they will experience similar emotional difficulties and stressors in, say, the period leading up to their exams. You can explain how the exercise is helping you and suggest that it might benefit them too.

But does mindfulness assist children and adolescents in learning to cope with the difficulties of life? There is a growing body of opinion that this skill, learned at a young age, may bear fruit in terms of mental health. In the USA, the MindUP programme funded by the Hawn Foundation (created by actress Goldie Hawn with the assistance of experts in the field) has been rolled out in many elementary schools, for students around ten years of age. This pro-gramme has been audited for effectiveness and shown to have positive effects on behaviour, mood, learning, capacity to deal with emotional distress, adapt-ability and stress.

There is increasing interest in the potential of providing such school-based mindfulness programmes (at the primary and secondary levels) in Ireland and the UK, and some schools have actually introduced them into their curriculums. But there is no nationally directed initiative yet. One of the concerns has been that, whilst there is a large body of anecdotal evidence to back up this approach, there are insufficient scientifically researched large studies to definitively support its widespread introduction. To deal with this deficit, such studies are now in progress, particularly in England. Some of the research already performed looks promising (see Kuyken et al in the bibliography). In time, mindfulness will hopefully become a core element in assisting teenagers in learning how to cope with stress, anxiety and some of the lower-grade depression symptoms so common in this group.

If it were introduced, it would be a great opportunity to discuss with students just what emotions are, where they come from, what happens when we become emotionally distressed and how mindfulness might be a simple skill to deal with the latter. It would be the opinion of both authors that introducing such programmes with built-in safeguards and regular auditing might eventually make mindfulness a key screenager life skill. In the meantime, I cannot recommend highly enough the introduction of the three-minute breathing space into the lives of both parents and screenagers.

I will now hand you back to Enda, who will take us through the other four categories.

Category Three: Meaning

The search for meaning lies at the mysterious heart of the human experience. Some might search through a set of spiritual beliefs, while others might search through science, art, literature or music. Still others might try to find it through more humanistic pathways.

My own experience has shown me, however, that if you remove the superficial differences between, say, all the different types of spiritual or humanistic beliefs out there, you will find that they are all trying to direct us toward a similar 'port' by guiding us to live a similar type of life. Each ideology encourages us to practise tolerance, accept ourselves as imperfect beings, accept life as it is and remove ourselves from the centre of our universes.

Learning to give up the belief that we are at the centre of our own personal universe is crucial to our own human development. Although we did not deal with the middle-age phase in Chapter Two, it is interesting to note that Erikson argued that during our own middle age we need to practise giving back to the next generation. To do so, we need to stop focusing on ourselves. If we don't, we will remain self-centred, which will result in unhappiness.

Developing an altruistic attitude toward others is an essential component in happiness. I often quote a colleague who says, 'If I want to have a miserable day, all I have to do is give myself my complete undivided attention.' So a key element of our search for meaning and, indeed, happiness itself has to include altruism – where we are putting the needs of others above our own.

Neil Bernstein is a psychotherapist who has worked with adolescents for years. In his fabulous book *Treating the Unmanageable Adolescent*, he argues that learning to be able to understand other people's feelings is the single most important skill adolescents need to learn if their disruptive behaviour is to be resolved. Unfortunately, trying to teach an adolescent this skill when they are firing from both barrels at their parents and the world is extremely difficult. I find that they have to be well down the road of recovery before I can even think about introducing the concept.

All adolescents will blow off from time to time. You did it, I did it and I'm even sure that Harry had the occasional blow-off from time to time. Teaching adolescents how to understand how others feel in different circumstances is not to try to turn them into altruistic saints. Learning to recognise other people's emotions is vital in learning how to recognise our own.

We learn how to recognise, express and regulate our own emotions by reaching out and learning how others do it. In all my years of working as a therapist I can't ever remember having to see a child for therapy who was a member of the Scouts, the Order of Malta or St John's ambulance corps or any other youth organisation with a philosophy of helping others and learning to put others' interests in front of our own.

The time to learn these skills is not when we get into trouble, but when we are growing up. As somebody told me once, the only thing you need to understand about God is that you're not it! Once we learn this, the rest is fairly straightforward, since it involves learning by Good Orderly Direction. Of course, we can't teach what we don't know. If we want our children to be able to learn this skill then, as parents, we need to learn and be able to practise it ourselves.

A common thread that I hope you pick up in his book is the importance of the environment in which we raise our kids, as it is only in a validating environment that they can grow healthily and learn the necessary skills that will be vital when they come up against the outside world.

So we each need to look at our own family environment. Is it one where everybody is respected as they are? Where everybody is listened to? Where problems and difficulties can be discussed in a non-judgemental way? And where everybody is allowed to contribute and feel that they belong? Or do we just dictate to our kids what we expect from them, dismiss their expectations of us as irrelevant and leave it up to the fairies to teach them how to do things?

Category Four: Activities of Living

All through adolescence and early adulthood, children are faced with situations where they need to learn skills to deal with what they encounter. We now need to tackle the skill that I regard as the daddy of them all, the one everybody complains about, but nobody ever seems to do anything about. And that is learning how to use the washing machine.

Commonly written simply as 'A/L', activities of living are all the skills that need to be mastered as part of our daily lives. These include simple things like cooking, taking care of our personal hygiene and learning how to find something in the fridge without having to ask your wife where it is. (My wife made me put that last one in.)

They also include going to school or work, managing our money and taking responsibility for all the things we need to do in order to live. Even though they are regularly overlooked, activities of living are the very foundation of all life skills. Not only that, they are the vehicle through which we overcome adversity in our lives.

People often ask me how I teach people to cope with tragic and difficult things that happen in their lives. My answer is always the same. I ask them to tell me how *not* to cope with something. It's as if facing a situation and coping with it had a brother called 'not coping'. As if not coping were an option open to us when things go wrong!

When something happens to us and we have to deal with a difficulty that will take time to overcome, we wake up each and every morning and have to face the day with adversity sitting on our shoulders. We may not be 'coping' the way we think we should, but we are still living.

Adversity doesn't just magically whisk itself away so that you wake up some morning and it's not there. It is there in front of you every morning. Every morning you haven't a choice whether you will cope with it or not. Life continues regardless of what trauma you are carrying.

Neither do any of us ever 'get over' anything. Even Freud said that nothing in our lives is ever forgotten. He argued that every event remains in our subconscious to influence our reactions for the rest of our lives. What we regard as getting over something is, in reality, a phenomenon where, over time, we gradually adapt to a situation that has been thrust upon us. Over time, we get used to the new world we are living in. Gradually, if we do the right things, the pain lessens, and the memories fade and are replaced with new ones from our new lives. Harry will be sharing with us later the experiences of parents who have lost children to suicide, and there can be no better example of the fallacy that we should be able to get over things than surviving such a tragedy.

If you want the pain to lessen, then you have to continue engaging with everyday living. For example, in recovery from depression, I try to tell people that the hardest yet most important part of recovery is getting out of bed and facing life. There are twenty-four hours in the day. We sleep for around eight of them. That leaves sixteen hours that we need to fill. I remember being told that personal recovery from adversity is dependent on the positive actions we take each day.

For example, when you lose a loved one, the hard part is not getting through the burial. The hard part is when everybody else has gone home and you are left on your own to face life without your loved one. It's then that you need the resilience to be able to carry out all the tasks of daily living. It's only by facing life each day and carrying on with your own A/Ls that you gradually heal and adapt to your changed circumstances.

It is not a good idea to leave learning how to carry out our own A/Ls to times of emergency. Trying to learn A/L skills during emergencies is like trying to get fit by entering and trying to run a marathon on your first day of exercising. Life, and adapting to situations, just doesn't work that way. The time that you need to learn A/L skills is when you are in a safe, secure environment, like your own home. Only by learning as we are growing can we perfect our coping skills and deal with life's adversities when they happen.

Please trust me on this one. As we shall see in the chapter on depression, getting out of bed and tending to your normal mundane activities is both the hardest and most important part of recovery. You cannot get better lying in the bed. Taking care of your own A/Ls is how you manage the crap that's going on in your head. Learning to focus your head on what's going on in the day is crucial. Having a method that will provide a platform whereby you can focus your brain on the reality of daily living is vital if you are to be able to challenge the 'stinking thinking' that's going on in your head.

Perhaps then, the next time you are turning on the washing machine, having raided all the laundry baskets in their rooms, sorted the whites from the colours, loaded the machine and put it onto the right wash cycle, you might just ask yourself why you are deliberately limiting your kids' abilities to learn or practise carrying out their own A/Ls, which will be vital to their lives in the future. Because it's only by practising their A/L skills when there's no crisis happening that we can learn how to cope when something serious happens. Trust me, having to learn these skills when we have no option but to use them makes the journey of recovery infinitely harder.

As the national mental self-help group Grow puts it: 'It is not possible to "think" your way into right action, but you can "act" your way into right thinking.' Ninety-five percent of those actions that are vital to life are simple, daily living activities that most teenagers never seem to think about, because as every teenager knows, it's the Laundry Fairy who magically cleans their clothes and hangs them neatly in their wardrobe.

Category Five: Mental Health

Dr John McKinley, an esteemed cardiologist, was asked to speak to a group of physicians on heart attacks at a conference in 1979. As it was a medical conference, everybody was expecting him to talk about the latest treatments in the medical management of heart attacks. Indeed, the 70s were a very exciting time for cardiologists, a period during which some of the biggest breakthroughs in the treatment of heart attacks were developed.

John, however, didn't give the talk people expected him to give. Instead, he started to speak about his frustration with his own clinical practice and how illness was viewed by the medical profession. To illustrate his frustration, John used the analogy of feeling like he was standing at the edge of a fast-flowing river.

He kept seeing people in the water floating by. As each person floated by, he was diving in and rescuing them. However, just as he was getting them to the bank, and safety, another person would float by. John would dive in again and rescue them, but as soon as he would get them to the bank, another person would float by. And on and on it went. Dive in, rescue someone, get them to the bank, resuscitate them and send them on their way. John's frustration was that he was spending so much time rescuing people downstream that he had no time to walk back upstream to find out who was pushing them all in.

John was making the point that because he had to focus all his resources on actually treating heart attacks, he had no resources left to look at why people were developing heart problems in the first place.

Indeed, John's frustration was very understandable. You see, prior to 1970, people would only go to see their GPs or think about their health when they got sick. And, indeed, the health services were very much focused on providing care to people who were sick.

We call this 'tertiary' health care. The term 'tertiary' comes from a Latin word meaning 'third', i.e. at the end. To run a health service based on a 'tertiary' philosophy means to divert all your efforts to treating people who have developed an actual illness.

Early Secondary Care

The 1970s were a very interesting time for understanding health. During this time, people like Dr McKinley started to look much more carefully at the way we provided health care. Society was starting to realise that, if we could understand why illnesses occurred, we could hopefully step in and treat them as they were developing, rather than wait until a real problem occurred.

By diagnosing and treating illness at a very early stage, outcomes for people would be much better, and illnesses could be 'cured' before they had done any major damage. If you want an example of this, you don't need to go any further than the philosophy behind encouraging women to have cervical smears and the recent 'breast-check' programmes. Catch the illness early and we can cure it much more easily.

Nowadays, we call this 'early secondary care'. Or, to put it simply, catching and treating illness at a very early stage. When I started my career, it was this philosophy that was all the vogue. You can see it everywhere – in day hospitals and in the invention of CT scanning and MRI.

The next major step in our understanding of health and illness started to occur in the early 90s. During this time, health professionals began to put two and two together and thought, 'If we can make huge improvements in health by catching illness early, then why don't we seek to understand what is causing the illness in the first place?'

This led to the development of the 'primary care' philosophy. Primary care is focused on preventing illness, and it has been very successful. An example is the smoking ban that was introduced first in Ireland but has since been adopted in many other countries. Two other examples are awareness campaigns focused on the importance of tackling obesity, and vaccine programmes.

In the last ten years, however, this primary-care philosophy of illness prevention has started to develop into another philosophy. The idea now is that promoting health is not just about preventing illness but about improving the quality of our lives and improving our ability to cope with life's hurdles. So now, not only do we see adverts to promote giving up smoking, we see adverts that encourage us to exercise, lose weight and watch our cholesterol.

So what does this all have to do with mental health? Well, if we look at how the four principles of physical health care have mirrored our understanding of mental health, we find some shocking results. To explain what I mean by this, I need you to keep the four principles in mind as we look at mental health:

1. Tertiary Care: Treat illness when it becomes a problem.

2. Secondary Care: Diagnose and treat illness at a very early stage, before it becomes a major problem.

3. Primary Care: Take action to prevent illness occurring.

4. Health Promotion: Good health improves overall quality of life.

In the Ireland of the 1960s and earlier, the approach to mental illness was to admit the person to one of the various Victorian institutions that were utilised as psychiatric hospitals. There was very little understanding of mental illness and long-term confinement in a mental institution was about the only solution that existed. This all started to change in 1969, with the development of certain drugs which revolutionised how we treat mental illness. What these drugs did was to relieve some of the most serious symptoms of illnesses such as schizophrenia. The net effect of this was that, instead of having to lock people away to 'protect' them, we could 'treat' them in the community.

Over the next thirty years, all of the old institutions were phased out and psychiatric units were opened, attached to general hospitals. When people became mentally ill, they could be admitted during the acute phases of their illnesses. As their symptoms subsided, they could be discharged. Follow-up, support and treatment could then be provided in the community.

Whilst the development of what we call 'community-based psychiatry' was infinitely better than locking people up in institutions, it still had a problem. The psychiatric services were almost entirely based on a tertiary philosophy. Psychiatry focused all its resources on providing treatment to people who were already mentally ill. To make matters worse, the philosophy of only providing for a tertiary mental-illness-care service continued, and is still having a colossal impact in how resources for psychiatry are allocated.

We have to look to 2006 to find the next big change in how the mind and illness are understood, because it was in that year that some bright spark had the idea that if we could only catch mental illness at an early stage, we might just be able to prevent it from progressing.

This led to the development of programmes like DETECT. This programme focused on identifying teenagers in the very early stages of developing what is commonly referred to as psychosis. Doctors have found that by identifying psychosis at a very early stage and starting treatment, they can substantially reduce the progression of the illness.

This is probably the first time that the philosophy of early secondary care has been used in psychiatry. However, this is more than forty years after the importance of secondary care was established in general medicine. And if you think this is a damming indictment of mental health services today, then read on – the story gets worse.

After the importance of early intervention for people with mental illness problems was established, you could be forgiven for thinking that making the next step to understanding and adopting a primary care prevention strategy would have been fairly simple. I suppose it *should* have been simple.

Surely, twenty years after the importance of primary care prevention was established in physical illness, some genius would have copped on that, if we want to help prevent mental illness, we need to 'go back upstream and find out what's pushing them all in'. Well think again.

The Proof

If you want evidence of how far we are from understanding mental health, then you need to do no more than listen to 'experts' when they talk. For starters, it is very rare to find an expert who is able to differentiate between mental health and mental illness. Instead, the term mental health is used as a polite, politically correct term for mental illness.

So, let's say an 'expert' is asked something about mental illness. Instead of referring to someone as being mentally ill, they will say something like, 'That person has mental health issues.' Unfortunately, by failing to differentiate between the concepts of illness and health, professionals create a confusion that prevents people from gaining an understanding of what mental health actually is, why it's crucial to overall health and, most importantly, how to achieve it.

Not illustrating the importance of mental health and why it's worth working toward makes trying to 'sell' the importance of not playing the computer game sixteen hours a day very difficult. It's the same as trying to 'sell' the idea that eating a diet of red meat is bad for you without understanding the role of cholesterol in heart disease.

To further illustrate what I mean, I want you to try this simple test. I want you to tell me what I need to do to prevent myself from having a heart attack. Now, the last time I asked this question, it was to a group of students who were due to sit their Junior Cert exam.

As I stood there, I marvelled at the understanding that this group of fifteen- and sixteen-year-olds had of this question. They were all able to make a contribution. They told me that I needed to maintain a healthy weight, watch my diet, get some exercise, avoid smoking and drink less. One girl even suggested that, if my family had a history of heart trouble, I should be even more careful.

Isn't it marvellous to see how wonderfully successful physical health-promotion programmes have been? These days, we know so much about the causes of physical illness that it is possible to run very effective health-promotion programmes. I have to admit that it was one of these programmes that pushed me into giving up smoking twenty years ago.

In the next exercise, however, I want you to try to answer this question: 'What do I need to do if I want to prevent myself developing depression?'

And now I meet the silence. Wherever I go, and whenever I give lectures, I ask this question. I always get the same result: silence or, as we call, it 'the pregnant pause'. After about a minute, some people will tentatively say things like 'talk to others when something troubles you', or 'have good relationships' or 'don't get anxious'. Now, whilst these suggestions are all well and good, they are incredibly vague. They don't explain how to achieve better relationships or express our emotions or, indeed, how to get rid of anxiety.

This is because there are very few people who actually understand what mental health is, how to get it and why it is so important. I think it's incredible that something we spend so much of our time dealing with can be so very poorly understood.

So What Is It?

I would be the first to admit that trying to describe mental health is very difficult. Some years ago, however, I used an idea that I picked up from a mental health association brochure in which, instead of defining mental health, the author had described the characteristics of mentally healthy people.

I used this idea to develop a questionnaire which gives the user an idea of the components of mental health. I get people to mark themselves on a scale of one to ten on each characteristic, one indicating that they are hopeless at that characteristic, and ten indicating that they are paragons of virtue at it. I then get each person to give the questionnaire to a loved one and ask that loved one to score it based on how they see them.

Now, none of us have all the qualities all of the time, and the questionnaire shouldn't be taken very seriously. It does, however, give us an idea as to a 'port' we may wish to sail for. Have a look at these characteristics and see how they reflect both your own attitude toward yourself and how you want your children to be as adults.

How I Feel About Myself

1. I don't get overwhelmed by my emotions – fear, anger, love, guilt or anxiety.
2. I can take life's disappointments in stride.
3. I have a tolerant, easy-going attitude toward myself and others, and I can laugh at myself.
4. I neither underestimate nor overestimate my abilities.

5. I accept my shortcomings.

6. I have self-respect.

7. I feel able to deal with most situations.

8. I take pleasure in simple, everyday things.

How I Feel About Others

1. I'm able to give love and to consider the interests of others.

2. I have personal relationships that are satisfying and lasting.

3. I like and trust others and feel that others will like and trust me.

4. I respect the many differences I find in people.

5. I do not take advantage of others, nor do I allow others to take advantage of me.

6. I can feel I am part of a group.

7. I feel a sense of responsibility to my fellow human beings.

How I Meet the Demands of Life

1. I do something about my problems as they arise.

2. I accept my responsibilities.

3. I shape my environment whenever possible and adjust to it whenever necessary.

4. I plan ahead and do not fear the future.

5. I welcome new experiences and ideas.

6. I make use of my talents.

7. I set realistic goals for myself.

8. I am able to make my own decisions.

9. I am satisfied with putting my best effort into what I do.

Now ask yourself how you promote these qualities in your family. As we shall see in later chapters, if we lose many of the abilities listed above, we can inadvertently contribute to depression and anxiety. Some of these things we can't change, like our genes, but more of them we most definitely can, like our thinking and behaviour. Similarly, in overcoming anxiety and depression, it is these qualities that we need to 'grow'.

So what can we hope to achieve if we practise mental health exercise in the same way that we exercise physically? What's in it for us to practise these skills? Well, for starters, if you learn to practise these skills yourself, you will be in a position to teach them to your kids. By teaching these skills to your children, you will show them how to become mature and responsible adults with a great ability to be able to enjoy life.

Your children will learn both how to love and how to be loved. They will be able to recognise reality and adapt as necessary. By learning how to understand their emotions, they will be able to use them for their own good, without becoming slaves to them.

Laughter and peace of mind will be dominant forces in their lives. Fear and anxiety will be distant cousins. Their lives will not be dictated by fear and anxiety but, when they do experience these things, as we all do, they will be able to face them with courage.

Your children will be able to experience the vastness of life and delight in its paradoxes, mysteries and awe. They will pass on this attitude to their offspring, thereby teaching successive generations of children how to grow into mature adults and to experience these results for themselves.

Category Six: Education

Every year, I start receiving calls, usually from mums, asking me to see their son or daughter who's doing either their Junior Cert or Leaving Cert in June.

Curiously enough, though, it's nearly always around November that they ring. Rarely will I get a call to see Mary or Johnny outside of this month if the stress about their exams is their primary problem.

And do you know what? I find seeing and helping youngsters over the stress of the exams the most difficult therapy challenge for me personally. It's true, after thirty-one years in the job, you would reckon I've seen it all, but nowhere have I had to overcome my own difficulties more than when I see teenagers about their exams.

When I first see a youngster, I explain this to them. I explain that even so many years after my own Leaving Cert I still get knots of tension in my stomach when I see Leaving Cert season approaching. I've never gotten over it. My family still tease me about it, as they know how hard I found my own Leaving Cert.

So what's this got to do with your teenager? Well, in the above paragraph about exams, I've been very careful to not put 'Leaving Cert' and the word 'education' into the same sentence. This is because the Leaving Cert is to education as memorising a dictionary is to speaking a language. Or a pile of bricks is to a house.

And what is regularly referred to as rote learning is how most of us will have experienced school. Alas, for most of us, when we think of education we will use this memory to reflect our understanding of what education is all about. However, if we are to understand why education is so important to our teenage development, we need to change our understanding of education.

You see, the sixth-most-vital part of growing up mentally is to be found in education. Now, I'm sure nobody reading this will challenge or dismiss the importance of 'the three Rs' (reading, 'riting and 'rithmetic). And it's rare that I will see people who have a problem with trying to achieve these skills. If, however, we let ourselves be blinded with the attitude that all education begins and ends with the core curriculum subjects of the Leaving Certificate, then we run into trouble.

What teens need in order to win out in the Leaving Cert is what we call the 'learn-and-forget' system. This works on the philosophy of 'cram as much information into our minds as possible and then conveniently forget most of it by natural wastage when we have no use for it in our adult world'. You'll probably leave school with a Pentium 4 chip in your brain but, unfortunately, very little else.

Now please do not think for one minute that I'm against either the Junior Cert or the Leaving Cert, or against the importance of doing well in both. I'm not. I'm actually a big fan of them and regard the people who support the system as having a wonderful balance between the needs of youth for education and the realpolitik of life.

You see, no matter how bad you may think the combined Junior Cert and Leaving Cert cycles are, they are paragons of virtue compared to how other 'more advanced' countries try to programme their youth. The realpolitik of life is that there has to be some form of assessment of knowledge in society and, in the absence of having an actual assessment of educational skill that would work, we're stuck with it. However, no matter how much importance we attach to the learn-and-forget system, we need to find some way to balance memory with all the other aspects of education that are not as easily assessed by 'terminal examinations'.

What we do in Ireland is assign two separate years of the post-primary cycle to this realpolitik. In Third Year we get our kids, by hook or by crook, to memorise an enormous amount of knowledge and then assess their memory by making them do the Junior Cert.

We then give them Transition Year to experience a bit of real life and get a bit more maturity under their belts. Next, we gently reintroduce them to studying in Fifth Year, before chaining them to their desks again in Sixth Year and cramming into their brains all the information they need for the Leaving Cert. Finally, we torture them over the course of three weeks, during which they regurgitate all the information back to us in the form of the Leaving Cert.

Now, my comments may sound cynical and daft, which they are, but at least in our system, we are attempting to give our kids a few years to get to know the world, how it works and how to survive in it. These are First, Second, Fourth and Fifth years. So it's a mix of education versus memory-utilisation. And that's why I love the Leaving Cert. It's a unique Irish solution to a common global problem.

Most other countries in the Western world start their assessments of memory at around ten or eleven years of age. (Look up the 'Eleven plus' exam in the UK, for example.) After this first exam, the societies and departments of education of these countries continue their memory assessments by forcing their children to sit 'terminal' exams on a regular basis. They call this 'continuous assessment'. Continuous it may be, but I fail to see the relevance of what it is they are trying to assess.

In Chapter Seven, I will tell a story about Caroline, who was sixteen and whose parents contacted me from the USA seeking some advice in relation to this area. Now, if she were in Ireland, Caroline's parents would find supporting her much easier, as they would only have to worry about the pressure she would be put under in Third Year and in Sixth Year. Indeed, they would even have an option of giving her a 'gap year' in Fourth Year if they felt she was struggling, before introducing her to a gentle academic Fifth Year, during which she would get involved in lots of other things, like school plays and debating societies. Manage to get her momentum going toward the end of Fifth Year and then she would only have a hard, one-year slog in Sixth Year to get over the Leaving Cert, and Bob's your uncle. She would bounce out of school, hopefully with a certificate which would get her into the college course she wanted.

Unfortunately for Caroline, she is growing up under the USA's system. In this system, she faces Leaving Cert-type 'assessments' regularly throughout her school life, with the net result that, instead of been pressurised for Third Year and Sixth Year, she is under continuous pressure all of the time, as the next 'assessment' is always just around the corner.

What Other Types of Education Are There?

When I am asked to help a young person, I try to get that young person and his or her parents to understand that, whilst the Junior Cert and Leaving Cert are very important means toward an end, they are not ends in themselves. They have roles in our lives and must be mastered if we want comfortable lives, but they are not life itself. Understanding this is the foundation stone that success in both exams will be built on.

Indeed, both exams have other uses for teenagers and parents. Getting our teens over the bar involves us having to learn skills. As any parent who has had kids go through it will tell you, the Leaving Cert year is one year where all the rules change. It is the year when our screenagers have to learn that, to protect their long-term interests, they must put work before pleasure.

Of course, this is sometimes at the end of a gun barrel pointed at them by their parents. As my wise-cracking sister once told me, 'We live in a very democratic house here. They can do it with a row or they can do it without a row.'

To survive, parents must learn to keep their mouths shut, choose our battles and keep the real goal in sight. Having to park any issue that diverts them from that goal and to give up on the idea that we as parents should win every argument ensures that the Sixth Year is a pain in the ass for everybody in the family.

When teenagers come to see me, I try to get them and their parents to understand this. I work to try to give them all some perspective on what the Leaving Cert is all about. Once this is achieved, getting them to develop a common strategy to get the family over the Leaving Cert is fairly straightforward. The result of this is that tension and anxiety in the family is reduced. Reduced tension leads to fewer arguments, a more relaxed teenager, easier parenting, less stress over the exam and better exam results.

I start this process by asking the teenagers why they are doing the exam at all if they are getting so stressed about it. At this, I usually get dagger looks from the parents. However, I push on. Why put yourself through something that causes so much discomfort, I ask. Most times I just get a blank stare back. There they sit trying to think of an answer to a question they had never asked themselves. Believe it or not, most of us just accept the Leaving Cert as the way of the world, without ever asking ourselves why we are doing it.

Eventually, with a lot of soul-searching, they usually find that small little black box in their soul that regards the Leaving Cert as the 'be-all and end-all of existence' and believes that 'everything that you are and will be in the future will be dictated by your results in it'.

Get on well and it's, 'Yahoo! Aren't you brilliant?' Do badly and it's, 'Ah sure, it's only an exam and you did your best,' which is shorthand for, 'You're a failure and we, as your parents, haven't a clue where to go from here.'

Yikes, no wonder they are buckled by anxiety. Trying to face the Leaving Cert while believing that it is a global valuation of you is a sure way to become overwhelmed by November of Sixth Year – hence the visit to me.

What Is the Alternative?

So if you do give up the belief that the Leaving Cert is a global rating of you, what are you supposed to replace it with?

Well, to answer this in a meaningful way, let me tell you a story about a girl who lived next door to a very dear colleague of mine. I never met her, nor even got to learn her name. Outside of this story I know nothing more about her. Since I heard about her story fifteen years ago, I have never even discovered what she did with the rest of her life.

Old though the story is, this teenager has remained one of my greatest heroines, a role model for how I pray that my own children will turn out. She lived next door to my colleague and his memory of her was as a lovely, non-arrogant, confident teenager who always had a bounce in her step and a piece of chewing gum in her mouth.

On the day that the Leaving Cert results were released, my colleague met her coming out of her house. Calling to her, he enquired as to how she had got on, to which she replied that she had got 530 points. My colleague said that he was delighted for her and commented that she must be so thrilled and proud of herself, to which she turned a precocious eye to him and remarked, 'No, I'm pissed off with myself. I only needed 470.'

Real Education

I would have loved to have had that kind of insight when I was her age. At seventeen, that kid had sussed out exactly what she needed to get so that she would get what she wanted out of the Leaving Cert. To her, it was no more than a smash-and-grab exercise.

Believing this, she would have approached each exam with the goal of just grabbing as many points as possible. Of course, this attitude would have ensured that she would not have been stressed or anxious during her Leaving Cert, with the result that she was at her intellectual peak during it.

And that is the attitude that I try to get teens to adopt. It's not a measurement of them in any way. It's just a memory test, nothing more. It's an opportunity to grab as many points as they can. The more points they grab, the more opportunities will be open to them when it's all over.

What's the Real Benefit of Education?

There are other aspects to education that are rarely mentioned in the points race that is the Leaving Cert, aspects that are very important in life if you want to be happy and have a better chance of developing the characteristics of mental health that we looked at earlier.

We call this the concept of 'lifelong learning' and, as the name suggests, it has to do with accepting that life is a continuous journey for us all, and that in order for us to be able to grow during this journey, we need to accept that we will always be learning!

This kind of learning, however, is not the 'learn-and-forget' system like in school. Oh no, this kind of learning is all to do with learning the skills vital to us if we wish to survive in a mentally healthy state. As I mentioned earlier, Charles Darwin, the father of evolution, argued that the survival of a species is not determined by either its strength or its intelligence, but by its ability to adapt.

And guess what? The core skills that we need in order to be able to adapt to our changing lives are the same skills we need if we want to be lifelong learners.

Real education is about learning how to understand what's going on around us, identifying what we need to do in order to be able to adapt, and utilising our resources to protect ourselves. Learning to understand, however, has some little brothers that must be mastered before we can ever hope to understand. These include:

1. Learning to keep an open mind on most issues. If you believe

something to be true, that's fine. However, your outlooks – like everyone else's – are usually coloured by a million different factors, including your upbringing, culture and experiences. The skill is keeping in mind that, no matter how right you think you are, you might not be 100 percent right. Accepting this means that, if you see something that contradicts what you believe, you can look at it in a 'critical' way, re-examine what you believe and take in new evidence and ideas. You are then able adapt in whatever way necessary to cope with situations.

2. Before you can keep an open mind, however, you must first learn how to keep things you feel strongly about in perspective. One of the major factors in mental health is how upset you get over how little. Losing your head over your teen's messy room is all well and good. However, if you get hugely upset over something that is relatively minor (it's not exactly life-threatening, is it?), how are you going to react when something major happens? We call this 'emotional regulation'. What therapists look at is how little it takes to set you off and, when you do get upset, how long it takes for your emotions to settle back down.

3. Another big payoff in education is realising that you can't learn about everything. If you want to learn, you have to choose which topics are suited to you. Is what you are learning useful to you? Will it let you take advantage of opportunities? Will it tie in with your own abilities? And, finally, have you an interest in it?

Note that I have put interest last. That's because, if you put it first, then whatever you choose to study in college, when you find the parts that are not as interesting as you demand, you will lose interest and think that the course isn't for you. This will happen with whatever course you choose, as all of life's directions have boring parts to them.

As we learn, we see that we are very good in some areas and dreadful in others. We also see, however, that everybody else has similar good and bad characteristics – that everybody is right sometimes and wrong sometimes, just like we are. As we learn, we see that others are as flawed as we are. We start to see people in terms of the qualities that they have as opposed to the personalities they show.

This, I would argue, is the real purpose of education. To be able to change our beliefs, looking for truth and learning to see reality. Adapting and changing our lives and beliefs so as to be able to recognise and be able to live in our world.

As we progress through life, education evolves into learning to be able to understand our children, to be able to show them how to become lifelong learners themselves. To be able to change how they view themselves. And these are the very skills that are, as we will see, crucial to have in overcoming anxiety and depression.

Oh, and hands up anybody who has ever bothered to read Shakespeare after their Leaving Cert!

SECTION FOUR

Rearing a Screenager: Skills Parents Need to Learn and Practice

CHAPTER SEVEN
The Parental 'No Win' Trap

I have noticed that the concept of the invalidating environment and its effect on our emotional well-being has started to be accepted and understood more since I first wrote about it in *Five Steps to Happiness*. However, there is another area where it shows its ugly face that isn't so readily understood, but is essential for parents – especially mothers – to understand if they want to be able to deal effectively with their teenagers when they really push the boat out in being defiant.

To illustrate this, I'd like to introduce you to Caroline, who we mentioned briefly in the last chapter. Or rather, I'd like to introduce you to her mum, Karen. Caroline was a sixteen-year-old girl I saw for therapy some time ago. Saying I 'saw' her, though, might be a bit misleading, as I never actually met her in person. I don't even know how Caroline's mum found me, as they lived in the USA – but find me she did.

It always amazes me where people pick up my name. I've had people contact me from places I had never even heard off. Over the years however, one lesson I have learned is that, if a mum believes that you might be the solution to her cub's problem, she will walk through hell and hot coals to get you. Mums are like that.

I sometimes illustrate how mums have what I call 'an irrational instinct' toward their children. You see, instincts are generally there to help protect us. We instinctively eat, reproduce and run like the clappers if we see a lion who wants to eat us. So instincts are generally good things to have and we couldn't survive long if we didn't have them. Mums, however, have another instinct, one which doesn't protect them but destroys their health in the end. If a mum perceives something to be wrong with her cub, she cannot switch off the instinct that makes her try to find a solution.

Let's say that one of her offspring starts to get into trouble with the police. The mum will instinctively try to fix the problem. And if her cub keeps getting into trouble, she will keep searching for a solution. Over time, the more the situation deteriorates, the harder the mum will try to find a solution. We have an expression that you can carry a message, but you can't carry a body. Well, the less responsibility the cub takes for solving his or her own problem, the more the mum will try to fill in the gap.

And she will keep doing this, no matter how bad the situation gets. I see mums every day beating their heads against the proverbial brick wall, trying to sort out their cubs. These mums keep doing this until they (the mums) collapse emotionally. However, even though they are bloody and bruised, once they regain consciousness, so to speak, they head straight back to the wall and start banging their heads against it all over again. Eventually they become so punch-drunk that their own health starts to suffer. Their stress levels go through the roof and this affects their physical and mental well-being.

As a very elderly mum told me, mums will worry and try to protect their offspring 'from the day they are born to the day I die.' When all logic dictates that they should walk away, and indeed everybody else has walked away, mum will still be there banging away until she either finds a solution or dies.

I find it so frustrating when people fail to understand this. Continuously over the years, I've had to deal with conduct-disordered teenagers. Unfortunately, the advice many of their mums are given is to kick them out, as if kicking them out was simple and straightforward. Unfortunately, people's pseudo-psychology gets even more damning, as it implies that if mum doesn't kick her child out, she must be the cause or, at least, a significant part of the problem.

What many people, and indeed health professionals, don't realise is that asking a mum to abandon her cub is like asking her to cut off her own arm with a blunt knife. She just can't do it. Understanding this point is essential if you're going to be effective in tackling serious behavioural problems at home. I've seen mums who have had no choice but to break off their connections with their offspring. It's easy enough to spot them. They look completely broken. Broken to the degree where they have a haunted look that never goes away.

I try to teach that, if mums are to be expected to be able to take such drastic action toward their children, they will require five times as much support as they would have required to sort out their conduct-disordered teenagers in the first place.

However, you don't have to have a conduct-disordered teenager to have this invalidating environment and, indeed, there is no way Caroline could have been described as conduct-disordered. The invalidating environment crops up in every situation where humans interact with other humans.

'TALK TO SOMEONE'

Believe me, even in situations where people are trying to help each other, characteristics of the invalidating environment will crop up. To give you an example, let me tell you about a lecture I was giving during a secondary school's mental health week. Some of the ideas that the school had were really fantastic. However, one of the messages that the school was trying to get across was that, if any of the students were feeling down or anxious, they could talk to a number of designated students.

Now doesn't that sound like a brilliant idea? On the surface it is, and it would be in keeping with how experts suggest programmes like this should be run. But it's only on the surface that this suggestion actually works.

To illustrate what I mean, let's use an analogy with being a mum. One of the most common things I see in my practice is postnatal depression (PND). Now, as I explained in my last book, when a mum has a baby, it is normal for her to get stressed out of her mind, feel guilty that she's not being good enough and blame herself for everything. (Remember, a mother's place is . . . in the wrong!)

When PND sets in, instead of accepting that it is normal, mum starts to think she must be abnormal for being the way she is. She tries to compensate by trying even harder to 'get it right'. Of course, the more she tries to get it right, the more she sees herself getting it wrong – which then leads her to conclude that she is a total failure.

Now imagine you are feeling like this. That no matter what you do, you can't seem to be able to get it right. You feel like an utter failure and are terrified that that's how other people will see you. Imagine that you see a poster that says that if you are feeling down you can talk to 'one of us'. Accompanying the slogan is a photograph of a smiling mum who looks like she has just walked off a catwalk, holding a perfect-looking baby.

Think how you would feel. Yeah, you've guessed it – like crap. What we, as experts, have inadvertently done is say to you that if you're feeling bad, then you are somewhere that we are not. Before you can take us up on our offer, you will first have to accept that you are 'different', and in your mind that means that you are a failure.

We are also implying that in some way we are different to you, that in some way what you are feeling is different to what we feel. Of course, because we are so sensitive and such good people, we will 'reach out' to you. This implies that we are in a different world to you. And if your world is a 'failure' world, then our world must be a 'success' world.

Furthermore, with the best will in the world, we offer to get some help for you to look after the baby, because we know a mum who has six children she copes with marvellously. So marvellously, in fact, that she has enough room in her day to support you with your kids. The net result is the more we offer help, the more mum sees it as a testament to how much of a failure we see her as.

This same interpretation applies for the rest of us as well. If we are hurting over something that we cannot achieve, then telling us to 'reach out' to someone whom we see as achieving what we can't will only make us feel worse.

What we have done, unintentionally, is to introduce a barrier that actually makes it harder for the teenager to approach us. In fact, this barrier is worse for teenagers. Since teenagers view themselves by how they appear to others, the effect of sending the message that 'we're over here and you're over there' is to create a problem that is totally unnecessary.

SO WHAT SHOULD WE DO INSTEAD?

To illustrate how we should approach making it easier, I'd like to try a little experiment with you. As you read this book, I want you to imagine that you have a few kids and are really struggling with them. You're reading this book with all its wisdom. How are you feeling?

I would suspect that you are probably thinking to yourself that it must be easier for Harry and me to handle our kids. That because Harry and I know so much about psychology and psychotherapy that we have it all sussed and will turn out children who will become world leaders and win Nobel prizes all round.

Eh, well think again. You see, as I was writing this chapter I got speaking to Joe, the manager of the crèche my son was attending. As we spoke, we were laughing with each other over the fact that, because we work in the business of teaching and guiding kids, people think we must have all the answers. Joe has a two-year-old little madam who has just learned how to say 'no'! Mine is a four-year-old pocket rocket who grasped the philosophy of self-determination a long time ago.

And would you believe it, Joe finds it as difficult to cope with his kids as I do with mine. It's like the old expression about how, in theory, there should be no difference between theory and practice but, in practice, there most definitely is. (Or as Brendan Behan said, 'Critics are like eunuchs in a harem: they know how it's done, they've seen it done every day, but they're unable to do it themselves.')

Now imagine that you find yourself in the situation where you need to get professional help with your kids. What kind of therapist are you going to feel most comfortable with? One who sits behind a desk and gives off an air that they are an 'expert' or one who you know struggles just as much with their kids as you do with yours? Most of us will find it much easier to approach someone if we see them as being as mad, bad or sad as ourselves.

GEOGRAPHY CHANGES NOTHING

Working as a therapist in both Ireland and China, I have found that when you scratch the surface, we are no different to anybody else. In *Five Steps to Happiness*, I tried to illustrate this idea, that if you come to see me for a problem, you probably are nuts, but that no matter how mad, bad or sad you may think you are, you're no madder, badder or sadder than the rest of us.

If you want to be successful with your teenagers, you have to practise this concept of 'normalising' their experiences for them. Remember, the aim of being a parent is not to fix all your children's problems, but to show them how to fix them for themselves. And this concept becomes more and more important as you progress from being a parent to being a mentor.

About a year ago, I developed an approach to overcoming anorexia nervosa where, instead of seeing the girl on her own, I had mum sit in whilst we talked. Why? Well, the most difficult aspect of overcoming anorexia nervosa is learning how to let go of trying to be in control of everything you do.

As I write, seven girls have been through the programme. As their therapy progressed, I used their mums as examples of real women. Sure they probably get it wrong frequently, but so do the rest of us. And yes, even though mum is probably part of the problem, she has the skills to objectively look at where she is going wrong and is able to do what is necessary to correct it.

During the therapy, I show the girl how to understand her mum, that her mum is a flawed, imperfect woman who tries to cope with her world each day with only the tools she has, as much a victim of her own upbringing as the girl is of her upbringing. However, even though her mum is imperfect and gets a lot of things wrong, she has managed to get a lot right and has learned how to survive and be successful. As the girl engages, she starts to view her mum as an example of what real women are like. As the girl fails herself, she starts to realise that, in failing, she is becoming more and more like a real woman.

Gradually, both mum and daughter grow and change, and the effect on their relationship is colossal. They bond in a way that most of us can only dream of. Mum has become a real role model to her daughter, just like the lioness with her cubs.

COPING WITH OUR OWN FEELINGS

About five years ago, I was wandering around Tesco at about 9 PM with my then four-year-old son. I laugh when I think that before I became a dad I couldn't understand why parents would be in Tesco so late with their very young children. Then I had my own children and wasn't too long learning why!

As my son and I wandered through the aisles, I came across a little toddler having a temper tantrum. She was lying on the ground and, by God, was she giving it socks. I'm sure everybody in the shop could hear her. Her mum, however, was nonchalantly looking at the cereals on the shelves, ignoring what was happening on the floor beside her.

As I walked by, I caught her eye and gave her my best empathic, 'I know what you're going through' look. To which, with a tired smile, she remarked calmly, 'Sometimes it's just easier to live with the embarrassment!'

And isn't that the truth. Wouldn't it be lovely to have the confidence to be able to do what that mum did. That is, accept that you aren't perfect, fail in loads of ways as you stumble through life, do what you need to survive and let people think whatever they want.

THIS MUM WAS A REAL MEMBER OF THE RAGGY DOLL CLUB

The Raggy Doll Club is a euphemism for a theory that is at the heart of cognitive behaviour therapy (CBT). This theory is that, since the whole is far greater than the sum of the parts, we can't be measured as a person by either what we do or how we think and feel. Yeah, I know that sounds like a load of codswallop. However, it's also completely correct.

To describe this concept, I came up with the idea of the Raggy Doll Club. *The Raggy Dolls* was a cartoon series in the 80s, which was set in Mr Grimes's toy factory. When a toy came off the conveyor belt that was broken or had something wrong with it, a big hand removed it and threw it in the reject bin. *The Raggy Dolls* was about the adventures of all the toys in the reject bin. All the characters had something wrong with them, like Sad Sack, who was overweight. The philosophy that the creator of the programme was trying to get across to the children who viewed the cartoon was encapsulated in the storylines.

When I started running courses in low-intensity CBT for health professionals, I found that most of them found it very hard to grasp the concept of unconditional self-acceptance. When I explained it in terms of *The Raggy Dolls*, however, they grasped it much more easily at an emotional level. In fact, they loved the concept – hence the formation of the Raggy Doll Club.

So if 'you're not at ease with your knobbly knees or your fingers are all thumbs', then why not try it. Joining is quite easy. You're a member when you want to be, and you cancel your membership when you decide to. There are only four rules for membership. You must:

1. Admit that you're not perfect, that you never were and that you never will be. (But neither is anybody else.)

2. Admit that you've screwed up in a big way at least once in your life. (But so have most people. And for those who haven't, it's only a matter of time before they do, since it's not possible to go through life without screwing up sometimes.)

3. Believe that you can't be measured by your screw-ups as there is no measuring tool.

4. Believe that you don't have to accept other people's opinions of you, as their opinions of you are no more valid than your opinions of them.

Of course, if you want to cancel your membership, then all you have to do is start measuring yourself again or accepting other people's opinions of you. So hands up anybody who thinks they're not entitled to membership. I ask this to every class and every person I teach, and do you know what? After all these years I'm still waiting for someone to raise their hand. This is because we all kind of know that we're not perfect.

In Chapter Four, I made the bold statement that I've never had a teenager who didn't open up to me. How do I do it? Well, there's no rocket science about it. All I do is illustrate my own Raggy Doll credentials through my attitude and treat them with respect. Apologise to them on behalf of the adult world for not showing them how to understand and handle their world, and hey presto, they open up like flowers, revealing all the hurt and fear that they have bottled up but are afraid to talk about because they will be challenged for feeling the way they do or even punished for doing what they believe they have to do to survive.

A little application of my universal spanner (it'll fit any old nut that comes through the door) and situations start straightening themselves out. Oh, and showing the parents that I'm no better at the parenting lark than they are results in them opening up to the world of fear and uselessness that they feel but are afraid to show others.

THE RAGGY DOLL PARENT

In learning from all the excellent parenting books out there (via my wife, by the way), one thing I have noticed is how little they focus on the emotional well-being of the parents. Sure, they focus on the emotions parents have that are unhelpful in interacting with your kids. However, only some of them will try to reassure parents that to struggle with coping is perfectly normal and will pass as the teen gets older. (By which time you'll have a whole lot of other problems to face . . . or so I'm told!)

For the rest of this chapter, let's look at the two most common problems normal parents experience.

Guilt

After 'a mother's place is in the wrong', the next most-common whip I see parents apply to their backs is the concept of guilt.

Guilt is one of those emotions that headshrinkers like me regard as unhealthy and negative. The reason we label it as unhealthy is that, instead of helping us to find a solution, it actually prevents us from acting effectively, as it leads us to expectations of ourselves that are impossible to achieve. The underlying core belief behind guilt is that we must know what to do in each situation and be able to do it.

This leads us to demand of ourselves that we must have a solution that fits in with a vague idea of what we believe the solution should look like. This vague idea of what the solution should look like leads us into a situation that, no matter what vague goal we manage to achieve, we should be finding a solution to some other aspect.

As we sink further and further into the hole, instead of solving the problem we use up all our energy in flogging ourselves, which doesn't solve anything.

Shame

Shame presents its ugly head when we believe that if people see the real us they will think we're mad, bad or sad, and that we must accept their opinions of us. Whilst shame is usually not as prevalent as guilt (except in mums with postnatal depression), it can result in parents taking actions that are detrimental to finding solutions.

For instance, if parents think their youngster's depression is somewhat shameful, they may avoid seeking help, as they will be afraid of what people may think. If they do feel this, then I can guarantee you that – whilst they may think that they are hiding this attitude from their teenager – their teenager will pick it up. This results in the teenager believing that they're somewhat shameful, which only goes to reinforce their own belief that they are weak/a failure/screwed up and less worthwhile a person than everybody else.

CHAPTER EIGHT
Unlocking Our Parental Minds

There is an old saying in the property industry that there are three things which are essential in valuing a house. They are location, location and location. What this means is that by far the most important consideration in valuing a property is where it's situated. Once you have the location right then everything else is quite straightforward. The same can be said about promoting mental health in your kids. However, in this case, it's not location that's important. The three fundamentals that must be borne in mind if you want to be an effective parent are listening, listening and listening.

And believe me on this one, unless you have learned how to listen to your children's attempts at communication then you haven't a hope of solving any other issue for them. We have a saying that 'unless you learn to listen, you can't listen to learn'. Once you have learned to listen, you can then hear what your child is trying to communicate, even though they might not be able to fully understand themselves what they are trying to say. Remember, teaching them the skills to understand their world is initially *your* job. So unless you have learned the skill of listening, you can't teach any other skills to your kids.

Try to understand that the teen is trying to understand and communicate with their world, and to do this in the face of a barrage of conflicting ideals and the demands that are being made of them by society. The teen might gain some of this understanding in the later years of their emerging adulthood but, in the early years, their ability to understand what they are experiencing is extremely limited. That's why they need you.

Nevertheless, even though they may be very unclear of what they actually need and may make a total hash of communicating what they think they want, it is incredibly easy to teach them how to understand their world and communicate their needs when you know how to give them the necessary tools to do so.

Now you might be forgiven for thinking that the secret of listening is fundamentally 'keeping your own gob shut'. And, indeed, you would be right in thinking that, but if learning to listen was that easy and practising it was that straightforward, then there wouldn't be much need for a book like this, would there?

You see, before we can learn to listen, we have first got to dismantle our own prejudices and preconceptions. What do I mean? Well, when someone says something to us, we all pass what is being said through our own emotional crucibles. These emotional crucibles are made from all the experiences, ideologies and philosophies that have made us the people we are today.

Unfortunately, once what the person says is passed through the crucible, what comes out the other side is often at odds with what the person was trying to communicate in the first place. So effective listening and understanding is much more about us as parents overcoming out own issues, than about teaching kids how to communicate with us.

You see, our kids are *always* communicating to us. It's we who are unable to either recognise or decipher what it is they are trying to say. And if that weren't bad enough, we then expect our kids to be able to put all the pieces of their communication together using skills that neither they nor we have.

Combine that with the expectation that our kids should be able to understand our communication perfectly, and you are left with a communication mess that can go around in circles for years, never resolving and making everybody's life a misery. So before we can get to the bit about listening to learn, let's look at the most common barriers that we, as parents, make that prevent us from being able to listen in the first place

BARRIERS TO LISTENING

By far the most common error I see parents make – and, indeed, I often fall into this hole myself – is regarding listening and agreeing as meaning the same thing. When someone says something that we don't agree with, we feel that we must interrupt and argue the point with them immediately because, if we don't, then we are in some way agreeing with what they are saying.

As a therapist, this was the first insight that I had to learn when I was training, and it is the first thing I try to teach parents. When I first link in with a teenager, parents sometimes feel that, because I'm not challenging their little darling, I am in some way colluding with their child and believing everything that child is saying.

And this can get to an extreme from time to time, because the second-biggest error that many of us make is demanding that we must be listened to by our kids. Now, there is absolutely no problem with wanting to be heard. Indeed, now that I think of it, being heard is probably the most vital part of the whole process.

It's when, however, we demand that we must be heard first before we are willing to allow our kids to be heard, that the problem arises. When this happens I often find that the teen will adopt a 'dig their heels in' attitude (if they haven't already), with the result that the same arguments get rehashed over and over again, driving everybody nuts.

To illustrate what I mean, I want you to try this exercise for me. The next time your teen or partner gets grumpy, I want you to ask them to tell you what is going on in their head. Now, when they talk, I just want you to listen to what they are saying. The only time you are allowed to interrupt is to clarify something that they have said.

When they say they are finished, I want you to paraphrase back to them what you think they have said and ask them to tell you how accurate you are. Start with some simple thing that is upsetting them. By practising this, you will find that understanding what they are saying is quite simple. Not only that, but as you practise, you will find that you are able to understand more and more of what they are saying in bigger and bigger issues, even when they don't fully understand themselves.

As you become more of an expert in the art of listening, you will find that people become more and more willing to be able to share with you what's going on in their heads, no matter how daft it sounds. They will share things with you that they weren't even aware that they were feeling. When we feel that we are being accepted as we are and are not being judged by what we say, then we can really open up to the world of emotion we feel. Only then can we come to understand ourselves and the world around us. And that is exactly what you want your teenager to be able to do.

So, the next time your teen starts to moan or give out about something, why not try listening without giving feedback or challenging them – because trust me, it really works.

COMMON MISTAKES WE, AS PARENTS, MAKE THAT DISABLE OUR ABILITY TO LISTEN

Learning to listen takes lots of time and practice. The listening bit is the easy part, though. Even learning to paraphrase and understand what is being said isn't too hard to learn, either. Learning to keep one's big gob shut when all you want to do is strangle the little monster is the hard part. And even though lots of parents will deny that they sometimes have murder in their hearts, it's usually quite common and perfectly normal to see when your little dearest starts to explore how far they can push your buttons.

Now, please, please don't believe that I am in any way encouraging you to hurt your child or that I'm in the process of setting up classes in strangulation techniques. All I'm saying is that unless you learn to listen, paraphrase and acknowledge your own negative thoughts and feelings, you haven't a hope of surviving your kids – never mind understanding what they are trying to say or teaching them how to emotionally regulate.

So before we go on to learning how to promote mental health in our kids, let's take a look at factors that negatively affect our *own* mental health and our ability to listen to our kids. Because the skills that we have to learn and practise are identical to what our teens need to learn.

THE PATHOLOGICAL CRITIC

In the introduction, we looked at the concept of the pathological critic and how it can have a devastating effect on your kids if left unchecked. Well hold on to your seat, because the pathological critic doesn't just exist in your kids. It's part and parcel of *your* head too, and a totally misunderstood part of being a parent, especially for mothers. As I mentioned earlier, a very good colleague of ours has an expression that 'a mother's place is in the wrong'. Need I say more? This pathological critic that is so damaging has been found in every mum since time began, because all mums instinctively hold themselves responsible for everything bad that happens in their children's lives.

Even when there is no crisis occurring in your family, your emotional head will still scan everything about your kids like radar, looking for something to blame yourself about. I explained the nature of the pathological critic in the introduction. However, it is the pathological critic being present in *your* life as a parent that can lead you into behaviours and philosophies which don't protect your kids – i.e. overparenting – and end up creating a world for them which in no way reflects the world that they will face as adults.

When I worked in the USA, I remember having lunch with two colleagues: one was an Egyptian Muslim and the other was a New York Jew. We started to compare which society had the most intrusive mothers. By the end of the meal we had finally concluded that there was no difference between 'Jewish mother syndrome', 'Muslim mother syndrome' and 'Irish mother syndrome'. They all had the same characteristics. And you thought that cultures all have big differences between them, didn't you?

But before I start to illustrate overparenting and its consequences, I want to clear up some incredibly dismissive fallacies and beliefs about it. If I don't, then it will not be possible to explain in any meaningful way why it occurs or how to prevent it. So before we go any further, try to remember that:

1. Nearly every mother does it.

2. Whilst it is usually the first thing health professionals blame for your kids' difficulties, it usually is not as big a factor as they would like you to think it is.

3. I don't believe that the over-mothering actually causes your child's

problem. Rather, I have found that the over-mothering has evolved as a reaction to a developing problem in your child.

4. Solutions that are offered by both professionals and amateur psychologists in your life are usually overly simplistic and impractical.

5. There seems to be a belief that, if the mum just withdraws support, the kid will somehow magically figure out what to do and, even more magically, be able to do it.

6. Ideology is the luxury of those who don't have to sort out the mess. Because the advice-givers don't have to make their solutions work, they can have the luxury of having whatever ideology they want.

7. Because the buck stops with you, you don't have this luxury. You have to find something that will work.

8. Overparenting, therefore, evolves as an instinctive response by you to try to protect your cub, and occurs in the absence of an alternative practical solution.

So how do you counteract your own pathological critic? Because even though overparenting is fully understandable, it can smother your kids from learning how to cope with their world. So whilst you can't just switch off your instinct to protect your cub, you can change from being a smothering parent to being an effective teacher. We will look at how to implement the solution in a minute, but before we do, I need to explain one last thing.

BELIEFS

We are continuously scanning the world around us, trying to make sense of what it is we think we see. To do this, we use the two parts of our brain which Harry dealt with in the first chapter: the 'logical mind', the origin of which is situated in the front of your brain, in the prefrontal cortex; and the 'emotional mind', the origin of which is situated in the middle of your brain, in the limbic system. These two minds are in constant communication with each other.

If you want an example of this, watch for the next time you're on your own. Notice the internal dialogue that's going on in your head. You start to think about something and chew it around for a while, trying to make sense of it. This is your logical and emotional minds talking to each other. It's also why we say that at times we may be in two minds about something, a figure of speech which is more accurate than you probably ever guessed. 'Feeling the penny drop' occurs when our logical and emotional minds synchronise with each other. We call this our 'wise mind' (or 'insight', if you prefer).

We are constantly interacting with our environment using both our emotional and logical minds. Most of the time, we are unaware that we are doing it and it would be well-nigh impossible to be able to examine every thought and situation. To get around this and still succeed in getting some kind of understanding as to what it is that's going on with us, we usually take a few parts of what we see and guess the rest subconsciously.

Indeed, this is perfectly normal and works quite well most of the time. Sometimes, however, like weather forecasters, we can get it spectacularly wrong.

What happens is that, when something occurs in our lives, we start trying to interpret it. We then interpret our interpretation and keep throwing it around in our head until we come to a conclusion as to what it is we think we see. We call this our 'belief', and it is this belief that then dictates how we respond to the event. No problem so far. It doesn't do us any harm if we get it wrong at times, either. So what if you felt that the checkout girl in the supermarket didn't like you? You're not going to be seeing her very often, are you?

Unfortunately, however, when our misinterpretations crop up closer to home, like in our family, we can end up going off on a complete tangent that is based on incorrect assumptions altogether. Once again, this isn't too dangerous for us. Who hasn't had a row with their spouse where both of you were reading each other wrong?

There are times however, when we can get it spectacularly wrong. And when we do, we can keep reading it wrong, which can have major impacts on our relationships. This is because, if we come to believe something, our minds can start a process whereby we only see evidence that will agree with what we believe. Or as we put it, 'Belief-based attributions will dismiss disconfirming evidence.'

In a nutshell, what this implies is that, having come to believe something about our kids, not only will we look for evidence to support our viewpoint, we will actively dismiss any evidence that doesn't conform to what we already believe. And that is why learning to listen has a close cousin called 'keeping an open mind'. Not much point learning to listen to what you're been told if you just keep dismissing anything you don't agree with, is there? (Or at least that's what my wife keeps telling me!)

OPENING OUR MINDS

Did you ever hear the story about the girl who wrote home to her parents, saying that she had decided to give up medical school? Her letter went like this:

Dear Mum and Dad,

Please forgive me for writing this letter, but I've decided to give up medical school.

I understand that you have both slaved for most of your lives so that I could go to college, but I've just found out that I'm pregnant.

I know that I'm in my final year and that I would have a most promising career if I finished, but with the baby and all, I don't think completing college will be possible.

On a brighter note, the child's father promises me that he will get a job and look after me and the baby when he gets out of rehab. And the black eye he gave me last week was really my fault and just a sign of how much he loves me.

Now, having read the above paragraph, please ignore it as it's not true. It's just that I failed an exam and wanted to make sure you kept it in perspective.

Tongue in cheek the letter may be, but the message it sends out is very important.

I remember talking to a client one day about being a father. This gentleman was the same age as me. However, he had married very young and his four kids were all grown up. I, on the other hand, was a very late starter as a dad and had one very young child and another on the way. As we were chatting, he gave me a piece of advice that I still remember to this day and try to practise as best I can.

As he was walking out the door, he remarked that, as a dad, I would hear loads of things about how to handle my kids – some good and some bad. And, indeed, I would have good times and bad times with my kids but, no matter what happened, I should always remember, 'It's only a phase!'

How true his advice has proved to be. Over the years, I have seen all kinds of harum-scarum problems with adolescents and young adults and, in the vast majority of cases, the situations that brought them to me have ironed themselves out with minimal input.

So the practical skill all parents need to practise in order to be able to keep an open mind is keeping things in perspective. And doing that involves not 'catastrophising' everything that happens with your adolescent.

OTHER PARENTAL HURDLES

Letting your kids rant without getting into the ring with them is very difficult. Not interrupting them is equally difficult. I've never managed to find an easy way to practice this myself, as it is just a case of shutting up, sucking it up and smiling supportively as they tear your character asunder.

Until you had kids, you could never understand your parents. The same goes for your children. They will never fully understand the hurt you feel when they are criticising you until they are standing there whilst their children are blowing up at them. Try not to take it personally. As far as they are concerned, you are just a part of their life whose primary purpose is to feed them, give them money and stand out of their way when they are going out on a Saturday night.

There is one word that has to be banned when you are trying to carry on a conversation with your kids. That is the word 'but'. Putting the word 'but' into a sentence means that you are now going to dismiss everything you said before the 'but'.

LISTENING TO LEARN

So now that you have started to listen, the next skill to be mastered is interpreting what your adolescent is trying to say.

Parents will often tell me that their sons or daughters are throwing tantrums at home, often for no apparent reason. Of course, my usual response is to ask them what their kids are trying to say, what they feel they must go to such extreme lengths to make heard. For reasons discussed in Chapter Four, 'The Invalidating Environment', it is common for teenagers to oscillate from emotional inhibition in order to be accepted to extreme emotional states in order to be heard.

When I ask parents what their children are saying, though, most don't actually know. Similarly, when I ask the teens what they are trying to say, they often don't know either. So much for shouting being an effective form of communication!

So the first thing I have to do is create an environment where the teens can learn to express themselves without somebody jumping down their throats. Only by being able to speak freely without comment from others do they learn to read what's going on in their heads.

And believe it or not, in the vast majority of cases, when the teen gets down to what's really bothering them, it's usually something very understandable and fairly straightforward to sort out. The problem isn't what's bothering them; the problem is how they are trying to express it. Combine this with the parent's inability to listen and interpret what their teen is trying to say and you will see why everybody in the family is getting extremely frustrated.

If parents want to be effective teachers and mentors to their children, they must realise that they are a vital part of any solution that is devised. Of course, in accepting this, we all have to accept that we are probably a major part of the problem too.

This can be very hard to accept for most parents, including myself.

However, if we want to be able to navigate our way through our teenager's vulnerable years, then we have to accept that this will involve us changing our approach and philosophy in life also.

The only thing in life that appears in black and white is a newspaper. Learning to parent and mentor is as much about us changing our perspectives as parents as it is about our kids learning that survival in real life involves putting down the computer game and going out and finding a job.

If parents can't grasp this need to change, then there is no point sending our kids off for therapy, as it will start off with the wrong person sitting on the couch.

It's vital, therefore, that as parents we look at our own mental health. Before being able to teach our kids how to get good mental health, we have got to get more than a passing relationship with it ourselves. There's not much point shouting at your teen to stop shouting at you, is there?

Even though I practise a specific type of therapy, I believe that no matter what type of method a therapist uses, 80 percent of the solution will be determined by the relationship they have with the teen. Similarly, in parenting, 80 percent of the result will be determined by the relationship you have with your teen.

I remember some years ago Ray D'Arcy, the radio presenter, asked people to text in with the most memorable times they had with their parents as they were growing up. Loads of people contacted the station and, do you know what? Not one person mentioned that their favourite memory of their parents was the trip to Disneyland or the holiday in Barbados. No, every single memory was about incredibly ordinary daily activities like being curled up on the couch with dad or mum, watching a movie and pigging out on pizza, or sitting on the canal bank with dad, fishing.

And that's how simple it is. Sure, your teens will probably recoil in horror at the idea of spending time with you, but it's vital that you do. You may find that you only have a five-minute window in which you can teach them something but, in order to find that window, you may have to spend four weeks in close company with them.

Over the years, I have seen hundreds of teenagers and young adults for therapy. Occasionally, I have had to implement very complicated technical skills in order to get a result. However, in the vast majority of cases, all that has been required has been to use basic listening and teaching skills in order to stop major problems from developing. In the next chapter, we will look at these basic skills and at how all parents can adopt them.

CHAPTER NINE
Keeping It Simple

Whilst I am usually an adult therapist, I do see children and adolescents. Or rather, I try not to see the child at all but to see the parents and teach them what to do. It's a system that has worked well for me over the years.

I have a number of reasons for doing it this way. Firstly, my attitude is that if you can train a twenty-year-old to be a therapist, you can train a parent to sort out their offspring. Secondly, it's far less traumatic for the child/adolescent. However, I suppose the main reason is that, since the parents are in constant contact with their children whilst I will only see them once a week or so, getting a result is much easier and more straightforward if done through the parents. Equally, any solution must have the parents on board or the therapy will be doomed from the start.

Of course, if as a parent you accept that you are an essential part of the solution, then you've also got to accept that you're probably a major part of the problem. Nevertheless, try to accept that even if you are, you're no more of a problem than Harry and I are to our kids. Isn't there great security in that? Here we all are, doing the best we can with the tools we've got, sometimes getting it right and sometimes getting it wrong, just like our kids. We're all learning. They're learning how to grow up and we are learning how to be parents. In a few years, they will be learning how to be parents themselves. We're all lifelong learners.

GILLIAN

Gillian was a teenager whose parents had asked me to see her. However, when they suggested to her that she see me, she resisted for ages. She had been quite open to her parents about her anxiety before they mentioned me but had started denying that it was a problem once they had suggested she come to see me. On and on this went. Feeling anxious, denying it and getting angry with her parents for 'breaking' her trust by involving others in what she had told them confidentially.

As the situation did not improve over the succeeding months, her parents contacted me and asked if I had any suggestions that might help. I asked them to ask their daughter whether she would be willing to meet me once. I would do all the talking. If at the end of that hour she didn't think I could help, then she need never see me again.

With reluctance, Gillian agreed to come. Once she realised I was not going to bite, she started to relax. She volunteered that the real reason she didn't want to come was that she was afraid that I would tell her that there was something wrong with her. Of course, the only answer I could give her was that there most definitely was something wrong with her, but that there was no more wrong with her than there was with me.

Now, this might seem like a clever little anecdote. However, can you spot what I've done? By inferring that she is no different to me and is experiencing feelings that I had at her age, I'm normalising the situation for her.

I then hinted that if she hadn't come to see me over that problem, she prob-ably would have ended up coming to see me over another one. What I was doing was helping her to understand that growing up is full of situations that we need to learn how to overcome. Some of these she would be able to figure out by herself, and some she would need a little guidance with. Indeed, with some of them she would probably need expert help to learn what to do.

I've been using this method for years to get adolescents to engage, and have never seen it fail. As the teen engages, they see more and more that they have a problem, just like the rest of us, but *they* are not a problem. By adopting a 'we're all in the same boat' attitude, the teen can gradually start to open up and talk about what's going on in their head.

INVALIDATING THE PARENTS

The importance of adopting an approach like this is even more relevant when, as parents, we have to change the way we think and react to our kids. Understanding that we all struggle trying to rear our kids is essential if we are going to change the way we do so. If, as a therapist, I sit there silently giving advice to parents, they will spend so much energy trying to cope with the shame, embarrassment and guilt of having to come to see me in the first place that they will have little energy left to try to understand how to solve the problem. Knowing that I have as much difficulty putting theory into practice as they do will help them feel a hell of a lot more comfortable in looking carefully at where they're going wrong and what to do. It's a bit like the kettle calling the pot black, so to speak.

So if you're feeling a bit embarrassed or guilty because you roared at your kids last night, then just remember that I roared at mine last night too. Accepting that you make mistakes and letting your kids see this when appropriate can make it much easier to get them to accept that they also make mistakes. This philosophy attains extreme importance when we have to confront them over more serious behaviours and attitudes.

The secret to teaching your kids survival skills for adulthood is to 'hasten slowly, let them grow up gently'. In order to do this, we need to be able to show them how we change the way we view *our* world when needed.

PARENTAL CONDITIONS THAT HINDER GROWTH

There are, however, certain hurdles that, if present, have to be overcome if we are to create an environment in which our children can grow healthily. The first of these involves parents being more focused on their own issues than on their teens'.

At the extreme end are addictions which, if present, create havoc. But there are others that are not so apparent but equally cause havoc and prevent solutions from being found.

As we have seen, teens want to be able to talk to their parents. However, as

I explained, teens will only talk to their parents if they feel that they will get helpful responses. If they are afraid that they will be given out to, or that the importance of what they are experiencing will be dismissed, then they will clam up.

Indeed, parents can have so many misconceptions about teenagers and what they want that they become incapable of understanding their teens. Now, I could write a complete book on these misconceptions but, for the moment, let's look at the most common ones:

1. Teens rarely, if ever, expect to get their own way all of the time. They will, however, try every so often to push the boundary with you, just to see how far they can go. This is a very important part of growing up, as boundaries should get broader as we grow. If you think about it, their behaviour makes sense. How are we going to know where the boundary is if we don't push?

2. Children and teenagers want to be accepted for who they are, not for who you want them to be. Every time you compare them to someone else, asking why they can't be more like so and so or remarking on how good so and so is at the piano, you are under-mining their own concept of themselves and destroying their self-esteem – not encouraging them to try harder.

3. When your teens make mistakes, try to remember that they are Raggy Dolls just like you. Blowing your nut at them is just forcing them into their shells and making it much more difficult for them to open up to you next time – which, incidentally, may be the time they really need your support.

4. Similarly, when they do something wrong, then deal with the offence and let it go. Don't be tempted to keep all their misde-meanours in a file in your head so you can bring them into the next argument you have. If you do keep reminding them of past 'crimes', you will only put them into a position where they are serving a

never-ending sentence. Teens put into this situation will eventually stop trying, as they realise they can never win.

5. Practise what you preach. If you expect your teens to behave in a certain way, then you must behave in a similar way yourself. If you want them to acknowledge it and apologise when they do something wrong, then you must be willing to do the same. Remember, saying sorry does not make you vulnerable. It demonstrates that you are fallible, and shows your teens what to do when they are in the wrong.

6. Keep your word when you make a promise.

7. If you have to take your teen aside to tell them off, then do it in private. Don't *ever* tell them off in front of others. Teens view themselves by how they appear to others. If you tell them off in front of others – especially their friends – they will lose face and resent you. It will also severely knock their self-esteem.

8. My wife says that I have a spam filter in my brain. Whenever she is nagging me over something, she sees me switching it on. My eyes seem to drift and, whilst I still make the right sounds ('Yes princess' and 'Sure thing darling'), everything she says ends up in my junk-mail box. The trouble is that my wife's spam filter is just as effective as mine. In fact, now that I think of it, we all have spam filters in our brain. So don't get annoyed when your teen switches on theirs when you start nagging. Just stop nagging!

9. Never undermine your teen's anxieties and fears, no matter how silly they sound to you. They are very real and important to your teen. They are also a microcosm of what they will experience in adulthood. Your job is to teach them how to deal with their anxieties, which you can't do if you just pooh-pooh them.

10. Even though they will probably always remain babies in your eyes,

your teens are able to see what's going on around them. If there is a problem – if someone gets sick or you have a row with your partner – trying to hide it from your teens is sending the message that you don't think of them as worthy enough to tell. Just tell them what is going on. Most teens will accept this and will let you get on with dealing with it.

TURNING YOUR COMMUNICATION AROUND

And now that we've got those issues out of the way, we can look at what we can do instead. Once we have our listening ears on, we are more than halfway toward being as effective a parent as we possibly can be.

First and foremost, we need to keep our goal in mind. Remember, what we are trying to do is teach our children how to live in the world that they live in and not the world we live in. In order to do this, we need to be able to understand them. We can only do this by tuning in to *their* perspective, instead of expecting them to tune into ours (which, as Harry has explained, developmentally, they can't).

The art of tuning in can be achieved by finding common experiences that we can share. When parents and their offspring are with me together, I get the parents to talk about the first times they had their hearts broken. You wouldn't believe how many teens have never even thought that their parents had boyfriends or girlfriends before they met each other.

I remember one time being with a few other dads who had their teenage sons with them. We were telling stories around the campfire and the subject turned to the most difficult thing each of us had ever done. I think we all ended up agreeing, much to the teenagers' amusement, that walking across the dance floor to ask a girl to dance was everybody's most cringe-worthy experience One dad, however, turned to his son, looked him in the eye and said that no matter how hard he might think the walk across the dance floor was, it was nothing compared to the walk back if she said no.

Tuning in and sharing your own experiences is an absolute treasure tool when communicating with your teens. All too often, I see parents trying to sum up their stories with morals about what they think the teen needs to learn. Unfortunately, this has the result of ruining the real story, since teenagers immediately know when they are being told fairy stories.

Remember, life, learning and growing are journeys, not destinations. Your children will learn the most by watching you. Don't try to only show them what you think they should see, as they can read you like a book and will switch off if they feel that you are not relating to them.

Failing is normal. We learn the most from the mistakes we make, and from how we react to these mistakes. So learn how to laugh at your mistakes.

The goal is to support your children as they fumble through their adolescence and emerging adulthood, giving them the tools for life and showing them how to use them. And you can't do this if you are trying to present the perfect ideal to them. Identification gives universality, which demonstrates normality.

Combine this with showing them respect as equals, and you will never go too far wrong. Don't, however, expect them to respect you if you're not willing to respect them. As we shall see, respecting your children is crucially important when you want them to learn how to accept accountability for their actions.

Finally, try to remember that if you ask them a question and want them to answer, then expect to hear an answer you don't want to hear.

SETTING BOUNDARIES

There are a multitude of books that explain in step-by-step detail how to set boundaries with your teens. You will find that the common denominator in them all is the importance of consistency. If you want a quick assessment as to how consistent you are in setting boundaries, then you need look no further than at how much your kids nag and pester you for things you have said no to. If your kids never leave off with the pestering, then it most likely means that you're been inconsistent in how you interact with them. And if you are, then what you have succeeded in doing is teaching your kids that, if you haven't given in yet, then they haven't nagged you enough.

There is an art in setting boundaries. This art involves you understanding your child so well that you instinctively know what they need, in order to keep them safe as they mature. The boundaries need to be clear and consistent, yet flexible enough so that your teenagers can 'breathe' in them. Setting boundaries is like the Goldilocks story. You only run into difficulty when you set them too tight or too loose. And learning how to set them can only be learned, like everything else, by practice.

Boundaries involve a balance of power between you and your teenagers. This balance in power is fluid, however. As they mature, your teenagers need to learn how to replace the boundaries that you have set with boundaries that they set themselves, in order to be able to live in the big bad world out there. And they can only learn how to do that through practice. So during the growing years from twelve to twenty-five you will find that, as they get older, your role will evolve from parent (where you make 90 percent of the rules) to mentor (where you will teach them how to make and keep their own rules).

In earlier chapters, Harry explained that the years between eighteen and twenty-five are some of the most vulnerable for the emerging adult. Unfortunately, some genius decided that, when your kids reach eighteen, they are mature adults who can be let loose in the world unsupervised and given total freedom over their lives, and that they will have the skills to be able to set and keep appropriate boundaries for themselves. And we wonder why we have so much binge drinking, so many teenage car accidents, so many inexplicable murders and so much general mayhem in these age groups.

As teenagers reach emerging adulthood, the do not lick boundary-setting off the proverbial stone. Setting limits on our own behaviour is a skill that has to be patiently learned over the years. It is not picked up at the end of the rainbow as we leave school for the last time.

So why do we have so many out-of-control adolescent screenagers? Well, think of an adolescent who has arrived home late to his student flat after being out on the piss with his mates. He misses college the next day and knows in his heart that he shouldn't have gone out late. Now, let's say he's a normal, everyday youngster. How does he pull himself up and change his behaviour? I know! He grounds himself to his house for a week. Or he gives away his Internet to a friend with the instruction that he is not to be given it back until he has changed his attitude. He might even decide to bar himself from a few Saturday nights out, just to reinforce the lesson.

Well before you start to laugh, think again. We can only behave in a way that we have already learned. This is how boundaries are enforced by the majority of parents. When the emerging adult tries to set limits on his behaviour, he can only use the boundary-setting skills he has already been taught. And these are the only ones his parents have taught him. As I write this on a Saturday night, I wonder how many emerging adults are sitting in their student flat rooms with no Internet, grounded as a self-enforced punishment in order to learn how to behave on their nights out.

PUNISHMENT VERSUS LOGICAL CONSEQUENCES

Sounds ridiculous doesn't it? But it is how we try to enforce boundaries with our teenagers. If they don't do as we ask, then we ground them, take away the Internet or something else that we feel will 'teach them a lesson'. That is why so-called punishments don't work. They don't teach anything. Or, I must correct myself, they do teach something. They teach the teenager not to get caught the next time! So what should we do instead? Well, as luck will have it, the solution is a lot simpler than you may think.

Nowadays, therapists like me try to steer parents away from punishing their teenagers when they do something wrong. We try, instead, to teach them how to bring into effect the logical consequences to their teens' behaviours.

To explain what I mean, the next time you are driving your car in a fifty-kilometre-per-hour zone, ask yourself why you are not driving at one hundred twenty kilometres per hour. Well, if you're like the rest of us, you don't speed too much because of the possible consequences that you may incur if you do. You may have an accident, kill someone or just get caught by a speed camera.

The same goes for nearly everything else that we do. We don't go on the piss the night before we go into work because we don't want the hangover, or to let the boss see us. We eat healthily because we don't want to have a heart attack. I gave up smoking in 1995 because I didn't want to die before fifty.

Nearly every one of our actions is governed by our fear of consequences. If this is true for us as adults, then it should equally be true for our children.

STARTING EARLY

Setting boundaries involves finding a balance in power between our teens and ourselves. As they grow older, teens need to feel that they have power over themselves and the choices they make. If they feel they have no power, it will lead to power struggles.

And it is this that creates so much hassle in our homes. Finding the balance between your teenager's wishes and your responsibility for keeping them safe is a very fine line between you lying awake and feeling anxious all night and your teenager sitting sulking in their room because they weren't allowed go to a night club with their friends. As they grow from adolescents to emerging adults, boundaries that you set for them need to be age- and maturity-appropriate. This involves both you and your child sitting down and discussing where you can both win by finding a compromise.

In doing this, parents must support each other. This is true, even if parents are split up and have a lot of animosity toward each other. If you can't find common ground and agreement between yourselves as regards your children, then don't think that a therapist will be able to find some magical solution that will prevent the consequences for your kids. If there is one job I hate, it is teaching youngsters how to cope with their parents' destructive behaviour.

The time to start teaching your child to maintain boundaries is when they are young. Every right that we have in life is governed by a responsibility. This involves accepting accountability for the consequences if I don't respect that responsibility. In other words, if I exercise the authority to drive my car, then I have a responsibility to drive carefully and obey the rules of the road.

Similarly, if a teenager wants to exert their authority over when and how they do their homework, then they have to accept the responsibility of getting it done correctly and diligently. Or, let's say they want to go over to a friend's house, then they need to accept the responsibility that they will actually go there and not off to somewhere that they have been told not to go.

COLIN'S STORY

The power in this for parents is enormous. I remember a teenager called Colin asking me if he could go to a car show that was on the following Sunday. I asked him why he was asking me. He replied that he had asked his mum and she passed the buck by telling him to ask me. I gently told him that, because he was eighteen, he was legally entitled to do what he wanted and that there was no need to ask me. However, I also pointed out to him that, in our previous session, we had discussed his impending Leaving Cert and the importance of studying, as he hadn't done too much over the year.

He then asked me again if I felt that it would be OK for him to go to the show. I again repeated that he didn't need my permission to go as he was a free agent,. but that going to the show so close to his exams would rob him of a full day's studying, which might mean he wouldn't get the points he needed for college. Back and forward we went, him looking for me to make the decision that he could go, and me repeating that it was his choice to make. That he could either go to the show or get on well in his Leaving Cert, but that he couldn't have both.

What he was doing was looking to be allowed to go to the show, but with me somehow taking away the possible consequences for him. Eventually, he decided that even though he desperately wanted to go to the show, he needed to accept the responsibility of studying instead, as that was more important. To end the story, he didn't go to the show, did very well in his Leaving Cert and got what he wanted to go to college.

Let's say, though, that he was sixteen, and his parents didn't think he had the maturity to decide whether to go or not. They would say no. Colin would then have gone on a rant about how unfair they were and that they had no right to control him like that. This time, however, his parents would have the winning argument. They would explain that they would love for him to be able to go to all the car shows in the world and, indeed, would support him in whatever way they could. But that they were being prevented from letting him go because he was refusing to accept his responsibility with his authority. Namely, balancing going with the necessity of preparing for his exams! And that's how it's done – authority and accountability in equal measure!

THE REST OF THE LEARNING EXPERIENCE

That's not the end of the story. You see, Colin has acceded to his parents' wish that he not go to the car show, which has solved their problem. However, in acceding, Colin is left in a hole, as he hasn't got what he wanted. This means that he feels very uncomfortable, which to him is distressing. ('All my friends are there. I've been left out.') To a teenager this is about the worst thing that can happen to him, no matter how you try to reason with him.

The next lesson, therefore, is to teach him how to deal with the distress of having to go without, which is as big a thing to him as losing your job would be to you. So how do we go about teaching him what to do instead?

ENCOURAGEMENT

Sitting at home whilst your friends are all away somewhere without you is particularly painful for teenagers. I try to teach parents how to validate their kid's cooperation with the rules by changing the whole focus of their approach. This is called the 'catch 'em doing something good' principle.

STEPHEN'S STORY

Stephen was another youngster who I was asked to see some time ago. His parents reported that he was always in trouble in school and at home. His parents and his teachers all reported one incident after another. In fact, the most recent episode had occurred the day before his parents saw me. I asked them to tell me about the incident before that one, and they started to recount an incident two weeks previously.

Before they could recount the incident, however, I asked them to tell me what he was doing during the two weeks between the two incidents. They immediately started again to focus on his misbehaviour. I interrupted and asked again what he had been doing during the two weeks between incidents. And do you know what? Neither his parents nor his teachers could recount one thing that he had done.

Trust me, I see this every day: children in trouble and everybody focusing solely on the wrongdoing. Stephen had worked so hard to not misbehave that he had managed to go two weeks without a mishap. He was lurching between incidents without having any idea that during the two weeks he had been doing exactly what was expected of him. Nobody had ever said this to him or told him 'well done' for behaving himself. By the time I saw him, Stephen had absolutely no idea what he was meant to do. He could see that he was expected not to do something, but he had no idea what he was supposed to do instead.

TEACHING THE ALTERNATIVE

In Colin's case, his parents approached him and asked if they could speak to him. They thanked him for making the decision not to go to the car show. They told him that they understood how he was feeling and asked what they could do to support him staying home instead. The compromise was that, as he had studied all day, his parents funded pizza and a movie that he could watch with his girlfriend that Saturday night. Hey, I never said that bribery wasn't effective!

ATTENTION

All children and teenagers will respond to receiving attention. Unfortunately for us, that can often mean that if they don't get attention when they do good, they'll get our attention by doing bad. By adopting the 'catch them doing something good' approach, we're giving our kids what they need in a way that's much more pleasant for all. So setting boundaries is as much about us changing *our* attitudes as it is about our teenagers changing theirs. Kids will live up or down to their parents' expectations. If you praise them, they will live up to the praise. If you are overly critical, or always on their backs, then your kids will live down to your criticism. We call this the 'command storm', which speaks for itself.

SETTING BOUNDARIES

Setting boundaries and teaching your screenager how to keep them has got to be one of the most difficult tasks that any parent faces in rearing children. All of us, as parents, have some idea as to where we would like our teenagers to be, and setting boundaries is the platform by which we try to achieve this. However, if you want to be successful in getting your kids to keep within these boundaries, then there are some fundamental principles you must keep in mind. But before we get to that, I need to introduce you to a concept in psychology called 'intermittent reinforcement'.

To explain this in a way that you will understand, I need to take you to a field in Cambodia that is a no-go area due to the huge number of landmines left there as a legacy of that country's turbulent history. The trouble in clearing minefields is that, in searching for them, humans have an unhealthy habit of treading on them. Even dogs are heavy enough to set them off. So, having spent weeks and weeks, and lots of money, on their training, you might find that you lose everything the first day you try the training out for real.

Rats, on the other hand, are light enough to not set the mines off. They are as intelligent as dogs and have a sense of smell that is just as keen. How they are trained to do the job is very interesting and has a lot of relevance to how you try to train your kids.

INTERMITTENT REINFORCEMENT

Imagine, if you will, a minefield and a rat on the end of a lead. Off he goes in search of a landmine. When he finds one, he digs it up. When he does this, you give him a reward. All well and good so far. He trundles off and, when he finds the next one, you give him another reward. After a few more turns, he learns to associate finding a landmine with getting a reward, so he keeps looking.

This is all great as long as the rat keeps finding landmines. However, if he comes to a part of the field where he can't find a mine, he will stop. The reason he stops and gets lost is that, whilst he associates mines with rewards, he has also learned that no landmines means no rewards. Unless he sees the reward, he figures that there's no point in trying to find landmines. And that is why we don't train rats this way to find landmines.

How we train a rat is that we give him rewards when he finds landmines, but only until we have trained him to associate landmines with rewards. Once we have achieved this, we start to reduce the frequency of his rewards. We start by giving him a reward after every second landmine, then after every third and so on. By only giving the rat rewards intermittently, we are reinforcing the idea that he should keep searching even if he doesn't immediately find a landmine or get a reward (hence the term 'intermittent reinforcement'). By the end of the rat's training, we only have to give him the reward once in ten or twenty times for him to keep searching and searching.

So what's this got to do with you and your kids? Well if you haven't guessed by now, it's got a lot to do with how we train our kids to behave in a certain way. I remember being told that the three most important things to learn in assuming authority over something are consistency, consistency and consistency.

As I mentioned a little earlier, there's an easy way to measure how consistent you are with your kids. I call it the Nagging Index. The next time you say no to your kids, count the number of times they ask you again before they finally accept the word 'no'.

I have to admit that, whilst neither of my kids will nag their mother too much, they will keep nagging me, as they see me as a soft touch. So if mum says no, my eldest will just look for me. Once he finds me and is sure that mum can't hear, he will start the 'please' routine and will keep at it. Not that he gets his own way every time. In order for him to keep nagging me, all I have to do is give in sometimes.

What I've succeeded in teaching him is that, because I haven't given in yet, he hasn't nagged me enough. He has also learned that the word 'no' translates as 'not yet'. Of course, when I give in and he stops nagging me, I then get it in the other ear from my wife for undermining her and making her out to be the 'bad guy'. So there's no peace. You'd think I'd have learned by now, wouldn't you?

So now that I have asserted my expertise in getting it wrong, let's look at other principles in boundary-setting that I haven't learned either.

PRINCIPLES OF BOUNDARIES

Having illustrated the importance of consistency in your interactions with your kids, let me reassure you that there has never been a person who has got this 100 percent right. And, thankfully, neither do we have to. I have found that if you only manage to keep 'between the ditches' so to speak (neither too strict, nor too lax), you'll be OK. Remember, rearing your kids is a marathon, twenty-five-year journey, not a sprint. Combine this with practising what you preach, and you'll survive.

AUTHORITY AND ACCOUNTABILITY

As Harry and I have both explained throughout this book, the aim of parenting is to teach our kids how to survive in their world. In order to do this, your children need to learn how to be responsible and accountable in their dealings with it. And they need to start learning this at home.

I don't think that I need to drone on about this, because you will already know that, as they get older, kids need to learn how to become responsible. In their early years, we are in the parent role, as we have to act as our children's logical brains. As they get older, reaching their late teens and early twenties, we gradually relinquish the parent role and develop the skills to become mentors to them.

To try to make some sense of this process, I teach that parents can look at what authority they can give their offspring in four different ways:

1. At this level, the child can talk to us about what they are experienc-

ing and we, as parents, will try to come up with solutions for their problems. If, for example, our child tells us that they are being bullied by some older kids in their school, then we and the school have the responsibility to get it stopped.

2. This involves letting our kids come up with suggestions as to what they would like to do, e.g. asking them where they would like to go on the family holiday or what subjects they would prefer to take in school. The authority still remains with the parents, but our teenagers' wishes are taken into account.

3. As our kids get older, they need to be allowed to make more decisions for themselves. At the start, parents will give them the authority to make and carry out their decisions after discussing their choices with them, e.g. going to a party in their friend's house, planning a day trip to the city centre or borrowing your car.

4. As our children progress through their adolescence and into early adulthood, we progress into the mentor role. This role should be present from early childhood, though, as it entails teaching our kids how to analyse their choices and the consequences of these choices. In early life, this may be allowing them to choose where they would like to have their birthday party or, indeed, who to invite – or deciding whether to go to Spain with their friends after they finish their Leaving Cert. The main difference between this stage and the previous one is that, in this stage, we are allowing our adolescents to make their own decisions without having to seek our permission and without us telling them what decision to make.

Everything your children do will be governed by one of these four principles. As they get older, their authority over their choices swings more to numbers three and four. However it is vital to remember three points:

1. No matter what age they are, children need to have some authority over decisions affecting their lives.

2. Children need to understand that, with each decision they are given the authority to make, there are responsibilities they must understand and accept. For example, say you let them go to a party. The responsibility is that they recognise that there will be some people there who will be drinking. Your teen promises that they will not drink. If they adhere to this, then they can assume the authority about whether they go to the next one. If they don't assume the responsibility and end up getting drunk, then they have shown that they are not able to assume the responsibility that goes with the authority, so their parents have to make the decisions.

3. When setting boundaries, it is not enough to tell children what not to do. You need to show them what you want them to do, and how to do it.

MUTUAL RESPECT

If you want to get your kids to respect you, then you must respect *them*. If you ask them to do some chores around the house, you need to thank them for doing it. Similarly, if you ask them to do something and they make a hash of it, don't overdo the correcting or moaning because they didn't do it to your high standard. If you do, then all that you will achieve is reinforcing to them that they might as well not have done it in the first place. Ninety percent of the learning in a task is gained from the effort of problem-solving and not from the result. So praise the effort – if you get the result, then that is a bonus.

Lose the word 'but' from your vocabulary. Everything you say after the word 'but' will dismiss everything you said before it.

Share your own experiences with them. Don't try to brag about how you were able to deal with a situation so much better. You won't teach them anything positive, you'll only reinforce their own negative views of themselves. If you haven't had the experience, then you don't have the experience to share. However, whilst you may not have had the experience, you can show them how you access help in solving problems, as it's in the solving that all our growth occurs.

Now Harry is going to introduce us to the world of the distressed teenager.

SECTION FIVE

The Distressed Screenager

CHAPTER TEN
The Pendulum Swing from Health to Illness

In the first four sections of the book, we have been examining the concept of mental health in both adults and screenagers and how, as parents, we need to develop skills and pass them on to our teenagers and young adults. We now need to look at what happens when we swing from mental health through emotional distress to mental illness.

A common thread that Enda and I hope you will have picked up as you have read your way through this book is that mental health is a lot more than just the absence of mental illness. If screenagers are not growing up practising the six categories of life skills outlined in Chapter Six, they can start to drift into becoming mentally unhealthy. This is similar to being physically unhealthy. If I have become obese, I may not be physically ill, but I am not physically healthy.

All of us become emotionally distressed at intervals during our lives, as we respond to the many slings and arrows that life throws at us. This does not, of course, mean that we are mentally ill during such phases – rather, it means that we are struggling to deal with the emotional consequences of what is going on in our lives and how we are looking at it in terms of our thinking.

There can be little doubt that the adolescent phase of life is a most challenging period for all of the reasons already detailed, so it is no surprise that emotional distress is normal – even commonplace – during this stage. One only has to look again at the list of concerns that the Greenhills Leaving Cert students opened up to, to get an insight as to why this is so.

We can also, however, become quite emotionally distressed as a consequence of mental health conditions or illnesses arriving in our lives, particularly if these are causing us significant social and functional problems, as is often the case. Major depression and OCD are examples of mental-health conditions or illnesses that can cause us significant social and functional problems. As already discussed, 75 percent of mental illnesses will present before the age of twenty-five. So it is no surprise that emotional distress due to these illnesses is an important and common occurrence.

If, for example, as in depression, some of us, through a combination of our genes and environmental influences, do not learn to handle stress well, we may develop 'structural and functional' vulnerability which can start to unravel when our emotional and logical brains come under stress in our late teens and early twenties. When this happens, our emotional brain starts to go completely into 'negative mode', and our logical brain is unable to switch this off. The consequences can lead to significant emotional distress.

It is often as a consequence of such emotional distress that screenagers or their parents seek assistance from family doctors and therapists in understanding how to deal with the underlying problem.

When young people become emotionally distressed, they may drink more, refuse to get out of bed in the morning, pull out of school or college, use hash, eat poorly, self-harm, develop eating disorders, end up in conflict with parents and others, or attempt suicide.

In Chapter Eleven, Chapter Twelve and Chapter Thirteen, we will deal with two common causes of emotional distress in screenagers: anxiety and depression. These can be triggered by the adolescent finding that he is unable to adapt to the normal psycho-social stressors that we all encounter in life. However, they can also be the result of very damaging stressors that should never be viewed as 'normal', like bullying, or the result of unhealthy behaviours like drinking alcohol and taking illicit drugs.

What parents most want to know when faced with the young person who is emotionally distressed is, 'What do I need to do and how can I be sure I won't make matters worse?' The good news is that you hopefully will already have learned, earlier in this book, some of the techniques to be employed, and what follows will only be further suggestions to deal with more specific situations.

In Chapter Fourteen, we will discuss self-harm and suicide – the more serious behavioural consequences of our adolescents not being able to deal with such emotional distress.

I am now going to hand you over to Enda, who will explore how anxiety can cause emotional distress not only in our young people's lives, but in our own.

CHAPTER ELEVEN
Understanding Anxiety

I'm often asked by groups to give talks on mental health and various other topics. One of the most common topics I'm asked to talk about is stress management. When I meet a group, I play a little game with them to help them understand stress.

Since everybody is there to learn how to manage stress, it's a safe bet that my little game will work. I ask those who experience a lot of stress in their lives to raise their hands. Of course, nearly everybody raises their hand immediately. I then ask those who have a big problem with anxiety to raise their hands. This time however, only one or two people will raise their hands.

Next, I ask the group to tell me what the difference is between anxiety and stress. And now the silence descends on the room. After some initial hesitation, people gradually start to describe what they think the difference is, and the fun begins. Over the years, I've played this game well over a hundred times. So I'm sure you can understand that I have been given so many definitions that, if I tried to list them all here, they'd fill a book.

As the members of the group get more and more tied up in trying to differentiate between stress and anxiety, I intervene and suggest that the only definition that comes anywhere near the truth is that if you have a medical card you get anxious, while if you have medical insurance you get stressed.

ME AND YOU

Mildly amusing as the above anecdote is, there is a very serious message to be learned from it. You see, what the game shows is that, whilst nearly all of us are willing to be supportive, understanding and helpful to someone when they say that they are anxious, perish the thought that *we* would ever have to admit to getting anxious ourselves.

Is it any wonder, therefore, that people who are depressed and anxious find it so hard to reach out? Only 10 percent of communication is verbal. The other 90 percent is non-verbal. That is, we show our real attitude by the way we act, and it is this attitude that someone who's suffering picks up on, which causes them to withdraw even further into their isolation. So before we go any further in talking about anxiety, let me correct some of the more ludicrous beliefs people have about anxiety by making a few things clear:

1. Everybody gets anxious.

2. If, when you get 'stressed', you get incredibly frustrated and angry, this is just another manifestation of your anxiety.

3. The thinking patterns that occur in severe anxiety are the same thinking patterns that occur in every other kind of anxiety.

4. Only people who are terrified of being anxious try to convince people that they don't get anxious.

5. Anxiety only causes big problems when we experience it and don't know how to overcome it.

6. Experiencing anxiety and seeking professional help is all about having a learning need as opposed to being an 'anxious person', whatever that is.

7. It is rare to find someone who knows how they keep their own anxiety in check. They might know what they do, but they won't know precisely how they do it.

8. Unless you are able to admit that you get anxious and are able to normalise it as being part of everyday life, then you cannot help anybody who suffers from anxiety. You cannot expect someone to own up and face up to something that you are unwilling to admit to.

9. So if you want to be able to help your screenager overcome their anxieties and worries, you have got to learn how to overcome your own first.

10. The magic ingredient in being an effective parent is losing the 'you and they' attitude and replacing it with a 'we and us' attitude.

WHERE EMOTIONS COME FROM

In order to be able to understand why we get anxious, we need to look more closely at how we come to feel what we feel. As I explained earlier in this book, when something happens to us, we go through a whole series of interpretations of what the event signifies. As we interpret our interpretations, we gradually come to a conclusion as to what the event means for us. This is our evaluation/belief, and it is this evaluation/belief that causes our emotion.

If I am mugged, for example, I might interpret what is going on and conclude that the thief is going to kill me. I will then conclude/believe that I must protect myself. This belief will trigger panic, which will in turn enable me to run away or tackle the thief.

This emotional chain reaction happens instantaneously, and it does not occur only in emergency situations. As we go through our days, we are going through numerous chains reactions like this, all at the same time.

If you want an example, then think of this chapter the next time you're driving your car or walking somewhere. When we are on our own, we always have an internal dialogue going on in our heads. This is our brains interpreting our environment, trying to make sense of our lives and the world we live in. We don't consciously have to interpret each interpretation, as the chain reaction happens almost automatically.

THE EMOTIONAL BRAIN VERSUS THE LOGICAL BRAIN

When something happens to us, we process it in two parts of our mind. That is, we start interpreting it in two parts of our brain. One of these is the logical mind; the other interpretation 'chain' occurs in our emotional mind. Our logical brain tells us one thing, but our emotional brain can tell us something completely different.

As Harry detailed earlier, there is a greater flow of information from the emotional to the logical brain than in the reverse direction. So when our emotional brain is in conflict with our logical brain, our emotional brain nearly always wins out.

I like to illustrate this with GP trainees by asking them if they accept that our interpretations cause our feelings. This usually gets universal agreement. I then point out to them that, if they are willing to accept this, they should have no problem accepting that the next time their partner does something that annoys them, they are actually annoying themselves, since their partner is not triggering their feelings. Of course, nobody is willing to accept this even though I am actually correct.

As we go through life, these two minds are in continual communication with each other. When we are mentally healthy, we are able to find a balance between the messages we receive from these two minds. Finding this balance is essential to being happy, having good relationships and being able to cope with life's stressors.

ANXIETY

Anxiety is a normal, everyday part of us. Its function is to protect us by acting as an early-warning signal that something is wrong. Imagine, if you will, walking across the Serengeti twenty thousand years ago. You see a yellow tail swishing in the air. Do you stand there wondering whether it's a lion or do you get up the nearest tree to escape? You will get up the nearest tree, of course. You wouldn't last very long if you didn't, would you? Well it's panic/anxiety that prompts you to flee.

Unfortunately, however, even though it is perfectly normal and common to experience it, anxiety can develop a life of its own when it gets triggered. Why is this? Well, when we have escaped the potential danger, we are supposed to look back to see whether the lion was real or not. If we don't, we can end up blindly accepting what our emotional mind is telling us. Unfortunately, this can result in us finding more and more things to get anxious about and getting less and less able to switch the alarm in our heads off.

In *Five Steps to Happiness*, I explained in greater detail the different types of anxiety, why they occur and how to get rid of them. Here, I will just briefly describe the dynamics behind them. If you identify with anything I say below, you can find more information in *Five Steps*.

FOUR TYPES

In my clinical experience, anxiety usually manifests itself in four ways.

1. Ego Anxiety

In essence, ego anxiety involves a form of negative self-rating in which we struggle to achieve unrealistic internal demands we place on ourselves. I have always regarded this type of anxiety as being the flip side of depression. However, it can also be found in things like social anxiety and in any social situation where we get anxious. We will be looking at depression in the next chapter, so I'll talk more about it then.

2. The Secondary Problem/Abnormalising Anxiety

One of the most common difficulties I have found as a CBT therapist dealing with anxiety is where the person attending me has begun to believe they are abnormal for being anxious. This is often called a secondary problem (with ego anxiety being the primary one). Unless you can learn to challenge the thinking style whereby you start to believe that you are abnormal for feeling the way you do, it is impossible to relieve the anxieties listed below.

3. The Panic-Attack Cycle

I remember, years ago, spending nearly an entire weekend sitting in college trying to figure out a conundrum that had been set for us by our tutors, Brian and Paula. The task they had given us was to figure out the difference between the thinking pattern in someone who's getting panicky and the thinking pattern in someone who is having a panic attack.

As usual, the answer was staring us straight in the face. However, to be able to see the answer, we had to get out of our complicated minds and find our simple ones. As the weekend went on, the picture gradually started to develop for us. In panicky feelings, the person is able to identify what is triggering them; in panic attacks, the person is not able to find that trigger.

Of course, the next question was why the person was not able to identify the trigger in panic attacks. And, again, the answer was so simple that it was nearly impossible to see.

In *Five Steps to Happiness*, I used the story of a client of mine, Hilda, who had come to me for help with her panic attacks. Hilda's most recent panic attack had occurred in a post office. To help her see what was causing the problem, I got her to look at her story in a specific way. By getting her to look at the panic attack in this way, I was hoping to be able to help her understand what was causing the problem.

Hilda had spent years trying to figure out why she would panic in certain places and not in others. When we looked at it together, though, we found that the common denominator in all her panic attacks was not where they were happening, but what was happening when she panicked.

When we looked at each panic attack, Hilda realised that what was causing her panic was the fear of the anxiety itself. When she got the panic symptoms – dry mouth, racing heart, shortness of breath – she was mistakenly thinking that she was either going to die, go mad or run amok. Because she believed the symptoms of panic were dangerous, she was going to extreme lengths to prevent them. It was like trying to get a song out of your head: the more you try to get rid of it, the more insistently it replays itself in your head. Similarly, the more Hilda tried to avoid the anxiety, the worse it got.

And this is the simple insight that we fought to understand that weekend in college. The reason we can't identify what's triggering our panic is because, like Hilda, we don't realise that we are actually getting anxious about being anxious. Furthermore, this simple insight is always the cause of panic attacks, i.e. attaching danger to something that is actually a survival necessity for us.

Like Hilda, if you want to overcome panic attacks, you have got to stop running away from anxiety. If you gradually do that, your logical brain will eventually convince your emotional brain that the feelings are not dangerous, and it will switch off the panic.

4. Trying to Be in Control

This last type of anxiety concerns itself with believing that we must be able to achieve 100 percent in everything we do. Some people call this perfectionism. However, it's rarely the case that we try to achieve 100 percent in order to be perfect. When we play this game in our heads, we are trying to achieve 100 percent in order to just be OK. Furthermore, the more we try to get 100 percent control, the less control we find. Eventually, all we can see is our lack of control.

Learning how to accept the uncertainties and imperfections of life without getting anxious is the only way to overcome this demand for control. This is learning how to fail. Trying to be in control of things you have no control over has got to one of the most damaging philosophies to play with. It is the underlying dynamic behind health phobias ('I must be 100 percent certain I'm not ill'), work stress ('I must get everything 100 percent right'), exam stress ('I must be certain I don't freeze/forget the information') and, in its most extreme form, it is the thinking dynamic behind anorexia nervosa ('I must have the perfect body').

Teaching our children how to overcome anxiety and not be dictated to by their emotions has got to be one of the most important things we can do for them. Imagine if you had learned how to shut off your anxiety switch as a teenager, how massively this would have improved your quality of life. Well, it is possible to teach this to your teenager. All you have to do is practise what Harry and I are suggesting in this book. If you do, your kids will pick it up from you as naturally as you learned to live and breathe in your childhood.

Now back to Harry, who is going to explore what happens when depression appears in our screenagers, and how it should be managed.

CHAPTER TWELVE
Depression and the Screenager

After anxiety, Depression is one of the most common mental health conditions affecting adolescents between the ages of thirteen and twenty-five, often leading to significant emotional distress. Many parents struggle to know how best to assist their adolescents with Depression. There is a lot of confusion and uncertainty about what it is, how to diagnose it and how best it should be managed.

The period between fifteen and twenty-five is when a significant number of cases of Depression arise for the first time – so parents need to be aware of what the differences are between the common, normal emotion of depression that we all experience and the much more significant mental health condition Depression. The aim of this chapter is to try and help parents to understand Depression better, including its cause, presentation, frequency and normal course, as well as how it should be treated and by whom.

We will start by discussing Major Depression. Later, we will examine particular issues presenting in the adolescent and young adult period. Much of the initial information here has been covered by my book *Flagging Depression: A Practical Guide*. Readers who are familiar with it can move on to the next section. For those who are not, the following will hopefully shed some light on the area.

MAJOR DEPRESSION

The word 'depression' is regularly used by all of us in our everyday lives. This has led to confusion, as some describe it as an emotion and others as an illness. Periods of feeling down, sad or low are like anxiety – part of the human condition. All of us experience such periods following bereavements of loved ones, relationships or beloved pets, major disappointments and losses, illnesses, or stressful episodes in our lives. Such periods are usually of short duration, and we quickly bounce back to our normal selves. I often refer to this as 'depression the emotion, spelt with a little "d".

This distinction is crucial, as when many hear the term 'depression', this is what they assume we are discussing. Since most of us experience such feelings regularly, we can become dismissive of the term. Didn't we too feel 'depressed' and manage to 'snap out of it'? But depression the emotion has to be distinguished from a much more significant condition or illness called 'Major Depression' or, as we will call it for the rest of this book, 'Depression with a big "D".

DEPRESSION: WHAT IS IT?

Depression with a big 'D' is a physical and psychological illness affecting between 10 and 15 percent of the population. Nobody really knows the true extent of this condition in Ireland, but it is estimated that between three hundred thousand and four hundred thousand people may be affected by it at some stage in their lives. According to the WHO, 'Depression is the leading cause of disability worldwide, and is a major contributor to the global burden of disease.'

WHAT ARE THE MAIN SYMPTOMS?

The main symptoms can be broken down into psychological, physical and cognitive symptoms.

Psychological Symptoms

- Low mood every day, persisting for a minimum of two weeks, but often present for months or years

- Loss of self-esteem

- Anxiety

- Negative thinking

- Inability to feel pleasure in normally pleasurable activities

- Suicidal thoughts and plans.

Let's see how this is expressed by some sufferers:

- Low mood: 'I feel weighed down by hopelessness and sadness. It is a physical pain in my heart, and no one understands how terrible it feels.' —John

- Loss of self-esteem: 'I am ashamed of the weak, useless, boring, incompetent failure that I am. People hate spending time with me.' —Carl

- Anxiety: 'I am constantly on a high state of alertness and always feel under pressure. I cannot cope when something goes wrong. I sometimes feel panicky for no obvious reason.' —Peter

- Negative thinking: 'I cannot wait until I am dead. Then I will be at peace, the loneliness and hurt will be gone. I cannot go on, not like this. I have often thought of trying to explain how I feel to those closest to me: to share the pain. But what would be the point? After all there is nothing they or anyone else can do to help and I would only be burdening them with my troubles.' —Andrew

- Inability to feel pleasure (anhedonia): 'I can barely manage a smile any more. I'm sick of people telling me to "cheer up" or "it can't be that bad", but it is, and much worse than they can imagine.' —Paula

- Suicidal thoughts: 'The world will be a much better place without me. I am a burden on everyone and they won't miss me at all.' —Jack

Let's examine these in more detail:

- The low mood is not just having a bad day! It's like being in a dark hole or well with high walls all around, surrounded by darkness, with only a brief glimpse of light visible from down below. One can see no way of climbing out. It is a world of deep-seated emotional pain, a shrivelling up of our very soul. Mothers have often described it as a pain more intense than labour. Others have described days with it as seemingly endless, with no end to the arid wasteland within.

- The lack of self-esteem goes to the very heart of how the person feels about themselves. They feel of no value and, in some cases, 'invisible'. They believe erroneously that they are a burden to those around them and not worth knowing or interacting with. This explains why many people with Depression seemingly reject those closest to them, their family and friends. They are not really reject-ing them, though: they just don't want to burden them with the worthless person they feel they have become.

- The anxiety experienced in Depression is nearly always intermin-gled with exhaustion. So although the person may feel anxious, they are almost apathetic in relation to it. Some may present more acutely, with panic attacks, whilst others may experience an agi-tated, restless form of anxiety, with worrying as well as physical symptoms.

- Negative thinking is now known to lie at the heart of Depression. It is where the person starts to view themself, those around them and, indeed, the world itself through a dark, hopeless lens. It is this black curtain around the person that prevents them seeking out help. It is the source of much of the psychological pain and con-stant ruminations characteristic of this illness.

- Inability to feel pleasure can be partial but, in many cases, is almost total. Many will derive no pleasure from normal human actions and interactions such as eating, sex and social mingling. Many describe being out socially in crowds and desperately trying to show interest or enjoyment in what is going on but failing miserably. This is why many with Depression will misuse alcohol in such situations – to conceal how they truly feel.

- Suicidal thoughts are common in Depression. This knowledge is often a great solace for the person with this illness. Many cry with relief when asked, 'Are you, like so many with this condition, having thoughts of self-harm'? They are often ashamed for having such thoughts. It is a weight off their shoulders to realise they are a common symptom. However, if a person is actually starting to investigate or 'plan' how to end it all, then matters become more serious. This is a strong indicator that they are becoming significantly depressed. It is a real cry for help from the emotional brain, which should be heeded.

Physical Symptoms

- Fatigue
- Difficulty sleeping
- Weight loss or gain
- Loss of drive (including sex drive)

Let's see how this is expressed by some sufferers:

- Fatigue: 'The simplest of tasks drains me of all my energy.' —Mary
- Difficulty sleeping: 'I just want to sleep all the time.' —Thomas
- Weight loss: 'I'm just not hungry any more. Food does not look

appetising and it's too much energy to eat. Hopefully I will waste away into nothing.' —Catherine

- Weight gain: 'Eating has become a habit for me; it distracts me from how I feel for a while. Then I feel worse as I get fatter and uglier, but who is going to look twice at me anyway?' —Michael

- Loss of drive: 'It all seems like so much effort now, and I don't see the point.' —Maura

Let's examine these in more detail:

- The fatigue described by most people with Depression is not like the fatigue we feel after a hard day of physical or mental work. It is a deep-seated state of total exhaustion where even the simplest task becomes a major ordeal. It is actually a form of mental fatigue but will seem physical in nature to the person involved. As a result, they stop all forms of exercise in the mistaken belief that this will conserve their remaining energy. It intrudes into every area, makes their lives very difficult. People who suffer from Depression often try and avoid social contact, as it will mean 'expending energy they just don't have'. Students with Depression will often be thought of as lazy, as they can't study. Employees with Depression may be felt to be not pulling their weight. Young people (particularly young men) with Depression may cut themselves off from friends and stop taking part in sports.

- The sleeping difficulties so common in Depression come from bio-logical changes to sleep rhythms and, in particular, our dream sleep (often called 'REM sleep'). Normally we sleep for around eight hours per night. We do most of our dreaming in the second part of the night when well. But, in Depression, this pattern is turned back to front, and the person finds themselves waking up in the early hours of the morning and struggling to get back to sleep. It is difficult for them to fall asleep and harder for them to stay asleep. The result is that they feel completely exhausted when they rise in the morning and wonder how to face the day.

• The weight loss comes from the fact that the person may lose interest in food as they get no buzz or enjoyment from it. Weight gain becomes a factor if the person finds themself eating all the wrong kinds of food in a desperate attempt to try and lift their mood. The weight loss, in particular, is a real warning sign that something is wrong. With young men, this may be the only warning sign we pick up.

• The loss of drive is another significant physical symptom dominating the life of the person with Depression. Each of us has an innate drive which gives us the enthusiasm to carry out normal human daily activities. As a result of it, we eat, have sex and involve ourselves in work and hobbies. In Depression, this drive dries up and we lose interest in food, sex, work and hobbies. Our lives become arid and nothing matters. The loss of libido or sex drive causes difficulties within relationships, as the partner involved (unless they have some understanding of Depression) feels rejected and unloved. In reality, it is the illness which is driving this loss of libido. This loss of drive also explains the seeming lack of enthusiasm to take on new challenges at work.

Cognitive Symptoms

There is an increasing understanding and acceptance that Depression causes not just physical and psychological symptoms but also, in many cases, significant cognitive symptoms. These are now being seen as far more relevant than was thought in the past and are among the major reasons why both adults and adolescents with Depression really struggle with work, studies, exams and many of their everyday functions. These cognitive symptoms can give rise to difficulties with:

- Memory, both short-term and long-term

- Concentration and attention.

Let's see how this is expressed by some sufferers:

- Poor memory: 'I have become increasingly forgetful and have difficulty remembering the simplest of things, like what I did yesterday.' —Noreen

- Reduced concentration: 'I don't read any more. It is too much effort to make sense out of the words, and it is becoming difficult to pay attention to anything.' —George

Let's examine these in more detail:

- Poor memory is a cognitive symptom which causes many problems. The memory part of our brain is physically attacked in Depression. Depression itself interferes with both our short-term and longer-term memory production and retrieval. Many people who do not understand this illness fail to grasp that this inability to retain even simple short-term memories can be quite profound. This is why it can be difficult in some cases to deal with Depression using talk therapies alone, as the person may struggle to retain the information discussed. This memory difficulty can make it hard for, say, a woman to carry out her normal shopping and other chores and for a student to study for exams. It also explains why some people with Depression forget appointments and dates, which can interfere with their working and social lives.

- Reduced concentration goes hand in hand with the memory difficulties discussed. Most of us take for granted the capacity to focus and retain information we encounter. The simplest example of this is reading the daily newspaper, which we do without difficulty. In Depression, however, the words seem like a blur. Many will talk about picking up the paper and reading the lines but being unable to put them together and eventually putting the paper down, frustrated. This concentration loss is an important physical symptom for students as they can't focus on and retain the information contained in books and manuals. Once again, this may be construed as laziness. In reality, it is a result of Depression.

- It is also being increasingly recognised that there are other, more subtle cognitive difficulties experienced by many people with Depression, such as difficulties in making decisions, and in starting and finishing tasks. Along with difficulties with attention, concentration and memory, these contribute significantly to the functional difficulties of people with Depression. Nowhere is this better seen than in screenagers who are going through a bout of this illness.

For a diagnosis of Depression, there must be significantly depressed mood for more than two weeks, combined with at least four of the above additional symptoms, particularly difficulties with sleep, appetite and fatigue, and feelings of worthlessness, suicidal thoughts and a loss of enjoyment of life. In practice, most people will have the majority of the above-mentioned symptoms. If you can imagine living in a world where these are present in your life, day after day, month after month – seemingly endlessly – then you can imagine Depression!

DEPRESSION: WHAT IS HAPPENING IN THE BRAIN AND THE BODY?

When we are well, our emotional and logical brains are in harmony. When we are undergoing typical, everyday highs and lows, our logical brains have the ability to keep manners on our more disobedient emotional brains. This protective mechanism keeps us grounded.

When we are unwell, negative emotions overwhelm our logical brains – the classical example is Depression. At its most simple, Depression is a breakdown in the normal balance between the logical brain and the emotional brain. This results in the logical brain being unable to switch off the torrent of negative thoughts and emotions flowing from the emotional brain.

If we grasp this simple concept, then understanding this illness becomes much easier to grasp. It is this breakdown that gives rise to most of the psychological symptoms of Depression.

To understand many of the physical and cognitive symptoms, we need to realise that our emotional and logical brains, as explained in Chapter One, are connected by three mood cables, which operate like simple telephone lines. As a refresher, these are:

- The serotonin mood cable, which is involved in mood, sex, sleep, appetite, memory and impulsive behaviour, including self-harm and suicide.

- The noradrenalin mood cable, which is involved in energy, sleep, drive and concentration.

- The dopamine mood cable, which is involved in enjoyment of food, sex and anything else that gives us pleasure.

When we develop Depression, these three mood cables become underactive and lead to the following symptoms:

- Reduced activity in the serotonin mood cable leads to low mood, increased anxiety, an increase in suicidal thoughts, an increase in impulsive behaviour, and sleep, sex and appetite difficulties.

- Reduced activity in the noradrenalin mood cable leads to poor drive, poor concentration, fatigue and difficulty sleeping.

- Reduced activity in the dopamine mood cable leads to a reduction in enjoyment of life, particularly in relation to food and sex, and an overreliance on stimulants like alcohol.

The last link in the chain is that our emotional brain is in charge of our stress system. It exercises control through the adrenal stress glands – on each side of the abdomen, over the kidneys – and the main stress hormone produced by these glands, called glucocortisol. We now know that, in Depression, the emotional brain sends the stress system into overdrive:

- The adrenalin stress glands are overactive in Depression, occasionally doubling in size.

- The stress hormone glucocortisol is elevated, particular at night.

- This leads to an increased risk of significant physical consequences, such as heart disease/stroke (sticky platelets), osteoporosis, infections or diabetes, to name a few.

So what happens in Depression is:

- The emotional brain, often triggered by stress, goes into complete 'negative mode'.

- There is a breakdown in the normal ability of the logical brain to switch it off.

- As a result, the emotional brain causes the stress system to become overactive, producing too much of the stress hormone glucocortisol.

- This attacks the three mood cables, and they may become underactive.

- We get the whole host of physical, cognitive and psychological symptoms of this illness.

Don't worry about the details. Just remember this: Depression is caused by a breakdown in the ability of the logical brain to switch off the negative emotional brain, and it is most often triggered by stress.

MAJOR DEPRESSION: WHY DO WE GET IT AT ALL?

There has been an explosion in our understanding of Depression in the past ten years. This has been driven by our new understanding of the brain. In particular, information is emerging on how the brain develops and interacts with our environment at all stages of life.

The crucial links between the emotional brain and logical brain described above can be disrupted due to the following:

- The genes we inherit from our parents
- Being exposed environmentally to a family pattern of Depression or anxiety
- Significant stressors in our early childhood and adolescence, including any form of abuse, an addictive or invalidating family environment, an overprotective family environment, bullying, sexual identity issues or poverty
- Sex hormones, particularly in women (oestrogen and progesterone)
- Exposure to high levels of life stress
- The deleterious effects of alcohol/drugs, particularly at both ends of our lives
- Vascular changes in our brains as we age.

Current thinking is that many who will later develop Depression, through a combination of their genes and the environmental influences described above, are predisposed to not handle chronic stress as well as others. This may be because key pathways between the emotional brain and the logical brain have been affected during childhood and adolescence. This can make it more difficult for the logical brain to control the emotional brain when it turns negative.

When life throws up significant stressors such as loss, relationship difficulties, pregnancy, the postnatal period, sexual identity issues or financial problems, it exposes this underlying predisposition, and the emotional brain dives into a negative Depression mode. When this happens, the normal control of the logical brain seems impaired, and it becomes swamped by the negative barrage emanating from the emotional brain. If this happens on a number of occasions, then it takes less and less stress for the emotional brain to trigger future episodes until, eventually, simple negative thinking can start an episode.

Some assume that Depression is caused by our genes and others that it is purely environmental in nature. In practice, it is a balance between both. The stronger the familial incidence of Depression, the more at risk we are of developing it. But there will usually be some environmental triggers which activate the relevant genes.

WHEN DOES IT APPEAR FIRST AND HOW LONG DO EPISODES LAST?

Whilst children under twelve occasionally suffer from Depression, in general, it seems to occur from puberty onwards. Depression can appear at any stage of a person's life, but often occurs for the first time before the age of thirty, and often following periods of great stress. Twenty-five percent of sufferers will first show signs of the illness during their teens. By the age of twenty-five, this figure has reached at least 50 percent. This is now seen by many leading experts as a significant piece of information as it is increasingly felt that earlier diagnosis and treatment may reduce the incidence of further episodes. Others will develop Depression later, either after childbirth or following a major stress incident such as the loss of a loved one or a key relationship.

Episodes or bouts of Depression can vary greatly in duration, but the average period is six to twelve months. For those affected, this can seem like an eternity. Usually, the Depression will begin to lift after this period, but some will have chronic or persistent symptoms.

HOW OFTEN WILL AN INDIVIDUAL SUFFER A BOUT OF DEPRESSION?

It is estimated that 75 percent of those who suffer from a significant bout of Depression will undergo between one and four depressive episodes in their lifetimes. In 75 percent of cases, there will be another episode of this illness within five years of the first one.

It is also felt that each episode makes further ones more likely, particularly if the condition is not treated; this is probably for biological as well as psychological reasons. The bouts often occur after a period of significant stress. This is why it is important for people with Depression to develop coping mechanisms to deal with stress.

The remaining 25 percent of sufferers will experience constant bouts of low mood, alternating with periods of feeling relatively 'normal'. In this group, the Depression is likely to start in the teenage years and often needs only the most benign stress triggers to be reactivated.

The above information is absolutely vital for all of us, but particularly parents, to understand. There is a strong myth out there that if we develop Depression, we are depressed for life. This completely incorrect information is part of the cause of the stigma so often associated with this condition. The truth is that the vast majority of people with Depression will spend most of their lives well, with only occasional bouts of Depression.

WHY IS DEPRESSION MORE COMMON IN WOMEN?

We know that women are twice as likely as men to develop major Depression. There have been many theories suggested as to why this is. Here are some possibilities:

- The serotonin mood cable is 50 percent less active in women than in men. Since this cable is a key player in Depression and anxiety, this may predispose women to these conditions.

- Women are exposed to significant hormonal shifts during their lives – much more so than men. We only have to look at the incidence of postnatal Depression in women to see this in action.

- Women experience more stress in their lives. This may be in part because they play larger roles than men in rearing children and looking after elderly parents.

- There are significant differences between male and female brains, both in how they are hard-wired and how they function. For example, women are multitaskers, while men find it easier to concentrate on single tasks. This may put more stress on women.

- In a world where women have been encouraged to go out into the workforce and also fulfil domestic responsibilities, there is a risk of the stress involved triggering bouts of Depression.

- There may be genetic differences between men and women which predispose women to Depression. Until we have learnt more about the genes involved, we will have to wait and see if this is the case.

HOW SHOULD WE TREAT MAJOR DEPRESSION?

The most important message is that this is a completely treatable condition. After decades of confusion and uncertainty as to how it should be managed, a modern holistic approach is emerging. This is dealt with in *Flagging Depression* and *Flagging the Therapy*. For the purposes of our current discussion, though, here is a summary.

The holistic pyramid is composed of a solid foundation of empathy and lifestyle changes. On top of this, we add talk and drug therapies.

What Is Empathy?

Empathy is the ability to sense where another person is at emotionally. Everyone possesses this innate ability, but many may not recognise it. We use this skill in normal human interactions without thinking about it.

The person who is depressed and in distress must be careful to choose somebody with whom they feel an empathetic bond to reach out to for help. If such a meeting of minds is present, the sufferer is more likely to feel sufficiently comfortable to open up to this person about their hidden world of pain.

Some may have this bond with their family doctor, others with a therapist/counsellor, a psychiatrist/psychologist, a family member/close friend or a spiritual advisor. For many people with Depression, reaching out to this person is the first, most important, most difficult step of all.

What Are the Main Lifestyle Changes?

Because of the emphasis on the psychological rather than physical nature of major Depression, lifestyle changes are often overlooked. Yet their role in treating this condition is crucial. Let's examine the key ones.

Exercise

Simple exercise is one of the most powerful tools at our disposal to treat and prevent relapses of Depression. Increasingly, research is backing up this statement. Consistent, regular exercise positively regulates cognitive functions, mood, motivation, ability to cope with stress, memory, ability to plan and ability to problem-solve. It helps lift Depression, reduces feelings of helplessness and alleviates anxiety. It also improves the drive that is so often lacking in Depression.

Top research minds have examined what form, frequency, and duration of exercise is most beneficial. The following is the general consensus:

- Thirty minutes of brisk exercise, preferably three to five times a week, is ideal.

- Longer periods don't confer extra benefits.

- Any form of exercise is acceptable. Walking, jogging, weightlifting and swimming are all equally effective.

- If walking, it is advised to do so in the fresh air, if possible, due to the beneficial effects of daylight.

- Creative types of exercise like dancing and water aerobics are equally effective and have an extra social dimension.

- If there are difficulties with motivation, then build up to the above ideal in small daily increments.

Many people with Depression lose interest in meeting others due to fatigue and a lack of enjoyment. If they interact with others while walking, jogging, dancing, swimming or going to the gym, this can only be positive. Again, exercise is the simplest and most powerful lifestyle therapeutic tool at our disposal.

Nutrition

A vast amount of information has been generated on this subject, as a visit to any bookshop will verify. Many claims have been made in relation to the treatment of Depression, in particular.

There is a clear place for proper nutrition as part of an overall treatment package, but there are too many unreasonable claims, which have not been scientifically validated. I counsel a 'healthy dose of common sense' when reading much of the dietary literature out there.

Having reviewed the research, I recommend the following:

- Eat a sensible mix of fresh fish (particularly oily types like salmon, mackerel and tuna), eggs (especially free-range), meat, vegetables, cereals, nuts, flax seeds/oils, grains and fruit.

- Prepare your own food. Avoid fast food and highly processed packaged food.

- Eat even if you can't see any point or pleasure in the task because of Depression. Your brain cannot run without fuel.

- While you should remember to eat regularly, also remember to avoid using food as a crutch when feeling down or anxious.

- Avoid high-stimulant drinks like coffee and Coke, which many with Depression and anxiety use in abundance.

- Avoid high-sugar 'hits', as bouncing blood sugar is not helpful to brain function.

- Avoid extreme diets sometimes recommended by alternative 'experts', which often exclude key nutrients/supplements.

- The main supplements accepted as playing roles in the treatment of mental health are omega-3 fish oils, and the key B vitamins folic acid, B6 and B12. All of these have been extensively investigated and there is substantial evidence to support their use as part of a holistic package, particularly in Depression.

- I recommend taking a B-complex supplement daily, as well as five hundred to one thousand milligrams of and omega-3 oils (particularly EPA).

Alcohol/Substance Abuse

It may seem unusual to include alcohol and illegal substances like hash, cocaine and ecstasy in a discussion on the treatment of Depression, but dealing with the misuse/abuse of these substances is of great importance. Adult brain pathways, as we have already discussed, are not fully formed until the age of twenty-five or thirty. The developing brain is extremely sensitive to alcohol and the drugs named above.

The misuse of alcohol is almost endemic in young people between the ages of twelve and thirty, so these pathways are open to being disrupted – increasing the risk of illnesses like Depression. Depressed teenagers or adults may use alcohol to treat associated emotional and physical symptoms. This sets up a vicious circle: Depression causes low mood, so we use alcohol (a depressant) to lift it, causing a further drop in mood, and so on. Without breaking this pattern, it can be difficult to treat Depression.

Since the misuse and abuse of alcohol is a common coping mechanism in Depression, it is vital to be honest enough to examine and face up to our behavioural patterns here. Because we live in a society where alcohol is socially acceptable at all ages, it is understandable that it is the port we turn to in the storm of Depression. But we must remember that it can lead to further drops in mood and, more seriously, to significant risks of self-harm and suicide.

In Depression, I recommend abstaining for a three-month period, or at least until your mood is fully recovered. Many who try abstaining come to understand the power of alcohol's mood-lowering effects and decide to quit altogether. If addicted to alcohol, cease using it permanently.

The misuse of hash and cocaine, though less common, is prevalent and equally disruptive, increasing risks of psychosis and Depression. There is particular concern about their use by people under the age of fifteen. The use of illegal drugs has to permanently cease, otherwise all therapies will struggle. I have seen some people transform their lives by facing their 'demons' in this area. It is particularly important for young people to take this step, as their brains are so vulnerable to long-term damage as a result of misuse.

Talk Therapy

Talk therapy (often called 'psychotherapy') is the treatment of psychological distress through talking with a specially trained therapist and learning new ways to cope, rather than using medication alone to alleviate distress. It is done with the immediate goal of increasing self-knowledge and awareness of relationships with others.

Talk therapy helps people become more conscious of their unconscious thoughts, feelings and motives. Its long-term goal is to make it possible to exchange destructive patterns of behaviour for healthier, more successful ones.

It has been recognised from the beginning that talk therapy is a crucial part of the recovery process in Depression. This is because negative thinking, as we have seen, is such a powerful emotional force in the life of the person with this condition. They have to learn new ways to challenge these thoughts or they will really struggle to get better. There are also many underlying stress triggers and early negative life experiences which may initiate a bout of Depression. Talk therapy helps us deal with all of these.

The type of talk therapy used has been shown to be less important than the empathetic bond between the therapist and the person in difficulty. There are many different forms of talk therapy, including counselling, psychoanalytic psychotherapy, cognitive behaviour therapy (CBT), behaviour therapy, inter-personal therapy, supportive psychotherapy, brief dynamic psychotherapy and family therapy. Whilst all of these can be very helpful in the management of Depression, CBT is probably – from a research and practical point of view – one of the most useful. Let me briefly explain what it is.

Cognitive behaviour therapy is a form of talk therapy which is gaining increasing popularity in the treatment of Depression.

- 'Cognitive' refers to mental processes such as thoughts, ideas, per-ceptions, memories and beliefs, and the ability to focus attention, reason and problem-solve.

- 'Behaviour' refers to what we do and, just as importantly, what we avoid.

- 'Therapy' refers to a particular approach used to deal with a prob-lem or illness.

CBT is based on two simple, profound concepts:

1. Our thoughts influence our emotions, which, in turn, influence our behaviour. So what we think affects what we feel and do.

2. It is not what happens to us in life but how we choose to interpret it!

CBT helps us to challenge negative emotions, thoughts and behaviours associ-ated with Depression. It is very much rooted in the present moment. Understanding CBT is as simple as ABC!

'A' stands for 'activating event', an event that sets up a particular chain of thoughts, emotions and behaviours. It can refer to an external event (present or future), or an internal one such as a memory, a mental image, a particular thought or a dream. A useful way of examining the activating event is to divide it into: the 'trigger', the actual event that starts the ball rolling; and the 'inference' we assign to the trigger, how we view the event. In many cases this involves assigning a 'danger' to the triggering event. 'Why is it bothering us?'

'B' stands for 'belief', an all-encompassing term which includes: our thoughts; our demands on ourselves, the world and others; our attitudes; and the meanings we attach to internal and external events in our lives. It is through these that we 'assess' the trigger, as described above. They are the lens through which we focus on our internal and external worlds. In practice, they often present as demands we make of ourselves – some reasonable, others not!

'C' stands for 'consequences', an all-inclusive term which includes emotional and physical bodily reactions experienced secondary to the emotions activated, as well as behavioural responses which result from A and B above.

Let's examine an example of this in action: Due to sit his driving test in two days, John becomes very anxious. If we were to do an ABC on his problem, it would look like this:

Activating Event

- Trigger: his upcoming test.

- Inference/danger: he might not pass his test.

Belief/Demand

- 'I must pass my test. If I don't, then I will be a failure.'

Consequences

- Emotion: anxiety

- Physical reactions: stomach in knots, tension headache, constant sighing to relieve tension

- Behaviour: stops eating as a result of his stomach being upset due to anxiety, wonders if he should find an excuse to cancel the test.

In Depression, the therapist will challenge the sufferer's irrational beliefs ('I am worthless' or 'I am a failure') and the sufferer's unhelpful behaviours, such as isolating themself from others or not exercising.

What About Drug Therapy?

Another (often controversial) form of treatment for Depression involves the use of medication. Some maintain that antidepressants are simply placebos, which work by tricking the mind into believing it is getting better. Others compare their use to taking paracetamol for a headache: it deals with the symptoms but not the causes. Some believe that they are addictive.

Users of antidepressants often complain that medications make them feel numb, eliminating some of the symptoms of Depression, but also leaving them unable to experience happiness. Another common argument against the drugs is that they are having no discernible impact on suicide rates and that, in some cases, they may even be increasing the risks of suicidal acts.

So what is the truth? Antidepressants are extremely useful as part of a holistic therapy package for the treatment of Depression. Many find themselves feeling so physically exhausted, so lacking in concentration, so negative and apathetic about themselves, and are struggling to just plain survive!

As we will be examining later, antidepressants can be invaluable in helping the person become functional again. Many CBT therapists and counsellors with experience of dealing with Depression quickly realise that it is hard to help a person deal with their negative thinking and emotional difficulties when they are feeling so poorly.

Combining drug therapy with a sensible lifestyle plan can help the sufferer reach a point where they can genuinely embrace talk therapy. A useful way of looking at this is that drug therapy helps them feel better, so that they can involve themself in talk therapy, which helps them get better!

Research has strengthened the clinical impression that Depression is often best treated with a combined approach of drug and talk therapies, allied with lifestyle changes.

THE FOUR-STEP APPROACH TO MANAGING A BOUT OF DEPRESSION

In *Flagging Depression: A Practical Guide*, I laid out four simple steps in the management of a bout of this illness. Before leaving this chapter, let's summarise them.

- Step One (now): Accept that the symptoms you are experiencing are due to Depression, make the decision that you want to start the journey of recovery and find a guide for the journey (often a GP or therapist).

- Step Two (0–2 months): Feel better. This involves lifestyle changes such as exercise and ceasing the use of alcohol, supportive counselling and, in many cases, starting a course of drug therapy.

- Step Three (2–8 months): Get better. This involves continuing the above, but with more emphasis on talk therapies such as CBT and on dealing with life-stressor issues.

- Step Four (9+ months): Stay well. This will often involve coming off the course of medication, continuing the lifestyle and other changes, and finishing up CBT or other talk therapies. The real aim of this step is to try and reduce the risks of relapse.

For those who would like to know more, I refer them back to the relevant books. But the key message here is that most bouts of Depression are quite easily treated with the above four steps.

Let's now examine how all this information can be applied to screenager Depression, and what parents need to know about this condition.

CHAPTER THIRTEEN
What Parents Need to Know About Depression and Screenagers

Parents reading this section will probably fall into a number of different categories:

- Some may have a young person between the ages of thirteen and twenty-five who is suffering from Depression and need advice and assistance on how best to help them.

- Some might like to know more about the warning symptoms in this age group so that they can spot Depression in their child if it appears. In particular, they would like to know the differences between the 'moody blues' of normal adolescence and more significant Depression.

- Some may have a personal or family history of Depression and be concerned about the possibility of their own child developing the condition.

- Some may have queries about the link between Depression and self-harm and suicide.

Here are some of the common queries we get from parents that we will try to answer:

- How do I recognise Depression in my teenager or young adult son or daughter?

- How do I distinguish it from the normal 'moody blues' of adolescence?

- What are the main causes of it in young people?

- Is it caused by genes, peer group issues, lifestyle issues or problems at home?

- How common is it in this age group?

- How will it affect the life of my teenager or young adult, particularly in relation to school or college?

- What are its links to suicide and self-harm?

- What is the best way to treat it, and what are the roles of drug therapy and talk therapy?

- Where should I go for help if my young person seems to be in difficulty?

- If they do get Depression, how long does a bout last and how often will they get it?

- If they develop Depression, will they have it for life?

- Do boys and girls present differently?

- If my child develops Depression, does this mean that I have failed them in some way?

- If one or both parents have a history of Depression, does it inevitably mean that their adolescent or young-adult children will develop it?

- As a parent, how do I manage the situation when my son or daughter is diagnosed with the condition?

- Why is it so common for Depression to develop on leaving home and starting college, and is there anything I can do to reduce this risk?

To answer some of these queries, we have decided to do a question-and-answer session on screenager Depression for parents. But before we begin, here is an important exercise that we would like all parents reading this book to do:

- First, find a quiet spot and sit down for the next ten minutes or so.

- Close your eyes and let your mind drift back to when you were a teenager between fourteen and eighteen, and then to when you were in your early twenties.

- Reflect on the times when you struggled, particularly your first relationships and the first time your heart was broken.

- Reflect on your grappling with issues to do with parents, peer group pressures, sexuality, body image, school and exam pressures.

- Reflect on the times when you felt down, anxious, embarrassed or hurt.

- Think of the roller-coaster ride of emotions that made up that time of your life, and the intensity of the experiences.

- Think about how often your self-esteem was in your boots.

- Think about how you coped with the stress of going to college for the first time or starting a new job after school.

This is often an excellent exercise to do, as it reacquaints us with who we were as adolescents and young adults. It also reinforces that it is 'normal' for teenagers to experience the full gamut of human emotions, including 'depression'. This is an important message when it comes to understanding our children during this phase. It is particularly common for adolescents and young adults to experience this emotion, and we need be careful not to abnormalise these natural feelings.

Key Point for Parents

If a teenager or young adult is diagnosed with Depression, it is critical that the parents do *not* abnormalise them by immediately regarding them as being 'different' or 'sick' or in some sense 'weak'. From the beginning, the approach must be that *they* are not the problem – *it* is the problem. The minute we abnormalise the young person with Depression, we have immediately created a secondary problem, which often becomes a greater issue for them than the condition itself.

Let's move on to answer some typical queries from parents.

Question: How can I decide whether my teenager or young adult is suffering from Depression or the normal mood swings of this age group? And how will it affect the life of my teenager or young adult, particularly in relation to school or college?

Harry's Answer: Parents hear so much about Depression that they are understandably concerned about missing the signs of it in their adolescent teenagers or young adults. This is also the period of life where screenagers are passing through secondary school or starting college, so parents are especially concerned about not missing out such signs.

We also know now that it is normal for adolescent teenagers – and, to a lesser extent, young adults – to be extremely labile in relation to their emotions. Parents will be familiar with the term 'moody blues'. This is used to describe periods when the young person goes into what appears to be a sulk, often withdrawing emotionally and becoming uncommunicative or even sullen with their parents, whilst still able to suddenly 'switch on' in the presence of peers.

So how can we pick out the young person in trouble? This can be a challenge not only for parents but also for trained professionals. There is little doubt that the better the relationship the child has with at least one parent in the family (often the mother), the more likely they are to open up if in trouble. In general, mothers have great natural instincts about when one of their brood is in difficulties. They seem to sense when something has changed. If they sense a problem, we would encourage all mothers and, indeed, fathers to sit down with the young person and open up a conversation. Later, we will examine how best to do this.

The following are some useful tips for parents on spotting possible signs of Depression in their children:

- Whilst most teenagers will go through bouts of the moody blues, these episodes are usually of relatively short duration, often lasting only for hours – days, at most. If observant, many parents will notice that these moods often relate to everyday issues including themselves or other family members.

- However, if these dark moods are extremely persistent, lasting weeks or months, then warning bells should start to ring.

- A key warning sign can be a persistent loss of appetite or loss of weight, which in some cases may be the only sign that parents notice – in young males, in particular.

- Some teenagers may reveal difficulties with attention, concentration, decision-making or working memory by falling behind in studies and failing exams when they have had no previous difficulties. These so-called 'cold' (not connected with emotion) cognitive difficulties are among the reasons that this condition can cause so much distress for young people developing it for the first time. There can be a number of reasons apart from Depression, of course, for having difficulty with studies and exams, but it should be kept firmly in mind as a possibility.

- Similarly, if at college a young adult screenager is struggling or falling behind (particularly in the first or second year), consider Depression as a possibility. If the young adult is very bright, then this may be masked, as they are intellectually able to compensate but, unfortunately, at a high emotional and physical cost.

Other possible signs include:

- Any evidence of significant fatigue which is of new origin.

- Any signs of difficulties sleeping. For example, the young person is wandering around the house in the middle of night or waking up early in the morning and is unable to get back to sleep. (Don't forget what we discussed earlier about what is 'normal' for screenagers in terms of sleep.)

- Any expressions of 'not wanting to be around' or any signs of self-harm or suicidal statements or attempted actions.

- A sudden tendency for the teenager or young adult to isolate themselves – often in their rooms – from either their family or their friends.

- Any increase in alcohol consumption which seems out of the norm.

- Any extreme emotional or behavioural changes, such as angry outbursts, which seem out of character – particularly in young males.

- The young person stops enjoying many activities they used to enjoy.

- A tendency for the young person to attach a so-called negative attention bias to everything that intrudes in their lives. This can involve picking up only negative comments about themselves and being unable to see any positives in relation to anything they engage in. Whilst all teenagers may exhibit these characteristics to some degree, those whose mood has significantly dropped may do so to a much greater degree. Experts like Professor Barbara Sahakian, who we mentioned earlier, feel that this may be a key warning sign, and one that in the future we may be able to pick out and measure, thus helping young people and their parents to deal with it before Depression actually arrives.

If there is a strong family history of Depression or bipolar disorder in either parent, then there should be a higher index of suspicion if any of the above symptoms seem to be an issue. Be very vigilant if there is any history of bullying in any form, or a sudden traumatic loss of either parent or a sibling due to trauma, suicide or illness.

If the above are also accompanied by a sudden increase in alcohol consumption, constant fatigue, sleep or appetite difficulties, weight loss or evidence of social withdrawal, then do not be afraid to sit down with the young person and try and open up the conversation – always asking about any thoughts of self-harm.

Question: If my screenager develops Depression, will they have it for life?

Harry's Answer: Many parents are almost afraid to ask this question, as they often have a stereotypical view of Depression being a lifelong illness and can't cope with the thought that their loved one would have to endure it for life.

The good news is that Depression is an episodic condition in the vast majority of cases. Most young people who suffer from it will experience their first bouts between the ages of fifteen and twenty-five, lasting for six to nine months. The current understanding is that most adults will then get between one and four bouts in their whole lives. Only a small (if very important) group will have persistent, regular bouts. Even in the case of the latter, they may be well in between episodes.

A lot of evidence is now building up, however, to support the view that the more aggressively we look for and pick up genuine Depression in our adolescents and help them deal with it effectively, the smaller the risk of recurrence becomes. The good news, therefore, is that if we can help our young person through a bout of Depression and help build in some preventative measures, we may be able to significantly reduce their long-term risk of relapse. This means parents – and older adolescents – need to have a good understanding of this condition. It also means that most of our young people who experience a bout of Depression will be back to themselves within a fairly defined time period, which should help both them and their parents in dealing with this issue.

Question: Is there a difference between how Depression presents in younger teenagers versus young adults between the ages of eighteen and twenty-five?

Harry's Answer: There are, indeed, some important differences. Depression is not common under the age of twelve. Up to the age of fifteen, children may not complain of many of the typical symptoms of Depression like an adult. Young teenagers of this age may be more likely to manifest an irritable, angry, apathetic and generally disruptive disposition. There is also a lack of interest in anything. Features of anxiety, such as recurrent abdominal pain, headaches and limb pain may also be present.

As teenagers approach the fifteen-to-eighteen age group, symptoms of Depression will start to resemble those of the adult, although young males may still present more with anger and irritability than obvious low mood. Between eighteen and twenty-five, the symptoms are for all intents and purposes the same as those in older adults, including: low mood; fatigue; cognitive difficulties; an inability to enjoy life, food and sex; negative thinking and suicidal thoughts.

Question: If I feel that my teenager or young adult is potentially suffering from Depression, what is the best way for me to approach them?

Harry's Answer: This is a question both of us are often asked. There are two common scenarios which may present.

The first and simplest relates to the teenager between thirteen and eighteen. In this scenario, the parent has not only the right but, in many ways, the responsibility to try and reach their child if they feel that he or she is in difficulty. This is often best done by sitting down with the child at an appropriate time and commenting that the child has displayed some signs of being quite down. The parent could also share that they too went through such emotions as a teenager. This often helps to normalise the symptoms for the child and may encourage them to open up about how they are feeling. If the young person feels that their parents both understand where they are at and actually care enough about them to try and help, there is a much greater chance that they will open up about their symptoms.

If that does not work, the next step may be to approach those who live in their teenager's world, such as close friends or a school guidance counsellor. Armed with knowledge gathered in this way, the parent can then approach the young person again. It can also be worth examining their mobile phones or Facebook pages, as many parents 'friend' themselves on such sites. There may be some evidence there of the child being in difficulties. Another possibility is to involve in the discussion somebody the child has had good relationship with, such as an older sibling or a grandparent.

It is often when a child has reached the young-adult stage (eighteen to twenty-five), however, that parents encounter the most difficulties in terms of trying to open up any discussion about Depression. In some cases, the young person may be attending third level and be more independent. Therefore, it can be both harder to recognise the symptoms and more difficult to approach the young person if they have developed Depression. This is because, once they are over eighteen, they are technically adults! So the parent's role has to change to that of a mentor.

The most effective approach may be to sit down with the young person and share with them your own experiences of anxiety and low mood whilst you were at college, if relevant. Once again, you can comment that you have noticed similar signs in them and are concerned about them. This may facilitate the discussion and allow them to open up. If they are clearly falling behind in studies or failing exams, then this might also be used as a route to discussing how they feel. If you have noted a major increase in alcohol use or that the young person is increasingly isolating themself from family or loved ones, then this too can be brought into the conversation. Other possibilities include checking their social-media sites and talking to close friends to get more information which can then be run by them.

Question: If my child develops Depression, does this mean that I have failed them in some way?

Harry's Answer: So many parents (particularly mothers) really struggle if their young adolescent is diagnosed with Depression. In some way, they feel that they have failed their child by allowing this to happen. Some will feel guilty that they have passed on some so-called 'defective genes'. Others will assume that there was something in the manner in which they reared their child that led them to develop this condition. Others with a family history of either anxiety or Depression will feel that they have passed on what they see as a 'weakness' to their loved one.

In reality, of course, each child is a unique person both genetically and in how they react to their environment as they grow and develop. As parents we can only do our best, love them and muddle through – and if they do develop a bout of Depression, be there to help them manage it in the most appropriate manner.

No parent consciously or unconsciously goes out of their way to create an environment where their young screenager develops a bout of Depression, so we must be quite clear that we have not failed them if it happens. This message is particularly aimed at mothers, who will generally be the ones most likely to rate themselves in this way.

Question: What are the major stressors in the lives of teenagers and young adults that predispose them toward Depression?

Harry's Answer: We have already detailed many of the significant stressors which affect the normal lives of teenagers and young adults. In the thirteen-to-eighteen age group, these include invalidating environments, bullying of any kind (including anti-gay bullying and cyberbullying), relationship difficulties, body-image difficulties, peer-group pressures, social-media isolation by peers, exam and future-employment concerns, school problems and issues arising from their home situations, such as separation or traumatic loss. An important but often missed stressor is simple acne, which can become a major issue for both sexes, but particularly young males.

In the young-adult phase, what often triggers Depression is leaving the safe home environment and trying to cope with the loneliness and isolation of starting third-level education, or taking up a new job at home or abroad. Significant alcohol and substance misuse, exam or work pressures, unemployment concerns and relationship breakdowns are other common triggers.

We have noticed a pattern of young adults reaching college and experiencing loneliness, difficulties with forming new friendships, relationship difficulties and significant financial pressures. This can lead to them getting into difficulties, with mood starting to fall and a lot of cognitive difficulties starting to appear. They often cope with these by isolating themselves and drinking excessively, which further lowers their mood. The final result is often them falling behind in their studies or dropping out of college.

Question: If my child has been diagnosed with Depression, what is the best way for me as a parent to cope with it, and how best can I help them deal with it?

Harry's Answer: Most parents panic if their teenager or young adult is diagnosed with Depression. As we have already mentioned, many fall into the trap of abnormalising the young person almost unconsciously. They suddenly treat the young person differently, tiptoeing around them, afraid to say or do the wrong thing and make their condition worse.

The elephant in the room is, of course, the unspoken fear of suicide. There is a strong link in the minds of many parents between Depression and suicide. This is quite understandable, as there is a genuine link. But in practice, as we see later in the chapter on suicide, the vast majority of those who go through a bout of Depression will never self-harm or take their own life. Many get fleeting thoughts of the latter, but never act on them. The fear that their child might go down this road, however, is a major reason so many parents become so anxious about how they should approach their screenager. This may end up with the young person feeling increasingly isolated, as they begin to believe that they are, in fact, abnormal and different to everybody else around them.

One of the most important things a parent has to understand and then pass on to their child in this situation is that the problem is not *them*, but *it* – the problem is not the young person, it is Depression. For if the young person feels that those close to them now regard them as being different or being a problem, they will withdraw further into themself, which makes recovery more difficult.

The first task for the parent, therefore, is to accept the young person where they are. The second is to avoid catastrophising the fact that their child is going through a bout of Depression. The third is to avoid treating them differently to other young people in the family. The fourth is to try and ensure that the young person feels that you will be there for them whilst they are dealing with the bout, no matter how difficult or frustrating this can be. The fifth is to try and ensure that lines of communication are as open as possible: this may significantly reduce the risk of self-harm.

If the young person is at college, do not be afraid to organise for them to take a year out on medical grounds if you both feel that they are struggling. If the young person feels you are supporting them and are with them in their difficulties, it can be a major factor in them recovering. Similarly, with teenagers, do not be afraid to suggest repeating a year if they feel it would help them recover more quickly from a bout. In all cases, this type of support can be invaluable.

It is very useful, if you are able to open up the conversation with your child, to listen to what *they* are saying about stressors. Once you both agree on what they are bothered about, you can work together to try and deal with the issues, whether they are due to bullying, relationship difficulties, exam or school pressures, concerns about sexuality or body image, or something else.

The old Irish adage that 'two shorten the road' can be quoted to them. And the evidence does actually show that once a young person feels that an adult is walking with them on the journey, recovery is more likely.

There are certain situations which can be especially difficult for some parents. One of these is when the screenager may seem to be 'shutting out' their parents, refusing to open up about how they feel, or involving themselves in fairly typical Depression-type behaviour, such as not getting out of bed in the morning, isolating themselves in their rooms or responding to many requests either angrily or by simply seeming to ignore the parent.

Many parents feel they are in a catch-22 situation in which they are afraid that if they say the wrong thing their son or daughter may become more depressed or impulsively self-harm. And yet, if they do nothing the young person may continue to isolate themselves. This situation is often even more complicated if the young person is between eighteen and twenty-five, under the care of a GP or psychiatrist and insisting that any conversations with the latter are totally confidential and not to be shared with parents. There are many parents who will be reading this book who will find themselves in this situation. They are often frustrated, exasperated, anxious and hurt.

Here are a few suggestions to deal with this situation:

- Don't be afraid to sit down with the young person and reveal just how difficult you are finding the situation.

- Tell them that you really care about them but need them to share with you the difficulties they are experiencing.

- Talk about times in your own life where you have struggled with bouts of being anxious or depressed and how you can empathise with them.

- If the young person is over eighteen, tell them that you totally respect their right to privacy, that it would be helpful for you as a parent and mentor to have some idea of how they are getting on in terms of mood and other symptoms, but that you will accept whatever they as a young adult decide to do.

- It is a good idea for each parent to approach the young person separately, as they may pick up different information, and they also may take different approaches to dealing with the issue.

Question: Why do some teenagers and young adults develop Depression whilst so many others of their peer group don't?

Harry's Answer: This is exercising the minds of many researchers. We know that, in general, screenagers suffer more from depression with a little 'd' due, in part, to natural brain development. For example, we noted earlier how the amygdala (stress box) is generally more active in adolescents. The importance of this is that adolescents, particularly boys, are more likely to misinterpret facial emotional expressions in adults. This can lead to many misunderstandings, as they are often misreading the signs that, say, parents or teachers are sending out. We also noted that at the heart of this difficulty was the poorly developed prefrontal cortex during this brain-development stage.

The result of the above is that teenagers and young adults are more likely to get significant episodes of being down or anxious – which is completely normal. But what happens when they start to suffer longer spells of being depressed, along with many or all of the physical and cognitive difficulties already discussed, and are therefore suffering from Depression with a big 'D'?

Well, increasingly researchers are looking at Depression occurring when the amygdala or stress box goes into total negative mode and ends up with the young person developing a negative attention bias. They can only relate to negative things in their environment, can only see the world through that lens. Key parts of the prefrontal cortex, already weaker in this age group, are unable to turn off the overactive amygdala. So the normal emotion of depression eventually becomes its more serious colleague, Depression.

We also know that one of the most likely reasons for this may relate to the stress system being overactive. Higher levels of glucocortisol (our stress hormone) and other stress peptides in the brain are now felt to be one of the most likely culprits for the amygdala turning more negative. We then find the whole 'FLAG' system in freefall, with the overactive amygdala firing the stress system to produce even more glucocortisol. A vicious circle ensues, as the glucocortisol hits the three main mood cables and all of the symptoms of Depression arrive.

But why would some young people develop this pattern while others don't? Well, there are many reasons, ranging from genetic susceptibility to growing up in a household where the mother or father had Depression and absorbing some of their negative attention bias patterns. Other reasons might include growing up in a house where the young person experiences what is for them an invalidating environment, or using alcohol or drugs at a vulnerable brain-development stage.

One of the most powerful and uncontested pieces of evidence comes from work done on all forms of abuse – particularly sexual abuse – which we mentioned earlier. We know that the stress system in such cases is dialled up to such a degree that the sufferer's hippocampus or memory box can even shrink in size. In such cases there is a very strong history of Depression occurring in the teens and in early adult life, with the hyped-up stress system being the vehicle through which this occurs.

The common denominator may be that anything that might interfere with the pathways controlling the normal flow of information between the emotional brain and the logical brain may increase the chances of the above pattern happening and Depression arising. So for those who present with significant Depression in their teens, there may already be a pre-set underlying predisposition which is then triggered by any one of the numerous stress triggers which arise during adolescence.

The real goal of much of the current research is, however, to try and see if some 'objective' evidence of real Depression is present in the mid-to-late teens, rather than the routine normal emotions of depression experienced by this age group.

We now know from research, for example, that younger members of some families with a history of significant Depression may even show evidence of negative attention bias on testing before Depression itself arrives at all. Perhaps this may be one future mechanism for picking out those who are more at risk. There is also recent interest in the concept of 'cognitive remediation', which would involve using special computer programmes to assist in counteracting such a bias in a form of biofeedback. But much work needs to be done before this will or should become a realistic form of preventative therapy.

We previously mentioned the recent research project carried out by Professor Barbara Sahakian's team in Cambridge, which was aimed at trying to come up with some measureable marker in the form of salivary glucocorticol levels to assist the more accurate diagnosis of Depression in this age group.

The more modern view of Depression is that, in some susceptible young people, higher levels of this stress hormone reveal an increased risk of developing this condition, particularly for boys. Hopefully, in the future, more accurate tests like this will assist us in trying to pick out of the large cohort of young people who complain of feeling low or depressed those who are genuinely more at risk of Depression, and come up with preventative strategies to reduce that risk.

This is critical, as it has also been shown that those who develop Depression in their teens, particularly those with an underlying family history, are more likely to suffer from recurrent bouts of Depression later on. There is an increasing view among experts that spotting and treating young people at an early age and correctly managing their Depression may, in the long run, reduce the risk of relapse. This is important because many people spend decades suffering from intermittent bouts of Depression which remain undiagnosed and untreated until their thirties or forties.

Question: Who is the best person to help my adolescent or young-adult screenager with their Depression?

Harry's Answer: The most surprising answer to most parents is that they themselves may be best placed to assist their adolescents. But what most parents want to know is whether the young person should seek help from a school or college counsellor, a general practitioner, a mental-health team, a psychiatrist, or a psychologist/therapist.

The first port of call for many young people may be a parent or school counsellor. The latter are a wonderful group of people who do excellent work in helping our young students deal with issues occurring on their journey toward adulthood. Equally important in the world of the screenager is information they can find on the Net. In some cases, this may be useful and positive, but in others it may be the opposite; there is information on the Net from groups like Aware, but there are also negative chat rooms and sites encouraging suicide and offering information on how to do it.

If the young person is suffering from depression with a little 'd', then some simple chats with the parent or a school counsellor may be sufficient. However, if it is clear that there are more-significant issues, as in Depression the illness, the best course of action is to accompany the young person to see the family GP. The GP will often know both the child and the family and can assess the degree of difficulties the young person is experiencing. In some cases, the GP may feel that referral to the local child-psychology service is warranted. In other cases, the GP may decide on referral to the local child and adolescent mental-health team, which can perform a full assessment.

The modern approach to treatment of significant Depression now involves a multi-disciplinary team, including a psychiatrist, a psychologist, a social worker and an educational expert. The team assesses the child's problems in different areas and isolates the environmental/psychological causes of their Depression. Once these causes are discovered, the team can deals with them.

This makes the child's environment favourable and free from stress. The difficulty with this approach is that it requires time, money, resources and organisation. In many parts of the country at the moment, this service is just not possible. Another quandary is the lack of child psychologists and other key members of these teams due to financial constraints. In more severe cases, the above approach may also include the child psychiatrist using drug therapy. This latter is a very controversial area, one we will deal with in a later question.

For young adults between the ages of eighteen and twenty-five who are suffering from Depression, the most common ports of call are either the college campus counselling or GP service, or the family GP or counsellor/therapist.

Question: What is the place of lifestyle changes in the treatment of Depression in the screenager, and how can I as a parent be of help?

Harry's Answer: Amidst all the discussion about the pros and cons of talk therapy versus drug therapy in the treatment of Depression in screenagers, there is a risk that lifestyle can get overlooked. But sometimes examining such issues and suggesting changes can be vital. This may involve examining the roles of:

- Exercise and diet
- Alcohol and substance misuse and abuse
- Sleep
- Technology and social media
- Significant stressors such as exam pressures, relationship difficulties, bullying and worries about the future.

Exercise and Diet

We have already discussed the fact that obesity is a major issue in our screenager and adult populations. Its links with risks of diabetes and Depression are increasingly being recognised. It is important, therefore, to look at both exercise and diet.

We know that thirty minutes of exercise can be very helpful in terms of treating and preventing Depression. For the young person it must be a form of exercise they find useful. It might be a good idea for one or both parents to offer to, say, go for a walk or a run, or go to the gym with their screenager – with young men, in particular.

It is important, though, for both screenagers and their parents to accept that fatigue and apathy are key components of Depression which can make it quite difficult for the young person to become involved in anything – never mind exercise. It is critical that the way forward must always be encouragement rather than criticism, as criticism will only increase the 'hot' cognition backing up their irrational belief that 'they are worthless'.

In terms of diet, it is critical that the whole household change to a healthy diet, not just the young person with Depression. This may lead to a good discussion in the house about the whole role of nutrition in relation to physical and mental health. We have already dealt with the dietary changes recommended.

Alcohol and Substance Misuse and Abuse

Whilst both exercise and diet are extremely important in terms of helping to manage a bout of Depression, the most important lifestyle change is often to do with alcohol and substance misuse and abuse.

Like many other doctors and therapists, we have observed that, in a significant number of cases, Depression in the screenager group is associated with excess alcohol consumption or the misuse of (or addiction to) drugs – particularly cannabis. We have already documented in the chapter on the developing brain just how damaging these substances can be, especially when taken before the age of fifteen. But this is also an issue right up to the age of twenty-five and beyond.

There can often be a vicious circle, with significant alcohol or drug use leading to changes in the brain, resulting in the appearance of Depression, which the sufferer tries to cope with by increasing their use of substances, and so on. In other cases, Depression appears first in the life of the screenager, who then tries to cope with it through significant misuse or even abuse of alcohol, or drugs such as cannabis.

It is vital for both screenagers and their parents to understand that treating a bout of Depression in the presence of, say, significant alcohol misuse is going to be very difficult. So the first tip for parents if their teenage child or young adult has developed a bout of Depression is to try and tease out with them just what their intake is. Sometimes being honest about our own intake of alcohol and how it can affect our mood might be a way of opening up the conversation.

From a practical point of view, if the screenager does admit to significant misuse and agrees to try and stop, it is often worth waiting for around six weeks for the effects of the substances on the brain to gradually diminish before deciding if true Depression was the issue, rather than the direct depressive effects of the substances themselves.

Sleep

Another key lifestyle issue for the adolescent is sleep – particularly for the thirteen-to-nineteen age group. We know from our earlier discussion that if they are sleep-deprived from getting less than nine and a half hours of sleep per day, their risk of developing Depression increases dramatically. So a simple preventative measure might be to encourage them to get enough sleep.

Once again, there can be a vicious circle: the screenager becomes sleep-deprived, which, along with other causes, leads to a bout of Depression, which causes further sleep difficulties, which increase mood problems, and so on. In other cases, the screenager develops Depression, struggles with sleep problems and ends up unable to get out of bed in morning. This latter scenario is one of the most common and most frustrating issues for many parents, who simply do not know how to handle this situation. Here are a few ideas:

- Try to ensure that your screenager is getting sufficient sleep, especially when they are between the ages of thirteen and nineteen.

- Try to avoid criticising your adolescent with Depression for struggling to get out of bed in the morning, as it will only increase a sense of self-loathing.

- Empathise with them as to how difficult it must be for them and try and encourage any small efforts they are making to improve the situation.

- Try and see if they are agreeable to letting you help them by, say, opening their curtains in the morning or calling them at an agreed time.

- Consider getting a 'dawn simulator' to both help their mood with an early morning light surge and get them to wake up earlier.

Technology and Social Media

The next lifestyle issue which is often overlooked in the management of Depression is the role of technology and social media in the creation and maintenance of a bout of Depression. This may involve parents of adolescents with Depression examining:

- How the young person is accessing information about their condition – both positive and negative.

- Whether technology and social media are making them more isolated from their friends and peers.

- Whether there is significant cyberbullying present that may be the major trigger for the bout of Depression developing and continuing.

- Whether – as in the case of 'Facebook depression' – the young person may be struggling to match up their online persona (which they may see as ideal) and their real-life persona (which they may see as boring and worthless). This may lead those at risk to develop an irrational belief that they are 'worthless' and dive into Depression.

- The use of sites that are not particularly interested in the mental health of young people, only in encouraging them down the road of comparing themselves socially with their peers.

- The significant risks of adolescents who are feeling very down involving themselves in negative chat rooms or, more seriously, sites which encourage suicide.

- The fact, discussed in Chapter Three, that the average time spent with technology and media is seven and a half hours a day. This means screenagers may miss out on vital one-to-one, face-to-face dialogue.

Parents may not have really thought about or examined the whole area of technology or social media in relation to their adolescents, and therefore they may be particularly at sea if Depression arrives. So the first piece of advice is to try and talk openly from the beginning with your screenager about how best to engage with this technological world in a healthy manner. There have to be some simple rules for this agreed between you and them, particularly those in the thirteen-to-eighteen age group. Parents have to make a real effort here to try and stay at least some way up to speed on the most recent social-media sites. Screenagers will always be way ahead of parents, no matter how hard we try, but we do at least have to stay on their coat-tails.

It is very helpful if, apart from setting guidelines for our screenagers in relation to time spent on technology and social media, we discuss with them as much as possible our own concerns about the negative effects of it on our own lives. Often, if we have done some of this homework when things are going well in the lives of our young people, it will be easier to reach them in this area if Depression arrives.

In particular, we need to discuss with them:

- The dangers of confusing online personas with real personas.

- The dangers of cyberbullying. Try and share some personal experiences of when you were bullied at school or by peers, or even later in life, at work. This will allow you to empathise with them as to how horrible it must be to be bullied online, where far more people are spectators to the discomfort and humiliation. This might possibly open up a line of communication so that, if it does happen to them, they will come to you, as they will feel that you will understand.

- Positive mental health sites like Aware – and the risks of negative sites. Again, this is often best done when the screenager is doing well, rather than after Depression arrives in their lives.

- The amount of time spent on technology or social media. Relate it to your own life, examining with them whether it is helpful for either parents or screenagers to spend such significant amounts of time on technology or social media. Try discussing what other areas of life you are both missing out on.

- The difference between being depressed with a little 'd' and Depression itself, and how the web can regularly confuse these situations. This gives you an opportunity to discuss your experiences with the former when you were a teenager and young adult. Once again, if this is done when the young person is well, it may be very helpful to them if Depression does arrive.

Significant Stressors

In earlier chapters we examined how adolescents have to deal with a number of important, stressful situations in their young worlds. As parents, it is crucial to remember that we too went through the roller-coaster ride of emotional highs and lows in relation to just the same kinds of stressors whilst at the same age. So we have huge reservoirs of experience that we often don't tap into to assist our screenager as they are going through similar traumas.

In terms of Depression, there are a number of very common scenarios that may trigger a first bout. These include:

- Relationship difficulties
- Exam pressures at school and in college
- Starting college – particularly if it involves leaving home
- Bullying in all forms
- Sexual identity concerns
- Losing key family members or close friends through illnesses, accidents or suicides
- Invalidating environments.

Let's examine these issues and discuss some brief tips as to what might help the parent and the young person perhaps avoid the pitfalls before Depression arrives – or help them come through the experience if it does.

Relationship Difficulties

We all remember the high when we fell in love for the first time and the low when the relationship did not work out. The teenage and young-adult brain, as we discussed earlier, exaggerates both highs and lows. So when a relationship breaks down – which is a completely normal experience – adolescents may experience significant depression with a little 'd'.

Whilst this is usually self-limiting (everything changes with the next exciting encounter), a small group of more vulnerable young people may struggle to cope with the stress, triggering a bout of Depression. Now the screenager is not only struggling with the emotional loss of a precious relationship, but also experiencing typical Depression 'hot' cognition (associated with emotion) of 'I am worthless', along with the other physical, emotional and cognitive difficulties.

When the screenager is trying to deal with this stressor, parents can be incredibly helpful by sharing their own often very painful experiences. This helps to normalise the experience for the screenager and may give them a road map out of the crisis. As part of a total holistic package to treat their Depression, dealing with this key stressor might be crucial. And it can be a great bonding experience for the screenager and their parents.

Exam Pressures

Many parents really emphasise that they would never put pressure on their teenagers or young adults to perform well in school and college exams. Part of the problem here is that this may not be the message the young person is picking up from their parents. It was interesting to observe how the Greenhills Leaving Cert classes we discussed in the introduction felt a sense of pressure from their parents' expectations – so this is an important issue for them.

Apart from parents, students put pressure on *themselves* to perform well in exams and also feel subtle pressures to do as well as their peers. Many will be experiencing pressure from all three: parents, peers and – most of all – themselves. If they start to struggle under the weight of expectations then, if they are vulnerable, their mood may drop significantly and Depression may arrive.

In the case of college, there are a number of different scenarios which may give rise to exam pressure. Some may have been spoon-fed at school and struggle to cope with the course itself. Some cannot deal with the sense of personal responsibility and isolation often experienced at college. Some, particularly the 'high-raters' or the more intellectually gifted, may set their bar too high, struggle to cope if they can't reach it, and end up developing Depression as a result. Others may consume too much alcohol as a coping mechanism and find their Depression deteriorating further.

As a parent, the key is to try and tease out the issues for each individual screenager and examine how best to help them to deal with them. Above all, both adolescent and parents must try and become pragmatic about the whole exam process. If the professionals helping your young adult sort out their Depression feel it is desirable, the screenager should not be afraid to take time out from school or college on medical grounds and return to finish the task when they are feeling better.

Starting College

For some young adults, this can be one of the biggest hurdles of their young lives to date. The Leaving Cert class we already discussed detailed the most minute detail all the issues they had about this process, belying the concept that they were already 'mature' and would be well able to cope with this change. I was astounded by just how much they had considered all the potential difficulties even before they had arrived in college. Clearly it was a source of significant anxiety for them.

It can be a time of great loneliness and isolation for many young adults, during which they miss out on the support and camaraderie of both their school friends and their families as they step out into the real world. Many find the whole change too intimidating and may, if vulnerable, end up with Depression. The complex picture for many screenagers starting college can include a lack of structure, difficulties making new friends, a lack of money, the necessity of doing part-time work to pay bills, long commutes, poor accommodation, uncertainties about whether they have taken the right course, the challenges of dealing with the virtual world of social media, a fear of failing crucial exams, the struggle of dealing with new sexual relationships and coming out.

It is hard for parents to properly prepare screenagers for this new world of freedom, where they have to take personal responsibility for themselves in college whilst often lacking both sufficient life skills and financial reserves. But a combination of parents sharing their own experiences whilst at college before their adolescents start their courses and keeping in close contact with them during their first year may ward off many potential serious consequences. Depression is more likely to be identified at an earlier stage and then appropriately managed.

Bullying

It is clearly important that any form of bullying be identified quickly and firmly dealt with. This is one place where parents can play an important role in helping screenagers. Parents should be particularly careful to try and spot any evidence of bullying – whether physical, verbal, sexual or cyber – particularly in the thirteen-to-sixteen age group, where it can be especially damaging to the physical and mental health of young developing teenagers and their developing brains.

This is one area where suicidal thoughts or attempts may occur if the young adolescent feels totally trapped. If a young person does come to a parent, the parent should start by validating how the young person feels and then investigate with them in detail just what is going on and what steps can be put in place to deal with it. One may say that bullying has always been with us, and it has, but there is greater scope now via social media for bullying to be unrelenting and seemingly endless. Both authors have seen some serious suicide attempts where it has gone unrecognised.

Sexual Identity

The whole area of sexual identity, which can include the sexual confusion so common for teenagers as well as the more difficult area of young screenagers who are genuinely gay or lesbian either coming out or being bullied, is another major stressor which can lead to many vulnerable young people developing Depression. In more serious cases, it can lead to the world of self-harm and suicide.

The advice here for parents is that, if you feel this is an issue for your teenager or young adult, make every effort to bring it up in discussion and strongly validate whatever position they are adapting. If it is simply confusion over sexual identity, be sure to explain to them just how difficult you found this whole area yourself when you were their age. That one step may assist them greatly in working out their own sense of sexual identity. If they are clearly gay or lesbian, it is quite likely that many parents (especially their mothers) will have had strong suspicions even before they open up to it.

This may be a seminal moment in their long-term relationship with you. If you validate and accept them with an open and warm manner, then they will feel free to share problems with you from then on. If you take the opposite approach, it may have the opposite effect.

Losing Key Family Members or Close Friends

Another major stressor which may trigger a bout of Depression in a young person is the loss – through illness, accident or suicide – of a key family member or close friend. This may be especially so in the early or mid-teens, when young people are very vulnerable to such traumatic losses.

The loss of a sibling or parent at this tender age can be a huge disruption to the young person's inner emotional world. If this is due to suicide, in particular, it can be a major stressor which may trigger Depression in those who are vulnerable and, in some cases, self-harm attempts. Of course, many adolescents will experience such traumatic occurrences and manage to deal with them without significant problems – but a sizeable minority may struggle.

Many parents who have lost a partner or a child to an illness such as cancer, an accident or suicide will spend a lot of time worrying about the possibility of one of their children developing Depression or attempting self-harm as a result. It is vital for such families to get proper help and counselling. It is also very wise for the parent to share with the young person their own sense of loss and confusion over what has happened and, in this way, give them the opportunity to ventilate how they feel.

Invalidating Environments

These are a significant stressor, which Enda has already dealt with in Chapter Four.

Question: What is the role of drug therapy in the treatment of Depression in screenagers?

Harry's Answer: This is one of the most controversial areas in the management of Depression, especially in young people between the ages of fifteen and twenty-five. There are many parents who are concerned about the use of medication whilst the brain is still at a vulnerable stage of development – especially under the age of eighteen.

Other parents have been affected by the persistent links between the use of antidepressants and an increase in suicidal thoughts, which led to the placement of the so-called 'black box' warning on the information attached to antidepressants. This warning originated from research done in the States that identified an increased level of such thoughts in young people put on these drugs, especially those under twenty-five.

Still other parents are concerned that we are medicalising what is just a normal phase of emotional development in adolescents, and believe that talk therapy is the only way to help young people deal with Depression. Finally, some parents wonder, if drug therapy is to be considered, what the safest drugs are and, most importantly, who should prescribe them.

To try and deal with all of these common and very sensible queries from parents, we will break screenagers up into two groups.

The 13–17 Age Group

We know from Chapter One that the emotional brains of teenagers in this age group are being pruned, and that their logical brains are less developed. The result of this, as we saw, is that the young teenage brain is very vulnerable at this stage to the use of medications and substances. So, clearly, the decision to use medication is a serious one and must be made by somebody with a lot of experience. In general, the family doctor is not the best person to make such a decision and is usually happier to refer the young person to a specialist centre.

Many parents are very uneasy about their children going onto medication at this age. Each case has to be dealt with on its own merits, but here are a few useful guidelines:

- It is probably best if the decision as to whether drug therapy is required be made by a child-and-adolescent psychiatrist as part of a mental-health team.

- In most cases of Depression referred to such teams, the modern approach, following careful assessment, is to approach the situation by first using talk therapy, usually involving the parents as well as the young person.

- If antidepressants are used, it is usually only when the psychiatrist feels that a more severe episode of Depression is present, and that talk therapy on its own will not be sufficient. This may include situations where significant suicide ideation may already be present.

- The safest drugs for this group are the SSRIs. The most common and safest of these is fluoxetine (Prozac), and there is a lot of experience built up on its usage. In the USA, Escitalopram (Lexapro) has also been accepted as potentially helpful. The evidence for many other drugs is scarcer. The doses for screenagers are usually smaller than those for adults. The young person is assessed regularly, particularly in the first month or so, as the evidence shows that this is the time when increased agitation or suicidal thoughts will appear, if they are going to.

- Overall, the general view is that antidepressants have a moderate success rate at best in the management of Depression in this age group. This is not surprising given the stage of brain development in this group.

- If antidepressants are used, then talk therapy will continue as an integral part of the process.

- Contrary to what many believe, drug therapy is not addictive and is usually only used for six to twelve months. In some individual situations it can be very effective, helping the young teenager to become more amenable to talk therapy. In many cases, their suicide ideation may be eliminated as their mood lifts.

- The best advice for parents is that, if the specialist feels antidepressants are appropriate, that advice should be listened to as long as all the safety measures are built in to the decision.

- If antidepressants have to be used, it doesn't make either the parents or the young teenager 'failures'.

- In most cases, it is not a question of medicalising normal feelings of depression or low mood in this age group. It is more that these have merged into Depression, which is now affecting the emotional, physical and cognitive work of the teenager, who is now struggling to function. This may, for example, be making it very difficult for the teenager to survive at school.

- Although suicide is not a common consequence of Depression, it is still a significant risk in a small number of cases where mood is very low. In such cases, even though there may be a risk to using antidepressants – in the first month in particular – there may be greater risks to not treating it, such as suicide attempts as the young person feels increasingly hopeless and desperate.

- The research on which the 'black box' warning was originally based did not find an increased risk of 'actual suicide', but rather an increased rate of 'suicidal thoughts'. This is an absolutely vital piece of information, as many assume the opposite.

- In all cases, medication should be administered by the parents, and only a week's supply should be dispensed at a time.

The 18–25 Age Group

Things become a little clearer as we move into this slightly older screenager group. The brains of people in this group are slowly beginning to mature, becoming gradually more adult in type. The one added complication for parents is that, technically, the young person is now regarded as an adult and can exclude them from the decision to use drug therapy. This can make the situation for some parents even more worrying and complex.

In terms of who should make the decision as to whether drug therapy is required or not – the family doctor is usually the one who has to decide. In some cases, he or she may be happy to do so and may, with the agreement of the young adult, involve their parents in the decision-making process. In other cases, he may refer the young adult to the adult mental-health services for an opinion.

In all cases, lifestyle changes and talk therapy should be part of the therapy plan. If possible, if the bout of Depression is mild, antidepressants should not be the first option. But if the bout is more moderate or severe and the young adult is struggling to function, their use can be very helpful as part of a holistic package.

Here are a few useful general guidelines for parents:

- Antidepressants are most often prescribed by family doctors. In some cases, they are prescribed by adult psychiatrists.

- The safest group of antidepressants are the SSRIs. If they are not working, then referral to the mental-health team or the use of SRNIs is usually the next step.

- As with the younger age group, starting with a lower dose and gradually increasing it if needed is the usual approach.

- In a small group, there may be increased risk of agitation or suicide ideation, particularly in the first few weeks of treatment, but this can be monitored by regular assessment.

- As in all cases of severe Depression, there is a risk of suicide even if the person is not on drug therapy. Many young people who die by suicide have never been prescribed an antidepressant at all.

- Drug therapy should always be accompanied by lifestyle changes and some form of talk therapy.

- A course of antidepressants will usually last for six to twelve months. They are not addictive.

- Their role is to make the young adult screenager function better and be more likely to become involved in talk therapy. This is particularly important if the screenager is at college.

- With the agreement of the young adult, the medication should be dispensed weekly from a chemist and, preferably, administered by a parent for safety reasons.

Question: What is going on in the head of the screenager when they are suffering from a bout of Depression?

Enda's Answer: Everybody experiences ego anxiety, which I discussed in Chapter 11 of my book *Five Steps to Happiness*. It has to do with how we look at and measure ourselves as people. When we're well, we are able to balance any negative thoughts about ourselves that emanate from the emotional brain. However, when we get depressed, our thinking can get extremely negative. This thinking can cause our emotions to oscillate from extreme anxiety and feeling so down that we can't see any way out and feel hopeless.

These thinking patterns are a result of our emotional mind becoming a pathological critic. When our emotional brain goes into complete negative mode, the cognitive consequence can be that our thinking gets more and more self-critical. This emotional voice is one that constantly dismisses our feelings, oversimplifies our problems and constantly criticises us for failing to problem-solve. It's like having a boss in work who constantly flogs you and criticises you over everything, and who is there at your shoulder twenty-four hours a day, seven days a week.

Without expert help in how to argue the critic away, we will never do it. This is because the criticisms that are levelled at us by our pathological critic are always vague. Trying to argue against a vague criticism is like trying to box against our shadow. As we try to argue with it, the critic moves the goalposts and criticises us over something else.

Over time, our ability to cope with this critic diminishes, until eventually we collapse emotionally and take to the bed, refusing to get up, as we can't see any point in it. It's easier to sit in the hole than climb out and just be knocked in again. As this thinking pattern gets entrenched over time, the actual structure and chemistry of our brain starts to change. This cascade of 'failure' thoughts pouring from our emotional brain becomes constant in a way that we are unable to prevent.

Question: What is the role of talk therapy, and particularly CBT, in the management of Depression in screenagers?

Enda's Answer: CBT works by gently helping the person to recognise their thinking. Taking each thought in turn, we examine it to see if it is accurate.

Once we start to identify our 'stinking thinking', the therapist will gently show us how to switch each thought off. Each negative thought is challenged, item by item, piece by piece. In each session, we look at how we view the world, what we have concluded this means for us and, most importantly, how we are reinforcing our unhealthy thinking through our unhealthy behaviour.

Gradually our thinking clears, we start to engage with life again, we start to enjoy things and 'hastening slowly' we get well gently.

Question: What is the normal outcome for screenagers who develop a bout of Depression?

Harry's Answer: This is a very important question and one that concerns most parents whose screenagers are going through or have experienced bouts of Depression. The good news is that research has shown that the vast majority have completely remitted within a year. But there is a tendency for the Depression to return again, either in adolescence or early adulthood, with some research suggesting that one-third of sufferers may get a second bout within three years, and half within five years.

There is a lot of interest, as already detailed, in coming up with innovative ways of trying to reduce these figures by identifying Depression earlier. There is little doubt that success in this area might prevent the future adult from suffering an increased risk of recurrence. If there is history of a co-existent condition such as alcohol or substance abuse, or an eating disorder, or if the bout of Depression is particularly severe and starts at a younger age, then the risks of recurrence seem to be higher.

It would be quite common for many adolescents to experience a bout of Depression in their teens, in particular, and cope with it on their own. Such bouts will usually settle within six to twelve months. It is often only when a second, more severe episode occurs – often in their early twenties whilst they are at college – that they finally come looking for some assistance and open up to the previous bout.

The importance of all this information for parents is that screenager Depression comes in bouts, the first of which is often in adolescence, and that, no matter how challenging they are, these bouts will remit within a year at the most in the vast majority of cases. Sometimes this information can be very helpful in terms of helping parents and screenagers make it through such periods of distress. It may also explain why so many screenagers arrive in college and, within a year or so, develop a bout of Depression. In many cases, it may be that they have already gone through a bout in their adolescence.

This is why it is so critical that parents learn good mental health skills and pass them on to their young screenagers. The more these are developed from a young age, the more resilience the screenagers will build up to help them cope with the young-adult phase of life, with all its challenges.

Question: Is there any evidence that improving certain skills in adolescents and young adults in high-risk families can reduce the risk that they will develop Depression?

Harry's Answer: The good news is that there is some evidence that resilience in adolescents from families with higher risks of Depression can be improved by some of the skills Enda dealt with earlier. Three key potential targets are emotional-regulation skills, coping or problem-solving skills and thinking styles relating to negative attention bias. These are areas all parents can work on both in themselves and, indeed, with their screenagers. But for parents who worry about their offspring developing Depression because they themselves have suffered regular bouts, these are definite targets to work on.

One other important way of preventing Depression in such families (and indeed all families) is to work hard on interpersonal relationships, as there is significant evidence that high-quality, warm relationships with parents and other family members are the best preventative measure of all. This is why the earlier chapters are so important in developing such relationships and skills.

Now I will explore the world of self-harm and suicide amongst our screenagers.

CHAPTER FOURTEEN
Self-Harm, Suicide and Screenagers

A common reason for a parent to seek help for their adolescent screenager from either a doctor or a therapist is that the latter is self-harming, is expressing suicidal thoughts or has attempted suicide. For most parents, this feeds into their worst fears. They have invested so much love, time and effort into helping their child grow and develop that the possibility of losing them to suicide is almost too much for them to bear.

But this fear is now almost palpable amongst parents of adolescents who are between the ages of thirteen and twenty-five – even extending up to the age of thirty. This is quite understandable, as the topic of suicide amongst this age group is regularly aired on the national and local media, and not without some justification.

If we examine Central Statistics Office (CSO) figures for suicide which cover 2010, for example, we note that the highest suicide rate was in young men aged between the ages of twenty and twenty-four. Ireland ranks fourth in the world for rates of suicide between the ages of eighteen and twenty-four, and is also the fourth-highest for deaths by suicide in this age group in the European Union.

In 2011, ninety-five adolescents between the ages of fifteen and twenty-four died by suicide in the Irish Republic, according to the Samaritans 'Suicide Statistics Report 2013'. Eighty of these were male and fifteen were female. Another fifty young people between the ages of twenty-five and twenty-nine died by suicide that year – forty-four male, and six female. In total, one hundred forty-five young people between the ages of fifteen and twenty-nine died by suicide in that one year, of which one hundred twenty-four were young men. Each one of those left behind grieving parents and siblings who are still struggling with trying to understand why they did it.

But in some ways, this is only the tip of the iceberg. As we move into the area of self-harm (rather than suicide), the numbers rise significantly. A 2012 report from the National Suicide Research Foundation noted that the estimated total number of cases of self-harm which presented to hospital in 2010 was around twelve thousand, and that the number of hidden cases was probably in the region of sixty thousand. This adds up to the staggering figure of seventy-two thousand.

For the purposes of this book, the key finding was that – of the twelve thousand who presented to hospital – most were between the ages of fifteen and twenty-four, and there was still a significant number between the ages of twenty-five and twenty-nine. Between the ages of fifteen and nineteen, more girls than boys self-harmed, but the number of boys who self-harmed was still a significant number. Between the ages of nineteen and twenty-four, the situation reversed, and more boys than girls self-harmed; the girls were not far behind the boys, though.

What all this information adds up to is that our young adolescents are experiencing significant emotional distress and are involved in unhealthy behaviours as a consequence. It is no surprise that so many parents are anxious and are desperately seeking information and support as to how to handle the situation if it occurs.

The purpose of this chapter is to try and give parents as much information as we can to assist them in understanding more about the area, what is going on in the mind of the self-harming or actively suicidal adolescent screenager and, in particular, what to do if they are encountering such problems. We will also try and pick out some potential warning signs that might trigger intervention and suggest a model for suicide based on the concept of emotional distress.

SELF-HARM

Here are a few common questions that parents ask in relation to self-harm, especially if they have an adolescent who is engaging in this behaviour:

- What is self-harm and what are its links to suicide?

- How common is it in Ireland?

- What are the commonest ways to self-harm?

- What are common warning signs for parents to watch out for?

- What are the common causes in Ireland of self-harm?

- Why is my adolescent screenager 'really' self-harming?

- What is going on in the mind of the adolescent who self-harms?

- Most of all, what should I do if I discover my child is self-harming?

Question: What is self-harm and what are its links to suicide?

Harry's Answer: Suicide is 'a conscious or deliberate act that ends one's life when an individual is attempting to solve a problem that is perceived as unsolvable by any other means', according to 'Reach Out: Irish National Strategy for Action on Suicide Prevention 2005-2014'. Self-harm, on the other hand, is 'a deliberate non-fatal act, whether physical, drug overdose, or poisoning, carried out in the knowledge that it is potentially harmful', according to 2009's 'Introduction to Suicide and Self-Harm' by Navneet Kapur and Linda Gask.

These definitions clearly suggested a difference in terms of the main objective of the acts. Some consider suicide as the end point on a continuum which begins with self-harm. Those who believe this theorise that self-harm may precede suicidal behaviour because such behaviour may stem from an escalation of self-harming behaviour. This is sometimes referred to as the 'gateway theory'. It suggests that gradual exposure to increasing self-harm may lead to more serious suicidal attempts (Hamza et al, 2012). This makes sense in that it implies that the person who self-harms gradually becomes inured to the discomfort of the act and, as a result, may be prepared to escalate to suicide.

Others prefer to look at the lethality of the actual self-harm act before placing it on such a continuum, only including those in which there was clearly serious intent of self-harm. Experts have found 'a significant and meaningful association between the degree of suicide intent and the lethality of the attempt' (Horesh et al, 2012).

It is now felt that, overall, it is more useful to consider suicide and self-harm as two distinct entities with different causes and presentations, which require different management. This argument that self-harm is an entity on its own rather than a phase on the road to suicide is supported by Matthew Nock and Ronald Kessler, who examined in a 2006 paper whether we could divide those who self-harm into 'suicide attempters' and 'suicide gesturers' (see bibliography). The authors distinguished the two primarily on the basis of 'intent'. The former would self-harm with a clear intent to die; the latter would not intend to die but to communicate their pain to others.

Nock and Kessler also noted gender differences, reporting that 'men who engaged in self-injury were more likely to make suicide attempts than suicide gestures, whereas women were more likely to make suicide gestures than suicide attempts'. In other words, men were more likely to report an intent to die from their self-injury, whereas women were more likely to report that it was a means of communicating with others.

However, while the distinction between self-harm and suicide is, in practice, quite useful and relevant, we cannot ignore a key link between the two. Kapur and Gask, for example, noted that the rates of suicide following self-harm attempts were '0.5–2 percent in the year after an episode of self-harm (or 50–200 times the general population rate)' and that 'longer-term studies have found rates of suicide of 3 percent at 5 years and around 7 percent for periods longer than 10 years'. We should also not forget that up to 25 percent of suicides are preceded by an act of self-harm in the previous year. So self-harm, although clearly an entity in itself, must be very carefully assessed in each case to rule out more lethal intent.

Question: How common is self-harm amongst adolescents in Ireland?

Harry's Answer: We have already discussed the staggering number of projected cases of self-harm in Ireland, and the bulge in the figures between the ages of fifteen and twenty-four. Clearly, young people in this age group are most active in this area. Therefore, this subject is of key importance to all parents reading this book. We also know from the National Suicide Research Foundation study mentioned, in relation to these figures, that the highest rates of hospital-treated self-harm are among '15–19 year-old girls' and '20–24 year-old men'.

We get a clearer picture of the situation amongst our school-going adolescents from an excellent 2010 study which examined the factors involved in deliberate self-harm (DSH) in Irish adolescents (McMahon et al, 2010). This cross-sectional study involved 3,881 adolescents in thirty-nine schools completing an anonymous questionnaire as part of the much wider Child and Adolescent Self-harm in Europe (CASE) study. This study reported that 9.1 percent of Irish adolescents surveyed had self-harmed at some point, and almost half of those had done so repeatedly. They noted that research had shown that less than 20 percent of adolescents who self-harm attend health services, with 33 percent seeking assistance from their social circle and 50 percent not seeking any assistance.

Question: What are the commonest ways to self-harm?

Harry's Answer: There are numerous ways to self-harm, but the commonest are:

- Cutting
- Burning
- Pulling out hair
- Scratching skin
- Banging head
- Taking overdoses
- Attempting hanging
- Seriously abusing of alcohol or substances

Question: What are common warning signs for parents to watch out for?

Harry's Answer: There are numerous possible ways in which self-harm may present in your adolescent screenager, but here are a few common signs for mothers, in particular (who are usually more perceptive to changes in their children), to be on alert for:

- Cut or burn marks on arms, legs and abdomens
- A habit of wearing clothing that might be used to hide evidence of cutting
- Knives, razor blades, box-cutters or other sharp objects hidden in the bedroom
- A habit of remaining locked in the bedroom or bathroom for lengthy periods of time following difficulties at school or with peers, or significant family conflicts
- Reports from a significant adult – such as teacher or doctor – of cuts or burns on the adolescent screenager
- Reports from a sibling that the teen is self-harming
- Evidence that the teen's peers are cutting or burning themselves

Question: What are the common causes in Ireland of self-harm?

Harry's Answer: The commonest reasons for self-harm in Ireland relate to a wide range of social issues, such as:

- Bullying of any form, including cyberbullying
- Family or peer relationship problems
- Drug or substance abuse
- School or work problems

- Any form of abuse – particularly sexual, but also verbal or physical
- Financial problems
- Sexual-identity issues
- Anxiety and underlying Depression
- Significant emotional distress

The McMahon study mentioned earlier found that the factors related to the lifetime reporting of self-harm in school-going adolescents varied according to gender, with some factors affecting young people of both genders:

- For young males, the main factors were anxiety, impulsivity and school problems – mainly bullying and keeping up with school-work.

- For females, they were low self-esteem, relationship problems (particularly with friends and family) and forced sexual activity.

- For both, a history of taking drugs and being in contact with a peer involved in self-harm were important factors. This latter is very important, due to the copycat nature of both self-harm and suicide in this young, vulnerable group.

Question: Why is my adolescent screenager 'really' self-harming?

Harry's Answer: This is where we really get down to truly trying to understand what is going on when an adolescent in their teens or early twenties self-harms. It is also where we link three significant conditions together that cause so much distress in the lives of screenagers and their parents and families. These are:

- Eating disorders, including anorexia and bulimia
- Self-harm
- Substance abuse

The common denominator to all three is that they are often the behavioural response to coping with emotional distress. It is the latter that really lies at the heart of self-harm, particularly in relation to young people between the ages of thirteen and twenty-five.

Parents get really distressed when it comes to the surface that their adolescent – the child they love so much and have put so much effort into rearing – is self-harming. The problem is that they fall into the quite-natural trap of focusing on the behaviour and not the cause of the emotional distress which underlies it.

In the vast majority of cases, the young person is struggling to deal with emotions which are quite powerful, and trying to do so without having the necessary skills. So what are typical emotions which lie beneath the surface? Well here are a few common ones:

- Anxiety (this is probably the commonest)

- Low self-esteem

- Depression

- Frustration

- Shame (often peer-related)

Being a teenager or young adult in modern Irish society is extremely daunting and challenging. There are so many real issues that members of this group are trying to cope with and, due to modern technology and social media, they are doing this very much in view of their peers.

Although most screenagers have sufficient resilience to deal with such issues, others really struggle with the emotions that get thrown up as a result. Their response is to self-harm, but one might ask why this helps. Well, the answer lies, once again, in the brain. When they cut themselves, for example, the brain releases feel-good endorphins which give rise to feelings of euphoria, and this helps to numb the emotional pain. Unfortunately, for some adolescents, this gives rise to an almost addictive buzz, which is why they continue to do it even though it is usually painful.

So they end up in a vicious circle. They start with some normal teenager or young adult issues like the ones we have already discussed: relationship difficulties, school problems or bullying. They start to become very emotionally distressed, but do not have the coping skills to deal with this. Their response is to self-harm by, say, cutting themselves. This leads to an endorphin release, a buzz and a numbing of emotions. The young person finds short-term relief from the emotional distress caused by the issue disturbing them.

Most of this happens in silence, with parents and other significant adults unaware of what is going on. The result can be that the behaviour starts to become a repetitive, almost addictive behavioural response to dealing with their emotional distress. But the real problem is that the initial cause has not been dealt with, and the young screenager is unaware that there are other ways of coping with their distress.

This is why screenagers 'really' self-harm. In general, they do not have any significant mental illness and are usually not really focused on ending their lives by suicide. They are simply trying to cope with the emotional distress created by the very stressful world they find themselves living in.

Beneath the vast majority who self-harm as a form of emotional release, however, lies a small but important group whose self-harm attempts may actually be designed to end the pain permanently. We will deal with this later in the section on suicide.

Question: What are we doing in Ireland to try and reduce the incidence of self-harm?

Harry's Answer: Whilst the vast majority of screenagers who self-harm will never reach a hospital setting, there is strong evidence that those who do are a definite population whose attempts may be more serious and who can be reached. This is important, as we will see later; some of those who do attend will eventually go on to die by suicide. We also know that many will repeatedly self-harm and some will end up being admitted. It is also clear that, in the past, we have been unsuccessful in stemming this flow.

That situation is hopefully about to change, as Ireland has adapted an approach which has been shown in the USA to be very effective in reducing self-harm and suicide. It's called dialectical behaviour therapy (DBT). In Chapter Four on the invalidating environment, Enda mentioned Professor Marsha Linehan, a world-famous psychologist and therapist – it is she who is the originator of DBT. She initially developed the model to deal with patients with borderline personality disorder (which we will be discussing later) who were engaged in persistent self-harm. But it is now used as a model to deal with many other conditions which lead to emotional distress and self-harm, such as eating disorders and substance abuse. The approach is based on the fact that many who are repeatedly self-harming come from an invalidating environment and lack emotional regulation and interpersonal skills.

Linehan decided to put together a combined individual and group approach to the problem, involving four key facets:

- Mindfulness, which we discussed in Chapter 6

- Emotion regulation skills

- Interpersonal skills

- Distress tolerance, which is often called 'self-soothing'

The key to DBT is that it is much more of a behavioural therapy than a cognitive therapy, so it is very much a 'hands on' approach, which is very effective at providing a different solution to the person's problems, rather than self-harm.

Ireland has now adapted this approach into a new scheme called the 'Endeavour' initiative. It has trained seventeen teams to work in self-harm and suicide 'hot spots' around the country and is hoping to roll this initiative out to every part of the country and is training therapists to achieve this target. One trial of this approach in Cork showed a significant reduction in admissions for self-harm. This is a most welcome initiative, and one that will hopefully bear much fruit in time.

What the above is demonstrating, hopefully, is that to find the answers to self-harm and suicide, we have got to look beyond the traditional medical model type of approach, to the world of emotional distress. The necessity for this becomes even clearer when we move on to discuss suicide itself.

For parents, the success of this type of approach demonstrates the importance of creating validating environments, and teaching ourselves and our adolescent screenagers key skills, like the ones Enda detailed earlier. The stark fact remains that, despite this really excellent initiative, there are still over sixty thousand young people self-harming, most of whom will never come to the attention of 'the system'. A significant number of these belong to the screenager group, and many are in our own homes but we do not recognise them.

Question: What is going on in the mind of the adolescent who self-harms? What should I do if I discover my child is self-harming?

Enda's Answer: In order to assist parents of young screenager adolescents who are self-harming, let's now examine just what is going on in their emotional minds.

In my clinical experience, I have never met a teenager who was cutting and self-harming who actually had a problem with it. Their family may have a problem, but the teenager rarely does. They will regularly fail to see or understand what all the fuss is about.

Understanding this is fundamental to getting the teenager to stop. If they are normalising the behaviour as a valid way to self-soothe their anxiety, then we as therapists and parents have to adopt the same standpoint.

I usually start by reinforcing for the teen that cutting is a very effective way of managing discomfort. However effective it may be, though, there is one big cost to dealing with distressing emotions this way: it leaves very noticeable scars! I try to suggest to the teen that, if they are willing, I can show them a much easier way to self-soothe, which won't cost as much and doesn't scar.

As they engage with me, we look at what distressing emotions they are experiencing and what is going on in their life. Gradually, I introduce more effective ways to overcome distressing emotions, changing circumstances whenever possible and adapting to them when necessary.

The secret to helping your child is to adopt the same attitude as I have outlined above. Above all, don't panic!

SUICIDE

It is worth revisiting the definition of suicide that we used in the beginning of this chapter: 'a conscious or deliberate act that ends one's life when an individual is attempting to solve a problem that is perceived as unsolvable by any other means'. There is much to learn for parents from this definition, such as:

- In general, it is a conscious and deliberate action. This means that, most of the time, the person who dies has not acted in a totally impulsive manner, but has made a clear decision that ending their life is the only way to deal with their perceived problem. The debate as to whether suicide is more impulsive or planned is particularly relevant for the screenager group. We will return to this issue later.

- The second important concept is that the definition implies that the act is a clear attempt to find a solution to an issue which is bothering the person. In other words, they have come to regard themselves as a significant part of the problem and removing themselves is the only solution they can come up with.

- The last part, which is critical, is that the person who dies has come to believe, unfortunately, that there is no other way to solve the issue which is bothering them, and so suicide is the only option left.

In this section, I will try and tease out the conundrum of why so many young Irish adolescents and young adults up to the age of thirty find themselves in situations where taking their own lives is the only option they can find to deal with the distress they find themselves in.

First, I will examine what research has shown us, in general, regarding suicide. Then I will examine the Irish situation. I will propose a model of suicide based on emotional pain and then examine what is really going on in the mind of the adolescent who is in difficulty. I will also examine the concept of the 'suicide cocoon' and what parents might learn from it. Finally, I will examine possible warning signs and how best to deal with potentially risky situations which may develop with those adolescent screenagers we love and cherish so much.

I am conscious that there will be three main groups of parents who will be reading this chapter:

- The first group, the vast majority, will be parents who are concerned that their adolescent screenagers might for some reason become emotionally very distressed in the future. These parents want to know more about suicide and its warning signs so as to be able to intervene in time.

- The second group will be parents who have actually lost an adolescent between the ages of fifteen and twenty-five – or a young adult under thirty – to suicide. Both of us have met and talked to such parents and our heart goes out to them in their pain and grief as they battle to understand why it happened. I have done some qualitative research on just how losing a child of this age to suicide affects the parents left behind, and the information they provided was both heart-rending and invaluable. I will include some comments from them later.

- The last group includes parents who have adolescents who are suffering from significant mental distress for a variety of different reasons, and who may be concerned about the risk of suicide.

The needs of each of these three groups are different, but we will do our best to try and answer the main questions members of each group might have.

What Can Research Tell Us About Suicide?

In a major review in 2009 in the respected medical journal *The Lancet*, Keith Hawton and Kees van Heeringen noted that suicide was 'the tenth leading cause of death worldwide'. It is difficult to estimate the precise numbers who die by suicide, and they felt that this may be associated with variations in the manner in which such deaths are both reported and certified from country to country, which may mask the true mortality rates. They noted that the male-to-female ratio for suicide was between two and four to one in developed countries. They also noted that, in general, men chose more violent means, such as hanging or shooting, and women choose less violent methods, such as self-poisoning.

The complexity of suicide was illustrated by the variety of underlying major risk factors associated with it. In a major review of risk factors in developing and developed countries, Vijayakumar et al (2006) noted that some common universal ones included: youth and old age; lower socioeconomic standing; substance abuse; previous suicide attempts; recent life stressors such as interpersonal loss, conflict, or rejection; loss of employment; economic problems; incarceration or legal troubles; eviction; and being diagnosed with a terminal illness. In developing countries, they noted that being female, living in a rural area and having religious beliefs that permit suicide were of more relevance than in developed countries, where being male and suffering from mental illness was felt to be more relevant. Access to means was of importance in both, but the specific means could vary, with pesticides felt to be of more relevance in developing countries.

Turecki et al (2012), Hawton and van Heeringen (2009) and others, found that major risk factors included: genetic and familial factors; mental illnesses, especially mood disorders such as Depression and schizophrenia; substance abuse (particularly alcohol abuse); unemployment; poverty; traumatic early life experiences; personality traits such as impulsiveness; and recent acute life stressors. In a review of thirty-one studies involving 15,629 cases of suicide, it was noted that 98 percent had a defined mental disorder.

The link with Depression was noted to be strong, with more than half of those who died by suicide felt to have been suffering from a current episode.

Hawton and van Heeringen suggested that suicide in Depression is most likely to occur during the first episode. In relation to schizophrenia, it has been estimated that lifetime suicide risk is 4 percent to 5 percent, the risk being highest in the early stages of the disorder, with risk factors including secondary Depression, drug abuse, previous suicide attempts and poor adherence to treatment. Alcohol abuse, when paired with Depression, is strongly linked to suicide risk, particularly if linked to stressful life events such as relationship breakdowns.

In *Flagging the Problem*, we examined the neurobiological data that underlies suicide, which was gained by post-mortem studies and neuroimaging of survivors of serious suicide attempts. This can be summarised as follows:

- The prefrontal cortex or logical brain is malfunctioning, particularly a key section called the ventral prefrontal cortex, which we called the 'impulse-control centre'. This results in a lack of control by this part of the brain, which normally prevents suicidal thoughts and consequent impulsive actions.

- The serotonin mood cable, which supplies this part of the prefrontal cortex, is impaired. Many see this as the most important biological finding. It is sometimes linked to genetic factors, deprivation, childhood abuse, smoking or substance abuse.

- The limbic mood system or emotional brain is overactive, giving rise to a huge surge through the stress system. This is the source of many of the negative emotional thoughts of despair, as well as the feelings of hopelessness and helplessness, so prevalent in those at risk.

- The adrenal stress gland is often enlarged (in some cases it actually doubles in size) and overactive, releasing large amounts of the stress hormone glucocortisol. This may be the case for some time before the person's death.

This neurobiological data is very useful, as it points to the person who dies by suicide being in significant difficulties for some time before the actual act, with their stress system, in particular, being over active. It fits in very well with the model of suicide we will be presenting later, namely that of a response to severe emotional distress. It also fits in with the definite link with Depression, where the serotonin mood system is often underactive. Finally, it suggests that there may be a hidden sub-group who are more likely to significantly self-harm (with a view to suicide) who, for a combination of genetic and environmental factors, may be particularly prone to an under active serotonin mood system supplying the logical brain.

All of the above risk factors can be summarised as follows:

- Men are, in general, up to four times as likely to die by suicide. So simply being a man increases risk.

- In a significant percentage of suicides, there is a history of mental illnesses such as depression, schizophrenia and substance abuse.

- There are common neurobiological signs found on post mortem and on scanning which suggest significant pre-suicide stress.

- Social factors such as poverty, unemployment, homelessness, sexual abuse, traumatic early life experiences and significant current stressors are significant.

- Alcohol is intimately connected with many suicides.

What Lies at the Heart of Suicide?

Suicide attempts are often a mixture of a wish to annihilate oneself and a cry for help. This duality of wanting to be destroyed and wanting to be saved reflects the state of chaos and confusion that the person in distress exists in. Sometimes the cry for help is answered, others times the attempt is successful.

Whilst all of the above research gives us some background into many of the social, neurobiological and mental health difficulties that are so often prevalent in suicide, it does not give us real insight into what finally leads the person to make the ultimate decision. This insight is a key one for parents who would like to have a better understanding of the condition.

One of the greatest researchers of all time into suicide was called Edwin Shneidman (1918–2009). He spent his whole life trying to develop a deeper understanding of what led people to die by suicide. At the age of ninety, in his *A Commonsense Book of Death*, he made the following statement:

> My theory of suicide can be rather simply stated. There is a great deal of mental pain and suffering without suicide – millions to one – but there is almost no suicide without a great deal of mental pain. The basic formula for suicide is rather straightforward: introspective torture plus the idea of death as release. The key, the black heart of suicide, is an acute ache in the mind, in the psyche, it is called psychache. In this view, suicide is not a disease of the brain; but rather it is a perturbation in the mind, an introspective storm of dissatisfaction with the status quo, a dramatic (albeit self-destructive) effort to return to a status quo ante.

If we delve deeper, Shneidman believed that if one examined the psychological factors underlying suicide, the principal finding in every case was psychological or emotional pain, which he called 'psychache'. Antoon Leenaars, in a 1999 review of Shneidman's work, explained it this way:

> From Shneidman's perspective: The view of the psychological factors in suicide, the key element in every case is psychological pain: psychache. All affective states (such as rage, hostility, depression, shame, guilt, affectlessness, hopelessness, etc.) are relevant to suicide only as they related to unbearable psychological pain.

At its heart, suicide is a behavioural response to what is experienced by the person as a state of intolerable emotional distress, which they feel will never stop and will always be with them. To the person, such a decision seems perfectly 'rational', as they see no other solution to their emotional distress, irrespective of what the issues were which led into it.

That is why so many loved ones, friends and work colleagues find it so difficult to understand why somebody close to them would decide to end it all. They cannot understand how the person could not have seen that there were other, simpler, more obvious solutions to whatever was upsetting them. How could they hurt those left behind in such a manner?

To try an answer some of these questions and concerns, let's examine these concepts further.

The Suicide Cocoon

There is a common theme running through the narrative of suicide: often, all seems normal to the outsider. The person seems to have been in good form, following normal routines and showing no external signs of distress.

- 'We never saw it coming!'

- 'She seemed to be in great form!'

- 'It makes no sense, he was behaving so normally!'

- 'He had been a bit down and withdrawn, but had got over this and seemed back to himself!'

- 'There was nothing in the days and weeks before it happened that was out of the ordinary!'

- 'Why?'

So just what is going on, especially in the mind of the person in difficulty? At an excellent Console conference in 2012, I introduced the idea that when some people in extreme distress make the decision to end it all, they enter what I call the 'suicide cocoon'.

The function of a cocoon is to provide a protective cover, shielding the occupant from the outside world. In the insect world, it is to protect the larva before it breaks out and enters the world (birth). The tragedy of the suicide cocoon is that it has the function of protecting the 'decision' of the person to end their own life (death)!

Once in the cocoon, the person is in a different world, one we will explore later. Some may enter the cocoon hours or days before they die by suicide. Others may spend several months entangled in its deadly embrace. One survivor called the cocoon 'seductive', as once inside it, the 'pain' was gone. He was in the cocoon for several months before an almost-fatal suicide attempt.

We must remember that suicide is a behavioural act, and that all behaviour has a definite purpose. Behaviour starts with a thought, which triggers an emotion and a subsequent action, so examining a person's pre-suicide thinking is the key. Later, we are going to attempt to explore the mind of the person in difficulties, both before they enter the cocoon and while in it.

Let's show how examining a person's thinking pre-suicide might work out in practice. I am going to take an allegorical yet typical example, which highlights Depression. John is a screenager who is going to end his days in the suicide cocoon, dying by suicide in the next three months. Let's explore his thinking and behaviour during this phase, using a simple CBT based ABC approach.

John's Story

John is twenty-five and is suddenly made redundant by the company he had been working with. He has a history of Depression, suffering from two significant bouts – one in his teens and the second in his first year of college. He did not receive any assistance for the first bout but did attend a college counsellor for the second. His family were completely unaware of both episodes.

The loss of his job triggers a new bout of Depression, and his difficulties begin. He has been renting an apartment with his girlfriend, and now financial difficulties start to emerge. His self-esteem implodes. He starts to drink more to try and cope with how he feels but this actually worsens his mood. He withdraws more and begins to spend more and more time late at night on his computer.

The relationship begins to suffer and the silences grow longer. His mother is becoming concerned that John does not seem to be in good form but puts it down to the stress of losing his job – so do his siblings and friends. Finally, his girlfriend, who has no idea that he is suffering from Depression, thinking he is just moody as a result of losing his job, gives him an ultimatum: she will leave him if he doesn't snap out of it.

Let's explore what is happening in John's internal world. To do this, we are going to imagine that he was actually engaging at this stage with a CBT therapist and, between them, the following ABC developed:

Activating Event

- Trigger: Loss of job.

- Inference/danger: 'My whole reason for living has gone. I will never get work again. We are going to struggle to even keep the apartment. I have let everybody down. Even my girlfriend does not want to be around me.'

Belief/Demand

- 'Because I lost my job I am awful.'

Consequences

- Emotion: Depression.

- Physical symptoms: Fatigue, poor concentration, difficulty eating, trouble sleeping, lack of drive.

- Behaviour: Avoids other people, withdraws emotionally and fights more with his girlfriend. Drinks more, spends more time on his own on his computer, ruminates constantly, has some fleeting suicidal thoughts but no active plans.

John was distressed by losing his job and that stress triggered an underlying irrational belief that he is a failure. That triggered persistent emotions of depression, which begin to lead to a host of distressing physical symptoms such as fatigue, sleep, lack of appetite, sexual difficulties, poor drive, cognitive problems and an inability to enjoy life. It also triggered a host of unhealthy behaviours and ruminations, culminating in the appearance of a bout of Depression.

If John had been reached at that stage, his Depression could have been treated with a typical holistic package of lifestyle changes, talk therapy and possibly drug therapy. In particular, CBT might have helped him to challenge his unhealthy beliefs and behaviour. This would be a common example of routine Depression triggered by a stressor. Suicide is less likely to occur at this stage as there is no planning. However, a small number at this stage who misuse alcohol as a coping mechanism may impulsively self-harm and may, unfortunately, take their own lives, even though they were not planning on it!

The vast majority of people with Depression may have significant ruminations but will not move beyond suicidal thoughts. So what happens to John that leads to enter the suicide cocoon?

To answer this, we need to ask what is going on in his emotional mind that will lead to significant suicide plans and suicide itself. I believe suicide is triggered by a bout of particularly severe, relentless, self-critical, negative ruminations caused in this case by Depression. The ruminations caused by Depression trigger a more lethal secondary ABC!

Activating Event

- Trigger: The ruminations – 'I feel so miserable, it is always going to be like this. I am just a burden on others. People just don't want to be around me. I feel so incredibly distressed, overwhelmed and totally helpless.'

- Inference/Danger: 'The situation is hopeless, there is no way out of it, it will always be like this. How could I have let it come to this?'

Belief

- 'This is awful' and 'I am awful for letting it happen.'

Consequences

- Emotion: Depression.

- Physical symptoms: Worsening of all of the previous physical symptoms.

- Behaviour: Increasing withdrawal, ruminations on ending the pain and distress, investigation and planning (Internet sites) as to how this could be achieved, decision made.

John enters the suicide cocoon!

Inside his cocoon it is quiet. There is a calm acceptance of his fate, a sense of peace at last, a lift in mood now that the internal debate is over and the decision to end it all has been made.

The reason behind this decision is to end the relentless distressing ruminations. There is a sense of detachment from everyday life. Although still interacting with the world, John is now a spectator. He is able to disengage emotionally from all those he loves.

His logical and wise minds have been totally silenced. The cocoon allows him to dispassionately make the necessary decisions to end the distress. The reality of death or the effects it might have on those left behind is blocked out. It was like being on autopilot. John is now only a passenger! This is a different dimension – suspended in time and place from the normal world. His emotional mind has only one solution to what it sees as an endless horizon of distress, and that is to take his own life, for he has now 'become the problem'.

Unless something intervenes there can be only one outcome!

A major reason John does not inform those close to him of his decision is that they may try to divert him from the course of action he has decided upon. Keeping up a normal routine is essential if he is going to carry out his decision. The whole purpose of the cocoon is, after all, to protect the decision he has made!

John remains in his cocoon for four weeks. To those around him, John seems to be in much better form, making plans for the future, even visiting close friends and family members – who all comment on how well he is coping with his difficulties. Up to the end, his cocoon protects his decision.

He dies by suicide, leaving a grieving family, heartbroken parents and a stunned community. All assume it was just an impulsive, unplanned decision, taken after imbibing alcohol the previous night. Another casualty of the recession.

One of the lessons we can learn from John's story is that the constant ruminations that he was 'worthless' and that the distress was 'never going to end' were the real trigger that drove him into the suicide cocoon. It is controversial but essential that if we did get a chance to reach John within his cocoon we would firstly have had to empathise with his decision to end his life! (Even if we clearly disagreed with it.)

We have to enter his cocoon and take the battle to a different place. To empathise with his decision but suggest another way of achieving his objective – by stopping the internal dialogue. The battle is to help him see that there is another way to end the relentless ruminations that he is 'worthless' and that *he* is the problem. It is to help him see that his thinking is abnormal, not him.

As a community, we need to try and understand the suicide cocoon concept, so that we can be more watchful of those around us who are struggling with life's difficulties and who then suddenly seem to be in much better form, or who start giving away precious items. Recognition of such changes might help us to intervene earlier.

The concept of the suicide cocoon is one that might also help many grieving families to understand the events leading up to the suicide of a loved one. Hopefully, it will ease their burden when they realise that it was the cocoon that blocked the capacity of the person to comprehend the distress they would leave behind in their wake.

We need to assume that everybody who has made a serious attempt at suicide is still in the cocoon, unless proven otherwise! Even if they have been shocked out of the cocoon by the attempt itself, we need to intervene – with talk therapy, in particular – to prevent them from re-entering it! If a person can be helped to reshape their negative belief that they are the problem into a belief that their thinking is the problem, then the journey back to health has begun.

The two crucial ruminations that perpetuate Depression leading to suicide are: 'I am worthless!' and 'This distress will go on forever and I have no way of stopping it!' These thoughts may really lie at the heart of the emotional distress which Shneidman felt was the trigger for the behavioural response of suicide. To deal with these key ruminations, we will have to help sufferers to accept themselves as Raggy Dolls, and to help them to challenge their irrational belief that the distress will go on forever by showing them newer and easier methods to deal with the causes of their emotional distress.

A key question that is often asked and one which Shneidman himself tried to answer is: 'Does the person who dies by suicide actually want to die or do they just want to end the pain?' The general consensus is that most who seriously attempt suicide are actually ambivalent about ending their lives, often right up to the last second.

This seems paradoxical until one realises that it is the emotional distress that the person is trying to escape from and not life itself. This is why many who are fortunate enough to survive a very serious suicide attempt or who are thwarted at the last minute by circumstance are able, with assistance, to move on and live full and fruitful lives. Many are actually relieved that they were not successful and grateful that they did not end up causing lifelong distress to those left behind. This insight is vital, as it means that if we can recognise warning signs and intervene to help the person to a safer place where they can get real help to deal with whatever lies behind their distress, then another tragedy can be avoided.

Some might say that this seems contrary to the suicide cocoon concept. But we must realise that many will have arrived in the cocoon only hours or days before they attempt suicide and that, even within the cocoon, they do not want to die but rather to end the pain. If we can recognise those who have arrived in the cocoon (or are headed there) and assist them in trying to find other, healthier ways to end their distress, then many lives can be saved. Nowhere is this more relevant than in the adolescent screenager group.

Suicide and Adolescent Screenagers: What Parents Need to Know

With this insight into suicide in general, let's examine what is happening in the adolescent group, in which there is such a high rate of self-harm and suicide in Ireland.

In one major review of mortality among young people worldwide between the ages of ten and twenty-four, it was noted that suicide was the cause of death in 6 percent of cases. A review of World Health Organization global figures noted that the mean suicide rate for young people between the ages of fifteen and nineteen was 7.4 per one hundred thousand, with suicide accounting for 9.1 percent of deaths worldwide in this age group. *The Lancet* review mentioned earlier noted that the rate of suicide in males rises throughout the teenage years, and that contributory factors such as Depression, substance abuse and disruptive behaviour disorders are important. It noted that previous suicide attempts, family difficulties, abuse, homelessness, and sexual identity issues can contribute to increased risk, and highlighted the role of the media in copycat clusters.

Earlier, we reviewed the statistics for suicide in 2011 in Ireland. You will remember that ninety-five young people between the ages of fifteen and twenty-four died by suicide in the Irish Republic that year, eighty of whom were young men. This is a typical example of just how many wonderful young lives are lost each year to suicide. We clearly have a major problem with young men, in particular, feeling that they have no other solution to the problems they are encountering.

In 2012, the number of deaths by suicide in that age group dropped to seventy-four. For 2013, the provisional figure was fifty-seven. Although provisional figures are often lower than final reported figures, this is encouraging. But there is still concern – as Paul Kelly of Console often highlights – that these may not be revealing the full story, as some deaths which may have been due to suicide are not recorded as such for many reasons. These statistical cold figures still translate into so many heartbroken families and parents whose lives have been destroyed by the loss of an adolescent they so loved.

The National Suicide Research Foundation studied the methods used by those who died by suicide between 2004 and 2010. The Foundation found that 72 percent of young men under thirty who died by suicide died by hanging, 9 percent by drowning, 8 percent by poisoning and 7 percent by firearms. It found that 58 percent of young women under thirty who died by suicide died by hanging, 19 percent by poisoning and 16 percent by drowning. What this shows is that the methods used in this age group were extremely lethal and the objective was clearly to take their own lives.

With so many young people – particularly males under the age of thirty – dying by suicide in Ireland, and in such extreme manners, we clearly have to examine in more detail what factors are responsible for creating the levels of emotional distress underlying this self-destructive behaviour.

Some parents reading this section may wonder why we are covering the topic in such detail. Many will feel that it is not relevant to their own families. But if a new infectious illness began to strike down one hundred forty-five adolescents and young adults between the ages of thirteen and thirty every year then there would be a furore of demand for information on the condition, its causes, who it might affect, how to recognise its warning signs and how to prevent it. Yet all over Ireland, in villages, towns and cities, young screenagers are dying and many more are making very serious self-harm attempts and we, as a society, seem to be failing them. So although, as a parent, it may not be especially relevant to you at this moment, it seems prudent to learn more about the subject.

It is only when one talks to parents who have lost sons or daughters to suicide, many of whom are receiving assistance from wonderful groups like Paul Kelly's Console, that the full impact of adolescent suicide on those left behind can by comprehended. These parents are devastated beyond words, and spend decades asking why.

To give some examples of just how devastating such a loss can be, I am including – with their kind permission – some statements from Irish parents on the experience of losing an adolescent to suicide:

- 'It's . . . it's just half of me is gone. I just I can't explain it. I can't explain how I feel. It's your worst nightmare, it's your worst everything.'

- 'There's never a day that goes by that you don't . . . it's with you last thing at night, and with you first thing in the morning.'

- 'I shouldn't have been picking the hearse for me son, they should have been picking it for me.'

- 'I'll just never mend. You go about the process your own way. You get dressed, you go out –you have to.'

- 'To think that he was in this dark place and he couldn't talk to me.'

- 'It's too hard, too hard.'

- 'I feel as if I failed some way.'

- 'It was an awful waste of life . . . If he had only come to speak to maybe, possibly not me but maybe somebody else, and put his problem out in front on the table as such and discussed it with somebody.'

- 'I feel I should have been able to see it.'

- 'If I could end the pain – I don't mean like doing anything – I'd often say, "If I keep walking out the road but bringing the pain with me."'

Apart from actual suicides, it is also important for parents to realise just how many 'close calls' there are each year in relation to adolescents who survive significant suicide attempts. These include attempted hangings, overdoses and drownings, as well as night-time single-vehicle road traffic accidents, in which the intention may have been to end the distress in a way that would be put down as an accident.

Many parents who have lost screenagers to suicide would join with us in beseeching fellow parents to:

- Learn to recognise emotional distress in their adolescents and young adults.

- Learn key warning signs that might help them recognise emotional distress.

- Know what to do if they do identify emotional distress.

- Learn how best to talk to adolescents, both when they are well and when they are in difficulties.

- Try to teach their teenagers and young adults key skills like emotional regulation and problem-solving as early as possible.

- Fight at a national level for proper resourcing for (and structural organisation of) suicide-prevention and assistance for parents left behind, as well as the groups that assist them.

Suicide and Adolescent Screenagers: What Parents Want to Know

Here are ten common questions parents ask:

1. Is suicide in the screenager adolescent normally planned or impulsive?

2. Why are so many Irish male adolescent screenagers and young adults dying by suicide?

3. Is it mental illness or life-crisis situations which lead to the emotional distress underlying suicide in adolescent screenagers, and what is the role of alcohol?

4. Why do screenagers find it so hard to come to their parents when they are feeling emotionally distressed?

5. What is the role of technology in screenager suicide?

6. What are the most common emotional and behavioural warning signs of possible suicide attempts in teenagers and young adults?

7. What are adolescent 'copycat suicides' and 'suicide clusters' and why should parents be concerned about them?

8. What should parents do to try to reduce potential self-harm or suicide risks in their adolescent screenagers?

9. If a parent feels their adolescent screenager is in trouble and talks to them about suicide, are they increasing the chances that the screenager may go ahead and make an attempt?

10. What should a parent do if their adolescent screenager admits to being very emotionally distressed and either openly or indirectly mentions self-harm or suicide?

Question One: Is suicide in the adolescent normally planned or impulsive?

Harry's Answer: In *Flagging the Problem*, I dealt at length with the question of whether suicide is generally impulsive or planned. The overall impression was that, in general, suicide is more likely to be planned than impulsive. When we focus on screenager suicide, however, the question inevitably arises, as adolescents are impulsive by nature, is such behaviour more likely to be impulsive than planned in this group?

In Chapter One, we dealt with how the adolescent brain slowly matures from the age of thirteen to the age of thirty, with the emotional brain only maturing by eighteen and the logical brain by twenty-five or thirty. We discussed the 'dopamine surge' between the ages of thirteen and eighteen, when the dopamine connections between the emotional brain and the logical brain are being strengthened, and how this dopamine surge within the teenage emotional brain causes adolescents to take risks and seek pleasurable activities without heed to the possible consequences. We also noted how this has been shown to rapidly increase in presence of peers.

We also discussed the gradual evolution of the 'impulse-control' pathways between the emotional brain and the logical brain, which slowly occurs between the ages of thirteen and thirty, and how this explained why adolescents gradually became less impulsive as they became young adults. This helps to explain some of the more impulsive behaviour seen in the thirteen-to-eighteen age group, in particular.

But what do all of these developmental changes mean in terms of suicide risk? Well, common sense would suggest that the younger the screenager, the more likely a suicide attempt will be impulsive. That is not to say that there isn't some evidence of planning even in the thirteen-to-sixteen age group, but more likely are impulsive attempts that are about seeking help or struggling to deal with emotional distress brought on by life-crisis situations such as bullying. In general, in such situations, the young adolescent does not have the emotional-regulation skills to deal with the issues causing them distress. They also often lack the problem-solving skills to know how to deal with emotional issues arising due to the absence of a mature prefrontal cortex or logical brain.

Both authors have seen such cases, where young adolescents of this age have seriously attempted suicide by hanging, overdosing or other means to try to deal with the harsh realities of cyberbullying, gender-bullying and personal problems at home or at school. What is most worrying in many such cases is that the parents often have no inkling of the distress which their loved one is undergoing and, therefore, have no way of intervening. The statement from some adolescents of this age group that they did not want to upset their parents by 'bothering them' with their difficulties, is perhaps the most chilling and worrying one for parents. For it shows the complete immaturity of the young screenager adolescent – they are still children!

From the age of seventeen onwards, however, suicide attempts are less likely to be impulsive and may involve more planning. The exceptions will usually involve the presence of alcohol or other substances which make impulsive gestures more likely. We will later examine the likely causes of the emotional distress which drives adolescent screenagers between the ages of seventeen and thirty to end their lives in such tragic circumstances. These range from mental illness to difficulties coping with life-crisis situations. By eighteen, we know that the risk-taking aspect of adolescent behaviour has reached its peak, but there is still an impulsive element to behaviour up to the age of twenty-five. In many cases, though, there seems to be a clear element of planning, whether it is the manner of death, the writing of a suicide note, the giving away of precious items or even the choosing of a location for the suicide.

We will later examine the role of alcohol and other substances in screenager suicides and it does seem to be the joker in the pack in terms of assessing whether the attempt is impulsive or planned. The higher the alcohol level, the more risk there is that the attempt – even if semi-planned – may have had an impulsive component at the end. If, for example, a young person in their early twenties is feeling very depressed and has suicidal thoughts and even some vague plans, they may not necessarily have reached the stage of the suicide cocoon. But maybe, out with friends and having consumed a significant amount of alcohol, their mood will drop further and the suicidal thoughts and plans will crystallise – with lethal consequences.

By the age of twenty-five or thirty, it would seem increasingly likely that planning will be involved in a suicide attempt. This is because the prefrontal cortex is almost mature and, therefore, more likely to overrule the emotional brain's distress.

We also have to consider the fact that some adolescents are, in general, more impulsive. Are these the ones who are more influenced by a peer's death by suicide? There is no doubt that copycat suicide is very much a reality, as cluster suicides of young screenagers have clearly demonstrated. One would be most concerned about the thirteen-to-sixteen age group, in particular, as they are developmentally more geared to be impulsive. So parents in such situations should be particularly sensitive to potential risks. It is also important to be on guard if some other member of the family – a parent or a sibling – has died by suicide. On certain occasions, there may be a greater genetic and familial tendency to impulsively deal with emotional distress in a self-destructive manner.

The message here for parents is that, in general, the younger the screenager adolescent, the more likely suicide attempts are to be impulsive; the older they are, the greater the likelihood that more significant planning will be present. This is important, as it can be very difficult to predict extremely impulsive behaviour in a young adolescent, but we may have a better chance of picking up planned attempts, as there may be a time lag between the decision to end the distress and the actual attempt. The latter is clearly a potential opportunity for intervention. The other message is to be particularly on guard if a thirteen-to-seventeen-year-old's peer or family member dies by suicide.

Question Two: Why are so many Irish male adolescent screenagers and young adults dying by suicide?

Harry's Answer: There has been intensive soul-searching amongst professionals, researchers and parents as to why so many of our wonderful young men between fifteen and thirty are dying by suicide. Some possibilities may be that:

- Men, in general, are hardwired from the womb to handle emotional distress differently to women. They are more likely to try to deal with such issues themselves than to seek assistance from others. It is, therefore, no surprise that young Irish males who do get into difficulties do not open up to those close to them.

- We also have to ask if, as a society, we have encouraged the idea that 'real men' don't show emotion. Or the idea that admitting any form of mental-health difficulty or emotional distress is a sign of weakness. Although some major sports celebrities admitting to mental illnesses such as anxiety or Depression has done a lot to counter this, there is still much to be done in this area.

- Young Irish males and their adult peers (us) misuse and abuse alcohol on a regular basis, both for pleasure and to counteract emotional distress. In *Flagging the Problem* there is a line graph showing that the more alcohol we consume, as a society, the greater the suicide rate. So Irish male screenagers who have learnt to deal with emotional distress through significant alcohol consumption are very much at risk of self-harm and suicide. All the research, unfortunately, backs up this negative relationship.

- Young Irish males are more likely than their female counterparts to misuse and abuse drugs, to end up in prison or homeless. All of these increase their risks of self-harm and suicide

- Seventy-five percent of serious conditions like Depression, bipolar disorder and schizophrenia develop before the age of twenty-five, so it is no surprise that most experts feel that many of the young Irish screenagers who die by suicide will have a history of one of the above, or suffer from substance abuse. Although young females develop Depression, for example, twice as often as their male counterparts, young males still die four times as often by suicide. It may be that if they do develop this condition they are less likely to seek help and also more likely to act on suicide plans and use alcohol as crutch. They are also more likely to handle secondary social and relationship difficulties more poorly.

• Young Irish males, in many cases, do not seem to handle relationship breakdowns well, often becoming extremely distressed by them. This raises the question of whether they lack the problem-solving and emotional-regulation skills to deal with such issues. Psychological autopsies following suicides in this age group regularly point to relationship breakdowns as being one of the common precursors, so this may be a potential area for prevention.

• Two of the most significant strengths of males – the ability to be single-minded in terms of planning, and the ability to complete tasks – may also be key to why so many young men die. Research has shown that if young Irish males decide to end their distress by attempting suicide, they are more likely than young women to use more lethal means and to be successful.

• Suicide is now seen by young Irish men as a definite 'lifestyle option' to deal with their problems. In the past, due to religious and cultural prohibitions, this was less true. But now, as religious belief in the adolescent group has significantly waned and there has been a reduction in the stigma of suicide, it has moved to centre stage as a potential problem-solving behaviour when emotional distress arrives. This is an extremely worrying cultural change, one which needs to be challenged head-on if we want to reduce the death rate in this age group.

- In the past decade or so, there has been a monumental power shift, with women quite rightly developing more autonomy in the areas of work and relationships. This has led to many young Irish males feeling almost dislocated in terms of what they see as their natural roles as fathers and bread-winners in families. Many have begun to struggle to see what their new roles should be in this fast-moving modern Irish society. This might be part of a general malaise amongst Irish males between the ages of twenty and thirty which contributes to suicide in this age group.

Question Three: Is it mental illness or life-crisis situations which lead to the emotional distress underlying suicide in adolescent screenagers, and what is the role of alcohol?

Harry's Answer: This is a complex question, as is the whole conundrum of suicide. In general, we know that in 90 percent of suicide cases there is evidence of some underlying mental illness. Yet there is also significant evidence that life-crisis situations seem to lie at the heart of many suicides. When we examine the adolescent screenager group, in particular, there is often evidence of both strands. So let's explore further. Let's examine the main mental illnesses felt to underlie many suicides between the ages of fifteen and thirty:

Depression
We have dealt with screenager Depression at length in the previous chapters. Here we will just mention its links with suicide in this age group. Many experts feel that Depression in some shape or form is present in up to 70 percent of suicides. Because at least 50 percent of cases of Depression will present before the age of twenty-five, it is not surprising that this condition is a common precipitator of suicide.

Young males, in particular, seem to really struggle with this condition. Despite the fact that they often hate themselves and feel completely worthless during a bout of Depression, they put on brave and unperturbed faces that do not betray how they are feeling. They don't believe they can be helped anyway, so they don't believe that talking about is worthwhile. Those suffering from Depression will often seem quiet and self-absorbed, but will also expend a great deal of energy in order to appear 'normal' when with their peers. Some will spend a lot time on their own, sometimes in front of computers/video games or listening to music – anything to blot out how they feel. They may live in this sombre limbo for a long time preceding suicide. It's when they cease to see a future for themselves and begin to review possible ways of ending their pain and emotional distress that suicide becomes a likely outcome.

It is important to stress, however, that although Depression does affect a significant number of our adolescent boys and girls, only a small number will reach a point where active suicide planning will occur. For the rest, some fleeting suicidal thoughts may be present but will not be acted out upon.

There are certain situations which may increase the risk, however: if the Depression is particularly severe or occurs early in the teenage phase; if there is a family history of suicide; if significant alcohol consumption is being used as a crutch to deal with distress; if friends have died by suicide; or if a significant relationship breaks down. But more on that later.

Schizophrenia

This is a complex illness which affects 1 percent of the population and is caused by malfunctions in some neurotransmitter systems, such as the dopamine cable, combined with structural abnormalities in the prefrontal cortex and limbic mood departments. Genetic contributions may combine with difficulties in the womb and delivery to cause these malfunctions.

Schizophrenia usually presents in the early teens or beyond. In this disease, a large amount of grey matter in the brain is lost between the ages of twelve and eighteen, which is why in *Flagging the Problem* we referred to it as the 'grey flag'.

It can cause damage to both the frontal cortex and limbic mood departments, resulting in a gradual withdrawal from reality. Delusions, auditory and visual hallucinations, paranoia and thought disorders are among the symptoms.

Up to 50 percent of people with schizophrenia also abuse alcohol or drugs. This group is more likely than people with schizophrenia who don't abuse alcohol and drugs to develop secondary Depression alongside their existing illness. This group are at a high risk of suicide, especially early in their illness. Despite their low prevalence in the population, they account for 10 percent of the yearly suicide statistics. The mixture of alcohol/substance abuse, Depression, and schizophrenia produces a lethal cocktail. That's why it is so important to detect symptoms of schizophrenia as early as possible and to have the adolescent's mental health managed by a specialist team.

It is important for parents to know that there is now felt to be a crucial link between the use of cannabis (which nowadays is so much stronger than it was in the 60s and 70s) and the appearance of symptoms of schizophrenia. The earlier in adolescence this substance is used, the greater the risk of psychosis developing; the risk is especially great if it is used before the age of sixteen. If you notice that your screenager has suddenly become very paranoid, consider the possibility that they are on this substance and watch out for other signs of schizophrenia.

Addiction

We know that up to 15 percent of those who die by suicide are victims of some form of addiction, whether it is to alcohol, gambling, or drugs like heroin, cocaine, amphetamines, benzodiazepine or sleeping tablets. It is not surprising, therefore, that those adolescents who start seriously misusing or abusing these substances – particularly from an early age – are much more at risk of self-destructive suicidal behaviour.

Addiction creates problems for the young person, both through direct biological effects on the cells of the mood departments and cables of the developing brain, and through the destruction of the fabric of their personal life. We dealt with the effects of some addictive substances like alcohol and cannabis on the developing brain earlier in the book. There is also a robust link between addiction and Depression, a fact that is only now being fully recognised.

Chronic alcohol and drug abuse destroys the life of the addict, affecting their health, relationships, employment and financial security. Drug addicts often will have to resort to crime to feed their addictions, ending up in conflict with the authorities and being incarcerated in prison, where their drug habits will worsen. Homelessness is also a likely outcome. An often unrecognised risk factor is head injuries, which are so common in this group due to falls and, in some cases, fights. Some experts feel head injuries may damage crucial parts of the brain, possibly increasing the sufferers' tendencies for destructive behaviour toward themselves and others.

All of these issues are commonly found in screenagers who seriously abuse alcohol and drugs, so suicide can be a significant risk for them.

Personality Disorders
There are two common personality disorders which can affect the adolescent screenager and which are associated with an increased risk of self-harm and suicide: borderline personality disorder (BPD) and anti-social personality disorder (ASPD).

BPD is most often associated with young females. Ninety percent of young females with BPD come from physically, emotionally or sexually abusive backgrounds. They have unstable self-images and difficulties with personal relationships. They suffer from impulsivity, have difficulty controlling outbursts of anger and making key decisions, and regularly experience sudden shifts in mood. They live in a black-and-white world, especially in their dealings with others. You may be their best friend one minute and dismissed the next!

Self-mutilation (cutting) is common, as are suicide attempts. They have a higher risk of Depression and anxiety disorders, regularly misuse/abuse alcohol and drugs and can be highly manipulative. This is the disorder that led Professor Marsha Linehan to develop DBT, which we discussed earlier. DBT is felt to be the only therapy which is effective in this condition.

People with ASPD, meanwhile, are usually in conflict with the authorities from early childhood, with difficulties at school, at home and with the law. They are violent, reckless and impulsive. They abuse alcohol and drugs and regularly assault others. They have a high incidence of both self-harm and suicide. It is quite likely that the prefrontal cortex is involved in ASPD, where a reduction in grey matter of up to 11 percent has been demonstrated in some cases.

The above list is by no means comprehensive. We have not included eating disorders, conduct disorders such as ADHD and, in particular, bipolar disorder. The latter is very well dealt with in *Flagging the Problem* and *Flagging the Therapy*, and parents who would like to learn more about this illness and its links to suicide should refer to those books.

Life-Crisis Situations

There are some common life-crisis situations which present in the lives of screenager adolescents who end up dying by suicide.

- Relationship breakdowns are an issue on every step of the journey from the age of thirteen to the age of thirty, and for males in particular. Relationship breakdowns can end up leading to serious suicide attempts, often abetted by alcohol. Young men can get jealous, hurt, angry and often significantly depressed as they struggle to come to terms with the fact that they have, in their minds, been rejected or replaced by somebody else. Young girls can sometimes self-harm as a coping mechanism to deal with this type of crisis.

- Bullying can be a powerful trigger for serious self-harm. This alone may be enough to significantly drop a young person's self-esteem and mood, and prompt them to attempt to end the hell their life has become.

- Difficulties with school, exams, pressure for points and uncertainty about the future are all significant stressors in the lives of our screenagers. Sometimes these can lead to crisis points and suicide or self-harm can be seen as the only way to deal with their distress.

- Sexual identity issues are significant stressors. The young person might be uncertain of their sexuality, fear the consequences of coming out or have concerns that they will be treated differently to their peers or even bullied because of their sexual preference. This can sometimes reach a crisis point where, once again, suicide may seem to the screenager like the only way out of their distress.

- Unemployment and a lack of hope for the future can also be powerful stressors. Sometimes losing a job or being unable to find one despite much effort can be issues for older screenager adolescents. If they come to view themselves as 'worthless' if they do not have a job or 'a future', then this may precipitate a crisis.

- Leaving home and going to college can be a key time of crisis. Suddenly, the screenager is cut off from the safe, structured world of their home, family and school friends and peers. They often end up doubting whether they have chosen the right course, but feel trapped due to financial difficulties. Some struggle to try to hold down part-time jobs, attend lectures and study all at the same time. Others end up misusing alcohol and other substances and get behind in their studies. It can be lonely, confusing and, in some cases, a very isolating experience. Mental illness difficulties may arise as a result. It is often the amalgamation of a number of these stressors that leads to a final crisis and suicide attempt.

- For those less-fortunate adolescents who end up homeless, through poverty or difficult home situations, or end up in prison, such life-crisis situations may end in the tragedy of suicide.

With all this knowledge in mind – let's now examine what is most likely happening in screenager suicide. It is probable that in many cases a confluence of events occurs.

For example, it is common for young adolescents to develop Depression between the ages of fifteen and twenty-five. This is also, unfortunately, the phase where they have to cope with the greatest changes they will probably ever experience in their lives. In some cases, life-crisis situations may trigger bouts of Depression – with bullying or loss as common examples of such stressors. In other cases, where they are actually struggling through a bout of Depression, the loss of a key relationship may be the life-crisis trigger for a suicide attempt as their mood plummets and they begin to seriously misuse alcohol to try to deal with the issue – further increasing their risk.

Sometimes a young adolescent may feel under tremendous pressure from either their parents or themselves to achieve educationally or at competitive sports. They then start to get very anxious, rate themselves as worthless and end up triggering a bout of Depression. The latter makes it much harder to study or succeed at their chosen sport. They then struggle further to achieve the high ratings they have set themselves, feel even more of a failure, and end up, through a combination of all of these factors, so distressed that suicide seems the only way out.

Another common scenario we mentioned above is the young screenager arriving in college, getting lost for all the reasons we discussed, triggering a bout of Depression, making further studies cognitively more difficult, taking more alcohol to cope and ending up with serious suicide attempt as they become overwhelmed.

At a later stage, an adolescent screenager in their twenties may be struggling to deal with a bout of Depression when they are made redundant from their job or break up with their girlfriend or boyfriend and end up with a significant further drop in their mood, prompting them to attempt suicide after using alcohol as a crutch. In other cases, the life-crisis events actually trigger a bout of Depression and the same vicious circle ensues.

A similar circle can be noted in adolescents struggling with sexual-identity issues or being bullied as a result of them. They may end up feeling hopelessly trapped, develop a bout of Depression, misuse or abuse alcohol as a coping mechanism and trigger a suicide attempt.

In other cases, the young screenager abuses or becomes addicted to alcohol or illegal drugs like cannabis, drops out of school or college, struggles to hold down jobs and to stay in meaningful relationships, ends up homeless or in prison and then enters a downward spiral leading to suicide.

Alcohol

We can't leave this discussion without mentioning the crucial role of alcohol as the accelerant fusing mental illness difficulties and life-crisis situations together to form an explosive cocktail leading to so many screenager suicides. Alcohol is effective in helping to forget life's problems and intense emotional pain. As a result, it is a drug that is easily abused when emotionally distressed and, in particular, when suffering from Depression. Alcohol sometimes offers the final motivation needed to drive a person to suicide.

Alcohol is a factor in more than 75 percent of deaths by suicide of males between the ages of fifteen and twenty-five. In one study in the north-east region of Ireland, alcohol was found to be present in over 90 percent of deaths by suicide of males under the age of thirty. It is particularly dangerous between the ages of fifteen and twenty-five, when its effects on the developing brain can be detrimental.

We know that the younger the screenager, the more impact even small amounts of alcohol can have. We also know that alcohol removes the natural protection normally provided by the young person's logical brain, which stops self-destructive behaviour. It's no surprise that the more alcohol consumption per capita increases, the higher the suicide rate climbs – particularly in the younger age groups. Even if not actually present at the time of the suicide, it may have been a factor in the days preceding the act.

The importance of this fact is that we, as a society, need to do whatever is required to try to make it harder for people under eighteen to access alcohol, and to educate our screenagers about to the links between alcohol, Depression and suicide.

What parents can learn from all of the above is that, in general, suicide in adolescents and young adults is rarely due to either a life-crisis situation *or* a mental illness; in most cases, it is due to a combination of both. This is important, as too many parents who have lost children to suicide only consider the life-crisis possibilities and spend many years berating themselves for not intervening. In reality, there is often some other underlying factor like Depression at play, and it is the combination of key-life stressors with this which ends up with the young person dying by suicide.

Other Key Points

- It's important to learn the signs and symptoms of Depression and to be constantly on the watch for any evidence of it in adolescents.

- Be especially observant during key life-crisis periods such as when the screenager goes to college, is approaching a major exam, is involved in a relationship breakup or loses a loved one to suicide, illness or an accident.

- Be aware of the dangers of alcohol and cannabis and their capacities to trigger and foster mental illnesses such as Depression and schizophrenia.

Question Four: Why do screenagers find it so hard to come to their parents when they are feeling emotionally distressed?

Harry's Answer: This is the question parents who have lost adolescent children to suicide struggle the most with. They so often had a wonderful relationship with their young adolescent son or daughter and were able to relate to them on so many issues. But when it came to the young person revealing that they were under significant emotional distress, this relationship seems to have broken down. There are probably a number of reasons for this heart-breaking situation:

- In a paradoxical way we, as parents, are too close to our screenagers to see them clearly. If you take a paper and hold it at arm's length you can see the print clearly. If you hold it right up against your eyes, it becomes a blur. And so it is with emotional distress in our screenagers.

- Young people are often really concerned that their parents will become distressed if the young people open up to how they feel. As one young screenager said following a thankfully failed suicide attempt, 'I just didn't want to bother my mother.'

- The young screenager will often not really recognise that the way they are feeling may be due to a condition like Depression and will accept that it is 'just them'.

- There is a natural pulling away from parents between the ages of thirteen and twenty-five, as adolescents try to make sense of their own worlds. So there is an increased reliance on peer-group support for assistance in life-crisis situations and in case of distress.

- Many screenagers who are misusing alcohol or substances at school or college are quite naturally very reluctant to open up about this to parents.

- Increasingly, screenagers are turning to technology to try and find solutions to their problems, and this quite often excludes parents

- The nature of some mental health conditions like Depression means that the sufferer is not going to seek help from anybody, including their parents, as they feel that *they* are the problem as they are just 'worthless' and of 'no value', so they don't want to bother anyone.

- In some cases, the adolescent lacks the language to open the conversation. In other cases, the parents may lack the skills to pick up on emotional cues or deal with the situation.

- In some cases, the screenager may act impulsively, not really allowing the parent any chance to reach them in their distress.

This does not mean, of course, that adolescents do not regularly turn to their parents when in emotional difficulties. A lot of research has shown that parents are still one of the most likely places for young people in difficulties to turn – the others being peers and the Web.

Tony Bates of Headstrong constantly reminds us that if a young person in difficulty can find even one adult person who they can open up to and relate to, they will often overcome whatever difficulties they are facing. So if you feel you are struggling to reach your adolescent and know someone else who might be able to – a sibling, grandparent, aunt, uncle, teacher or counsellor – then try to arrange for them to open up the relevant conversation with your adolescent.

Question Five: What is the role of technology in screenager suicide?

Harry's Answer: We have dealt at length with the impact of technology on the developing brain and all the positive and potentially negative effects it can produce. There is an increasing concern that the widespread use of social media and other forms of technology may be linked to some cases of adolescent suicide. Let's now examine that concern.

Cyberbullying

We noted earlier that the 2014 report 'Net Children Go Mobile: Initial Findings from Ireland' found that 22 percent of Irish children had experienced online or offline bullying.

Thirteen percent of thirteen and fourteen-year-olds said they had been bullied on a social networking site. Girls were more likely to have experienced bullying than boys; the figures were 26 percent for girls and 17 percent for boys. Twenty percent of girls and 11 percent of boys said they were upset by what had happened. So, from an early age, adolescents are at risk of this insidious form of bullying. In many cases, this risk continues into the late teens.

The major concern is that there is a clear link between cyberbullying and increased incidence in our screenager group of Depression, self-harm, suicide ideation and, in some cases, suicide. Bullying in any form has a devastating effect on its victims and also on its perpetrators. And the advent of the cyber world has greatly increased the potential range and severity of bullying. For example, if I am bullied by a few school peers, this is one matter, but when a whole group gang up on a child online, the effects are magnified greatly.

Cyberbullying occurs in many forms: through emails, instant messages and images sent to cell phones, as well as in chat rooms and on websites. The anonymity offered by the cyber world allows the bully to say or do almost whatever they want. This is harmful to the victim and desensitises the perpetrator – leaving both open to mental-illness difficulties. The biggest difference between cyberbullying and traditional bullying is that it doesn't just happen at school or on the way home. It goes on day and night, relentlessly, in many cases. Bullying has moved into the adolescent bedroom at 3 AM.

Some websites like Ask.fm, which has one of the biggest teenage followings in the world, have been associated with some high-profile suicides. These have helped to bring this matter out into the open. In these cases, there was evidence that the young adolescent who committed suicide had been exposed to a systematic campaign of cyberbullying.

It is quite difficult to accurately estimate how significant cyberbullying is in relation to actual suicide figures amongst adolescents, but we do know that it increases significantly the rate of Depression, self-harm and suicidal thoughts amongst this group. So it would seem likely to be a significant factor in some cases of suicide.

A new policy toward bullying – the 'Action Plan on Bullying' – has now been launched in schools and the initial impressions are very positive. It clearly lays out a policy on how to deal with both the victim and the bully in a manner that is much more non-judgemental than has been the case in the past. But this may not be enough to prevent children from being subjected to severe cyberbullying away from the school environment, so it is there that parents need to be more vigilant.

If you learn that your adolescent is being cyberbullied, here are a few practical pieces of advice:

- Most importantly, validate their distress and make it clear that you are going to be on their side and assist them in dealing with the issue.

- Advise them not to respond to the cyberbullying, as this often encourages the bully.

- It can be helpful to share your own experiences of being bullied at school, as this puts it into perspective for them.

- Ask them not to erase the messages or images, as they are proof of what is happening.

- Try with them to discover the identity of the bully.

- Work with them to see if there is some way to block the messages.

- If necessary, contact relevant messaging providers like WhatsApp, email providers or social networks.

- Immediately contact the school, particularly if the culprit turns out to be a school peer, as is most often the case. Schools have now installed excellent anti-bullying programs. Work with them to try and bring the cyberbullying to an end.

- It may be useful to liaise with the parents of your adolescent's school friends or classmates to see if they have any knowledge or have had experiences of a similar nature. This is particularly easy if parents exchange email addresses at the beginning of each school year, which is advisable.

- Consider exploring with your adolescent the fact that many bullies are very unhappy and that bullying is their cry for help, so what they are saying has to be seen in that context. This is most appropriate if the bully does turn out to be a school peer.

The main message for parents here is to spend time with their adolescents to work out in advance a strategy for dealing with bullying in any form and go through the risks of it happening through the cyber world as well. It is particularly important for parents of young female adolescents between the ages of thirteen and sixteen to be constantly vigilant in relation to this area. It will be virtually impossible to out-think them in terms of trying to remove such access, as they are usually adept at bypassing us. Of significant concern is the use of mobile phones in bedrooms after 11 PM. Perhaps an agreement could be reached that all their phones and iPads be left in a central location after that time.

Suicide Websites

In 'Net Children Go Mobile', one chilling statistic was that 9 percent of young people between the ages of thirteen and sixteen had encountered a site online discussing suicide. There is national and, indeed, international concern about the existence of these sites, but little has been done to counter their poisonous messages.

If an adolescent screenager is feeling very emotionally distressed or depressed, with significant suicide ideation, they are very vulnerable to the discussions which can occur on such websites, particularly in relation to methods that can be used to make suicide easier and more deadly.

Parents may struggle to prevent young people from coming across these sites by accident or finding them when in emotional distress. But we can have full and frank conversations with our adolescents about them and the danger they present.

Desensitisation and Suicide

Another important risk of technology is the increasing concern that exposure to violence and pornography (including rape) through TV, videos and games and online has begun to desensitise our adolescent screenagers. The epidemic of mass shootings in schools in the USA may have some of its origins here. There are many studies which show definite links between TV news violence, violent films and violent video games and increased aggression in adolescents which extends into their adult lives (Huesmann et al, 2006).

Evidence of a violence effect for news was found in studies of the so-called Marilyn Monroe Effect, which is when highly publicised suicides are followed by an increase in suicides among the populace over the course of the following two weeks (Huesmann et al, 2006). Some studies on this relationship suggest that news coverage of suicide produces a 2.5 percent increase in suicides.

It is hard to know whether this is contributing to our higher male suicide rate. The concern here is that if we become desensitised to violence, then it is much easier to consider self-harm and more violent methods of suicide if we are emotionally distressed. It is important for parents to be aware of potential links between our adolescents viewing violence and potential desensitisation, leading to an increased risk of violence toward themselves and others.

Question Six: What are the most common emotional and behavioural warning signs of possible suicide attempts in teenagers and young adults?

Harry's Answer: This is probably one of the most important questions that parents ask. We have to be realistic about the fact that, despite all our efforts and all the research, it is often hard to spot when one of our adolescent screenagers is in real trouble. In general, mothers usually have a built-in 'radar system' for sensing when one of their children is getting into difficulty. They should always listen to that inner voice and intervene if it is warning them that something does not feel right. The only mistake we can make is not to ask about the possibility if we feel they are in a bad space.

Parents should be especially watchful in high-risk situations, such as when dealing with adolescents who are:

- From a family with a strong history of Depression involving suicide attempts or actual suicide.

- From a family that has recently experienced a suicide, particularly of a parent or sibling.

- From a family that has recently experienced the traumatic death of a family member, particularly a parent or sibling.

- From a family coping with a family member experiencing addiction, abuse or relationship breakdown, particularly if acrimonious.

- Homeless, in prison, or trying to deal with addiction, Depression or schizophrenia.

- Going through a bout of severe Depression, having suicidal thoughts or planning suicide – particularly if they do not recognise the cause of their distress and have kept it to themselves.

- Suffering from the personality disorders BPD and ASP, especially if they are abusing alcohol or substances.

- Extremely isolated socially and are having difficulties forming relationships.

- Dealing with the breakup of a significant relationship – particularly if the adolescent is male, suffering from Depression or coping with heavy alcohol intake.

- Suffering from undiagnosed bipolar disorder, particularly during the depressed phase of the illness and if misusing alcohol.

- Gay or are struggling with coming to terms with their sexuality, and those who are being bullied as a result of it. One study showed that these people are twice as likely to attempt suicide as their heterosexual peers.

- Being bullied either traditionally or cyberbullied, and whose self-esteem and mood has fallen as a result.

- More impulsive and more prone to risk-taking.

- Seriously misusing or abusing alcohol or substances.

- Coping with key stresses: coming up to exams, losing a job, struggling with unemployment or dealing with financial difficulties.

- Feeling significant shame about something that has happened in their lives – i.e. being filmed in a compromising situation and having the video released online.

Parents should also be especially watchful when dealing with adolescents who:

- Have been exposed to a recent suicide of a peer-group member.

- Have self-harmed in the past, particularly if the attempt was more lethal in nature.

- Have a history of physical or sexual abuse. Professor Kevin Malone's report on youth suicide, 'Suicide in Ireland 2003–2008', noted that '20 percent of cases were known to have experienced either physical or sexual abuse and that 80 percent experienced this before aged 15.'

- Have major problems at school, academically or discipline-wise.

This list is not complete by any means, but most parents should examine it carefully and just keep an eye out for emotional difficulties at key times they might subsequently identify as high-risk.

It is important to note that in many screenager suicides there were warning signs – sometimes subtle and sometimes more obvious – which may have preceded the event. Parents who have experienced this tragedy can often recognise these afterwards, but may not have been aware of them beforehand.

The following list deals more with possible warning signs or behavioural changes which might allow parents to recognise when our adolescent screenagers are in trouble:

- Increased levels of agitation or violent outbursts of anger in an adolescent with known Depression.

- A sudden drop in weight or significant problems sleeping in an adolescent who has not yet been diagnosed with Depression, as these may be the only physical symptoms of this we notice.

- A sudden 'improvement' in mood in an adolescent who has clearly been very distressed with Depression – this may be a move toward the suicide cocoon.

- In students who are attending school or college, evidence of a decrease in hygiene standards, a sudden fall-off in performance or, more seriously, dropping out.

- A sudden deterioration in physical appearance and a lack of concern about this.

- Any sudden increase in the misuse of alcohol or substances.

- A really important sign is where the adolescent begins to withdraw more from family and peers, perhaps spending more time in their room on their own or on a computer.

- Any obvious statements or references to suicide, such as 'I would be better off dead' or 'I just want to die' or 'I can see no reason to live' or what may seem like an attention-seeking statement such as 'If I was dead maybe people would take me more seriously'. These should all be taken very seriously and explored further.

- Any indirect references like 'Don't worry, hopefully I won't be troubling you for much longer' or 'I just want you to know how much I love you – no matter what happens'. Once again, these should be treated seriously.

- Written diaries, obvious suicide notes, poems or stories suggestive of suicide or listening constantly to heavy-metal songs with such content.

- A real warning sign is giving away prized possessions, particularly to siblings or close friends.

- Any evidence of saying goodbye to loved ones, whether in person or on the phone, particularly visits to, say, grandparents with whom they have had good relationships.

- Any evidence of self-harm, even if seemingly insignificant, should always be explored further.

Question Seven: What are adolescent 'copycat suicides' and 'suicide clusters' and why should parents be concerned about them?

Harry's Answer: When a person attempts suicide trying to emulate another suicide which they have heard about either through local knowledge or through TV, newspapers or other forms of media (particularly social media), this is called a 'copycat suicide'.

When a number of similar copycat suicides occur – either at the local level or the national level – this is called a 'suicide cluster'. These should be of major concern to parents, as screenagers aged thirteen to twenty-five have been found to be particularly susceptible to this 'suicide contagion' effect.

Suicide clusters can be 'mass clusters', which involve suicides that cluster in time (irrespective of geography) and are felt to be influenced by media reports about, for example, suicides by significant celebrities such as Marilyn Monroe or Kurt Cobain. They can also be 'point clusters', which involve suicides that are close in time and, in some cases, space, often occurring within institutional settings such as schools, or within distinct local communities. Finally, if they happen around the anniversary of a particular suicide, they are called 'echo clusters'.

Professor Malone's 'Suicide in Ireland 2003–2008' report noted that:

> Assuming our dataset has elements of representativeness of youth suicide in Ireland, careful examination of our data, conservatively interpreted, has identified that 70 percent of younger suicide cases in Ireland may be exposed to a suicidal act in another within 3 months of their death by suicide.
>
> Across all ages, as many as 10 percent of suicide deaths in Ireland may be part of a cluster, and perhaps between 30–50 percent of suicide deaths under age 21 may be part of a cluster. Clusters may be small (3–5 deaths), medium (6–9 deaths) or large (10 deaths), and they are likely to have a profound impact at a family and community level.

There are many theories surrounding these suicide clusters. Most are now felt to be due to a form of social learning. This makes sense for, just as we discussed earlier, empathy can be both negative and positive. So if I am in significant emotional distress myself and read or hear how somebody else 'solved their problem' by suicide using a particular method, this may trigger me to imitate or emulate them.

The reason why adolescents are so vulnerable to this suicide-contagion effect relates to the relative immaturity of their developing brains, which have an increased tendency to react more emotionally than logically to events – particularly if negative. They are thus more likely to absorb the negative empathy messages created by the suicide, particularly if they are in a vulnerable emotional state.

There is increasing concern that technology, in the form of social media, is going to create new difficulties amongst screenagers, who are more likely to access data about such deaths through this medium and less likely to do so through TV or newspapers, where fairly strict regulations are in place on media reporting on suicide.

One of the other serious side effects of social media in this area is the creation of 'virtual online shrines' to deceased peer adolescents, where tributes pour in, sending out the dangerous signal that suicide is in some way an acceptable solution to dealing with emotional distress, one that will lead to your peers eulogising you when you are gone! There is much evidence that when the contrary message is presented through other forms of media – focusing on the huge devastation and hurt caused to parents and families when one takes this course – the suicide-contagion effect is greatly weakened.

The relevance of this information is that parents need to be particularly on guard if there is a death of an adolescent either at school or in the local community, or a death by suicide of a celebrity admired by their screenagers. Once again, there is much to be gained by having conversations about this with our screenagers before such events happen. Try to seek out and explore with them their views on the subject. This may make it much easier to intervene if such a death happens.

Question Eight: What should parents do to try to reduce potential self-harm or suicide risks in their adolescent screenagers?

Harry's Answer: Here are some tips.

- Read the advice that Enda has laid out throughout this book on how best to listen to and interact with your young screenager. This will greatly increase the chances that they will come to you if they are in emotional distress, as they will feel you will listen to them and take their concerns seriously.

- Try to encourage them to talk about the 'real issues' they may be worried about: school problems, relationships, concerns about sexual identity, exam pressures, fears about going to college, times they feel very anxious or down and don't know how to deal with these feelings, and so on.

- Try to validate their emotions, no matter how much you might disagree with their views. Accept them where they are and work from there.

- Try to have regular discussions with them on what to do if they do get emotionally distressed. Talk about what you do yourself.

- It is important not to be afraid to open up the whole discussion of suicide increasingly being seen as a solution to such problems and talk to them about how they feel about this.

- Become extremely familiar with the symptoms of Depression and, in particular, teenage Depression. Make your adolescents equally aware of the symptoms and how to cope with them.

- Watch out for any of the at-risk situations or warning signs we have already discussed.

- Discuss bullying, and particularly cyberbullying. Have a protocol set up in the house for what to do if it occurs – particularly for girls between thirteen and sixteen.

- Spend a lot of time and effort supervising your adolescent's cyber world and have regular discussions on the risks and potential dangers lurking there.

- Have frank discussions about the risks of suicide sites on the Web.

- Try to leave the door very open if you suspect there are gender-identity issues.

- Try to set clear ground rules in relation to alcohol. Be honest and don't be afraid to share with them your own experiences at the same age.

- Liaise closely with your screenager's school through teachers and counsellors, and also with your screenager's friends, as much as possible, to try and maintain a window into their worlds.

- If seriously concerned about younger screenagers, check out their phones, diaries, Facebook pages and any other possible sources of information. If you find something of concern, bring it up with them.

- If, say, as a mother, 'your antennae are up', bring up the whole area of emotional distress with your screenager, voice your concerns and link this into your own experiences at the same age. Do not be afraid to ask directly, 'Have you had any serious thoughts of self-harm?' It is better to ask this question before something tragic happens. In most cases, the young person will be relieved to talk to somebody about how they are feeling. If they say they have thought about self-harm, make sure you ask how they would do it. If they give a clear answer, then you must be very much on guard, as it means they have been seriously considering the possibility.

- Do not be put off if the screenager reacts angrily or seems to ignore your advice. They will often go away and digest it, and may come back later for a further conversation.

- If one of your screenager's peers commits suicide or a suicide cluster appears, it is very important to sit down with your screenager and discuss the reality of the death for the family or families involved. Discuss how there are other, much less destructive solutions to emotional distress. It is also important at such times to liaise with the school involved.

Question Nine: If a parent feels their adolescent screenager is in trouble and talks to them about suicide, are they increasing the chances that the screenager may go ahead and make an attempt?

Harry's Answer: One of the great myths about suicide is that if I ask a person whether they have thought about ending their life by suicide, it will in some way increase the chances that they will go ahead and do it. The implication being that we just put the thought into their head. In practice, nothing could be further than the truth. It is, in general, a great relief for the adolescent screenager to be able to unburden themself of the locked-in feelings of emotional distress and the quite frightening presence of actual suicidal thoughts in their emotional mind.

Question Ten: What should a parent do if their adolescent screenager admits to being very emotionally distressed and either openly or indirectly mentions self-harm or suicide?

Harry's Answer: The most common reaction is total panic, particularly if the parents have been previously unaware of their adolescent's inner emotional distress. But it is important that you have developed some knowledge about how to handle such an episode long before it occurs. Here are some useful tips:

- Always take any indirect or direct comments about suicide very seriously and make sure you make it clear to the young person that you are doing so.

- It is crucial to remain very calm on the outside, no matter how distressed you may feel. Your calmness and empathy will seem like a solid anchor to the young person, who may then feel able to unburden themself to you. However, if you react by becoming upset and panicky, the adolescent will clam up, as they will not want to feel that they are distressing you.

- Don't be afraid of opening up to your adolescent about periods in your own life, both as an adolescent and as an adult, where you felt yourself being overwhelmed and totally emotionally distressed, and to discuss how you managed to deal with these periods. This gives the young person an important insight into the reality that we all go through such periods but, with assistance, come out the other side.

- It is important to ask directly about suicide and discuss the fact that some people consider it the only solution to life difficulties and emotional distress, but that from experience you have learnt other ways of dealing with these things and would be happy to work with them on this.

- Try to ascertain if they have any definitive plans as to what they might do, and remove any possible means, such as tablets, ropes, sharp objects (knives or razors) or guns from the house.

- Try to focus in with the adolescent on the main cause of their emotional distress. Are they feeling very down? Are they being bullied? Are there difficulties at school, worries about exams or fears about leaving home to go to college? Are there any relationship problems or sexual-identity issues? Have they been traumatised by the suicide of a peer-group member? Are they struggling to deal with conflicts or separations in their own family? Have they been abused in any way?

- It is particularly important to go through with them the symptoms of Depression. If it is clear that these symptoms are present, discuss them and offer to attend your family doctor with them for further assistance.

- It is crucial that you try and get them to open up to drinking heavily or using substances like cannabis. If they do, it is important not to be judgemental, but to calmly explain why you would be concerned about this.

- It is also vital that you get a clear picture of what is going on in their cyber world. The reasons for their distress may lie in the world of social media. Be especially explicit about possible cyberbullying.

- Make it clear that you are happy to assist them in any way to help deal with these issues – not necessarily to solve them for them, but to be there as a guide and mentor.

- Once you have a clearer picture of what is causing your screenager to be so emotionally distressed, you will be in a better position to seek further assistance. The usual first port of call should be your family doctor. If your child is under eighteen, they may consider referral to the local child-and-adolescent team, if available. There, the young person can access help from a psychiatrist, psychologist or social worker, as appropriate. If there is evidence of any serious mental illness like Depression or schizophrenia, then it is vital to get a specialist's opinion.

- It is also wise, if the screenager is still at school, to link in with the school guidance counsellor.

- If there are obvious bullying, cyberbullying, relationship or sexual-identity issues, you can offer to walk the journey with the young person in terms of finding solutions to the problems which are in play in their lives.

- Other excellent resources include Console and Pieta House, where counselling can be urgently accessed if felt necessary.

One of the most frustrating and distressing issues for many parents who find themselves in this position is when the screenager is over eighteen and considered an adult. In many of these cases, the mother and father are 'blocked out' by the system of confidentiality.

The young person requests that only they can see the GP, psychiatrist or therapist, and refuses the parents access to any information which appears during these consultations. This is often as frustrating for the professionals as it is for the parents.

Ideally, you should try to reach an agreement with your screenager from the start that you will be involved in the process. Either you can attend with them or they can allow the professional to talk to you at the end of the consultation.

Conclusion

TAKING THE 'NON' OUT OF 'NONSENSE'

As I (Enda) admit in *Five Steps to Happiness*, I'm actually a very reluctant author. It's not that I don't enjoy writing – I do – it's getting me to sit down and start writing that's the hard part. I reckon that being a parent is somewhat similar. I love my kids, and could never see myself wanting to be where I was before we had them. I am a completely different person now compared with who I was before I met my wife and started a family. It's all the hard work that goes with parenting that I find excruciating.

At times, when I feel the steam coming out of my ears over some small infraction that they have committed, I think how wonderful it would be to live in Downton Abbey. I would have loads of nannies and servants to do all the hard work. They could sort out all the tantrums and deaf ears, break up all the squabbles, correct all the homework, and get their head around maths projects. Loads of people to do all the not-so-nice stuff that always seems to get in the way of the enjoyable parts of parenting that the books describe.

I could focus on all the warm, fuzzy bits, like watching them play together, feeling close to tears when I see my eldest protecting his little brother; or observing little brother looking for big brother to share his sweets with – before eating them himself. My head and my heart would be filled with all these 'Waltons' moments, making life oh so wonderful and fulfilling.

And then I am woken up from my dream by the sounds of them fighting over the remote and am snapped back to reality. As I trudge down the stairs to break things up before my wife loses her temper and is tempted to strangle them both, I realise that both my wife and I are those servants and nannies, and that it is our kids that are the lords of the manor, waiting to be served!

And the beat goes on. I often think that the reason I'm happier now than at any other point in my life is because I have absolutely no time to think about myself. Why am I happy? Well, for a person like me, who is generally selfish by nature, having no option but to put my wife and family first is the best place I can be, since the less time I have to think about me, the happier I become.

When I look over the last few years, I realise that nearly all my growth as a person has occurred during the bad times and not during the good times. And that's the way it is. So the next time I'm ready to collapse, I'm going to remember that I'm doing all of this for *me*. Well, that's the theory anyway. Totally out of tune with reality, but a nice way of showing why theory and practice have very little in common.

KEEP IT SIMPLE

While, in practice, rearing kids may be a constant struggle, in theory it is incredibly simple. In *Five Steps*, I admit that the reason why it took five years of nagging before I agreed to write it was because, in all my professional experience, the secret to being happy could be written on the back of an envelope. Similarly, the secret to being an effective parent can be summed up in three points:

1. Learn to listen

2. Learn to identify with your kids' experiences

3. Learn to teach them how to understand and live in their world.

Over the years, I have watched hundreds of parents overcome every kind of difficulty with their kids. And it is these same parents who have taught me how to cope with *my* kids. I have already shared with the reader what one particular dad told me, when my wife was expecting our first child, and I quote it here again as its message is so important:

Over the next thirty years, Enda, you'll be given all kinds of advice as to how to handle your kids, some of it useful and some of it rubbish. But no matter what you're told, or how difficult it gets, just remember one thing: it's only a phase. By next month, you'll have a whole new set of problems to deal with.

So the next time you feel at the end of your tether with your kids, remember this – the most valuable lesson I have learned from the hundreds of parents I've seen over the years – that if you can manage to come within an ass's roar of getting it right, your kids will turn out all right. Your kids will survive your hopeless parenting – just as you did your parents' hopeless parenting!

Now Harry is going to finish by sharing with you one of the most important messages in the book, namely the throwaway comment!

THE THROWAWAY COMMENT

If you ask any family doctor when, in any consultation, the most important revelation appears, they will often say it is when the person is at door, just about to leave, and turns around and says, 'It's probably not important, but I've just noticed the following . . .' They will often go on to say something like, 'I've noticed a lump in my breast' or 'I've been having a little chest tightness when I'm out walking, but I'm sure it's nothing of consequence'.

As I came to write a conclusion to this book with Enda, this thought came to my mind: the most important message in the book may be the one that I hope to finish with. My 'throwaway' message relates to what will remain when our adolescent screenager has successfully arrived, with our help, in adulthood and is striking out into the world and leaving us behind.

Guiding a child through adolescence and into adulthood is extremely challenging for the individual parent and, in particular, for their personal relationship with their partner. How often do we see parents, whose children have moved on, sitting in restaurants almost as strangers – spending long periods in silence or texting away on phones – as if something in the relationship has died? How often have mothers ended up living their lives through their children or husbands thrown themselves into their careers once their children have grown up?

The throwaway comment might relate to a parent whose screenager has become an adult but who stops at the door to comment: 'It is probably of no importance, but since my adolescent has moved on, I am no longer sure of what my role in life is, and I feel dislocated from my partner.'

Perhaps the most important message in terms of guiding our screenagers into adulthood relates to prioritising what should be most important in the whole process. This message might start to become increasingly relevant as more and more parents begin their relationships in their late thirties.

A very wise midwife in Holles Street Hospital made a comment to me more than thirty-five years ago, and it has never left me: 'Either the child fits in with the family, or else the child takes over the family!' What she was trying to impart was that children are really important in our lives but must not be allowed to *become* our lives!

Nowhere does this message become more important than during the ten-year period between the ages of fifteen and twenty-five. Many parents lose themselves and their relationships during this phase, as it can sometimes be extremely trying and traumatic, particularly if there are significant difficulties such as mental illness. For the parent who wants to come out of the 'adolescent phase' in one piece, the following setting of priorities, which centre on the word 'love,' are important.

PRIORITY ONE

As parents, we must first learn to love ourselves as individuals and to take care of ourselves in the following ways. We need to embrace the various skills that Enda detailed earlier: becoming physically and mentally healthier, practising mindfulness, finding meaning in whatever form, and becoming more altruistic. Above all, we must become Raggy Dolls in our personal lives and accept that we can only do our best – including when it comes to guiding our screenagers to safety.

PRIORITY TWO

Our second priority is our personal relationships. Not every parent will be in a longstanding, stable relationship: many will be rearing screenagers on their own. (Nearly a quarter of Irish children live in one-parent homes.) For those in relationships, I suggest that their second priority, after loving themselves, should be to love their partner and to invest heavily in their personal relationship during this crucial screenager period. If you don't believe me, then ask parents of adolescents with eating disorders or severe depression, or whose children have experienced significant self-harm or suicide attempts, just how potentially damaging it was to their personal relationship.

It is useful to regularly ask yourself where you see yourself as an individual and you and your partner as a couple at the end of the twenty-five-year contract that Enda mentioned in the introduction. Will you end up as survivors or as victims of the process? Try to bond even more tightly together as a couple if you want to survive the process in one piece. This is real love – not the romantic, fairy-tale version depicted in Hollywood.

Spend as much 'quality time' together as you can during this phase. Try to approach all problematic issues together as a couple and, above all, try to be a Raggy Doll couple, accepting that neither party is perfect and that our only job is to do our best in all situations. Become Raggy Dolls, and throw in a healthy dose of humour, and you will come out at the other end together, having grown and matured like a good wine!

PRIORITY THREE

If you have managed to put the other two priorities into practice, then the last one is in many ways the easiest. This is where we try to love our screenagers, even when they are trying our patience to the utmost. It really helps if we have become Raggy Dolls ourselves, both as individuals and parents, as this makes it easier to regard our adolescents as Raggy Dolls too – struggling to find out who they are in life. They are not perfect, and neither are we!

If we can learn to listen to them, interpret what they are really trying to say, and act accordingly, then they will, with our love and our best attempts as muddling parents, emerge, like caterpillars, to become wonderful butterflies that we can set free to go where they feel they must.

Bibliography

Ackard, D. M., Neumark-Sztainer, D. & Hannan, P. (2003). 'Dating violence among a nationally representative sample of adolescent girls and boys: Associations with behavioral and mental health'. *J Gend Specif Med*, 6(3), 39-48.

American Association of Suicidology (2004). 'Survivors of suicide' factsheet.

Ashtari, M., Cervellione, K., Cottone, J., Ardekani, B. A., Sevy, S., & Kumra, S. (2009). 'Diffusion abnormalities in adolescents and young adults with a history of heavy cannabis use'. J *Psychiatr Res*, 43(3), 189-204.

Barry, H. (2007). *Flagging the Problem: A new approach to mental health*. Dublin: Liberties Press.

Barry, H. (2013). *Flagging Depression: A practical guide*. Dublin: Liberties Press.

Barry, H. (2013). *Flagging the Therapy: Pathways out of depression and anxiety*. Dublin: Liberties Press.

Barry, H. P. (2013). 'Exploring the parental experience of living with the loss of a child to suicide'. Research thesis for master's in CBT.

Blakemore, S. J. (2008). 'The social brain in adolescence'. *Nat Rev Neurosci*, 9(4), 267-277.

Blakemore, S. J. (2012). 'Imaging brain development: The adolescent brain'. *Neuroimage*, 61(2), 397-406.

Blakemore, S. J. (2013). 'Teenage kicks: Cannabis and the adolescent brain'. *The Lancet*, 381(9870), 888-889.

Bloomfield, M. A., Morgan, C. J., Egerton, A., Kapur, S., Curran, H. V., & Howes, O. D. (2014). 'Dopaminergic function in cannabis users and its relationship to cannabis-induced psychotic symptoms'. *Biol Psychiatry*, 75(6), 470-478.

Brenhouse, H. C., & Andersen, S. L. (2011). 'Developmental trajectories during adolescence in males and females: A cross-species understanding of underlying brain changes'. *Neurosci Biobehav Rev*, 35(8), 1687-1703.

Cahill, L. (2005). 'His brain, her brain'. *Scientific American*.

Carskadon, M. A. (2002). *Adolescent Sleep Patterns: Biological, social, and psychological influences*. Cambridge: Cambridge University Press.

Casey, B. J., Giedd, J. N., & Thomas, K. M. (2000). 'Structural and functional brain development and its relation to cognitive development'. *Biol Psychol*, 54(1-3), 241-257.

Casey, B. J., & Jones, R. M. (2010). 'Neurobiology of the adolescent brain and behavior: Implications for substance use disorders'. *J Am Acad Child Adolesc Psychiatry*, 49(12), 1189-1201.

Cassoff, J., Knauper, B., Michaelsen, S., & Gruber, R. (2013). 'School-based sleep promotion programs: effectiveness, feasibility and insights for future research'. *Sleep Med Rev*, 17(3), 207-214.

Cavanagh, J. T., Carson, A. J., Sharpe, M., & Lawrie, S. M. (2003). 'Psychological autopsy studies of suicide: A systematic review'. *Psychol Med*, 33(3), 395-405.

Chaddock, L., Erickson, K. I., Prakash, R. S., Kim, J. S., Voss, M. W., Vanpatter, M., Raine, L.B., Konkel A., Hillman C. H., Cohen N. J., & Kramer, A. F. (2010). 'A neuroimaging investigation of the association between aerobic fitness, hippocampal volume, and memory performance in preadolescent children'. *Brain Res*, 1358, 172-183.

Choi, J., Jeong, B., Rohan, M. L., Polcari, A. M., & Teicher, M. H. (2009). 'Preliminary evidence for white matter tract abnormalities in young adults exposed to parental verbal abuse'. *Biol Psychiatry*, 65(3), 227-234.

Choudhury, S., & McKinney, K. A. (2013). 'Digital media, the developing brain and the interpretive plasticity of neuroplasticity'. *Transcult Psychiatry*, 50(2), 192-215.

Dahl, R. E. (2004). 'Adolescent brain development: A period of vulnerabilities and opportunities'. Keynote address. *Ann N Y Acad Sci*, 1021, 1-22.

De Bellis, M. D., Clark, D. B., Beers, S. R., Soloff, P. H., Boring, A. M., Hall, J., . . . Keshavan, M. S. (2000). 'Hippocampal volume in adolescent-onset alcohol use disorders'. *Am J Psychiatry*, 157(5), 737-744.

De Bellis, M. D., Keshavan, M. S., Beers, S. R., Hall, J., Frustaci, K., Masalehdan, A., Noll J. & Boring, A. M. (2001). 'Sex differences in brain maturation during childhood and adolescence'. *Cereb Cortex*, 11(6), 552-557.

Dooley, B., & Fitzgerald, A. (2012). 'My world survey: National study of youth mental health in Ireland'. Dublin: Headstrong – The National Centre for Youth Mental Health; UCD School of Psychology.

Dryfoos, J. G. B. C. (2006). *Adolescence: Growing up in America Today*. Oxford: Oxford University Press.

Eiland, L., & Romeo, R. D. (2013). 'Stress and the developing adolescent brain'. *Neuroscience*, 249, 162-171.

Feinstein, S. (2009). *Secrets of the teenage brain: Research-based strategies for reaching and teaching today's adolescents*. California: Corwin Press.

Forke, C. M., Myers, R. K., Catallozzi, M., & Schwarz, D. F. (2008). 'Relationship violence among female and male college undergraduate students'. *Arch Pediatr Adolesc Med*, 162(7), 634-641.

Giedd, J. N., Blumenthal, J., Jeffries, N. O., Castellanos, F. X., Liu, H., Zijdenbos, A., Paus T., Evans A. C. & Rapoport, J. L. (1999). 'Brain development during childhood and adolescence: A longitudinal MRI study'. *Nat Neurosci*, 2(10), 861-863.

Guerri, C., & Pascual, M. (2010). 'Mechanisms involved in the neurotoxic, cognitive, and neurobehavioral effects of alcohol consumption during adolescence'. *Alcohol*, 44(1), 15-26.

Gurian, M. H. P. T. T. (2001). *Boys and girls learn differently : A guide for teachers and parents*. San Francisco: Jossey-Bass.

Hamza C. A, Stewart S. L, Willoughby T. (2012) 'Examining the link between nonsuicidal self-injury and suicidal behavior: A review of the literature and an integrated model'. *Clinical Psychology Review*, 32 (482 - 495

Hawton, K., & van Heeringen, K. (2009). 'Suicide'. *The Lancet*, 373(9672), 1372-1381.

Health Service Executive. (2005). 'Reach out: National strategy for action on suicide prevention 2005-2014'.

Health Service Executive. (2010). 'HSE Framework for Action on Obesity 2008 –2012'.

Hopkins, M. E., Davis, F. C., Vantieghem, M. R., Whalen, P. J., & Bucci, D. J. (2012). 'Differential effects of acute and regular physical exercise on cognition and affect'. *Neuroscience*, 215, 59–68.

Horesh N, Levi Y, and Apter A. (2012) 'Medically serious versus non-serious suicide attempts: Relationships of lethality and intent to clinical and interpersonal characteristics'. *Journal of Affective Disorders,* 136 286–293.

Houses of the Oireachtas Joint Committee on Health and Children. (2009). 'The high level of suicide in Irish society'.

Hoven, C. W., Mandell, D. J., & Bertolote, J. M. (2010). 'Prevention of mental ill-health and suicide: Public health perspectives'. *Eur Psychiatry*, 25(5), 252-256.

Huesmann, L. R., & Taylor, L. D. (2006). 'The role of media violence in violent behavior'. *Annu Rev Public Health*, 27, 393–415.

Johnson, S. B., Blum, R. W., & Giedd, J. N. (2009). 'Adolescent maturity and the brain: the promise and pitfalls of neuroscience research in adolescent health policy'. *J Adolesc Health*, 45(3), 216-221.

Kapur, N., & Gask, L. (2009). 'Introduction to suicide and self-harm'. *Psychiatry*, 8(7), 233-236.

Kuyken, W., Weare, K., Ukoumunne, O. C., Vicary, R., Motton, N., Burnett, R., . . . Huppert, F. (2013). 'Effectiveness of the Mindfulness in Schools Programme: Non-randomised controlled feasibility study'. *Br J Psychiatry*, 203(2), 126-131.

Leenaars, A. A. (2010). 'Edwin S. Shneidman on suicide'. *Suicidology Online*, 1, 5-18.

Malone, K. (2013). 'Suicide in Ireland 2003-2008'. Dublin: 3Ts.

Mann, J. J. (2003). 'Neurobiology of suicidal behaviour'. *Nat Rev Neurosci*, 4(10), 819-828.

McMahon, E. M., Reulbach, U., Corcoran, P., Keeley, H. S., Perry, I. J., & Arensman, E. (2010). 'Factors associated with deliberate self-harm among Irish adolescents'. *Psychol Med*, 40(11), 1811-1819.

Melvin, G. A., Dudley, A. L., Gordon, M. S., Ford, S., Taffe, J., & Tonge, B. J. (2013). 'What happens to depressed adolescents? A follow-up study into early adulthood'. *J Affect Disord*, 151(1), 298-305.

Millman, R. P., Working Group on Sleepiness in Adolescents/Young, A., & Adolescence, A. A. P. C. o. (2005). 'Excessive sleepiness in adolescents and young adults: causes, consequences, and treatment strategies'. *Pediatrics*, 115(6), 1774-1786.

Moeller, S., Powers, E., & Roberts, J. (1988). '"The World Unplugged"' and '"24 Hours without Media": Media Literacy to Develop Self-Awareness Regarding Media'. *Scientific Journal of Media Education*, 45.

Murphy, E. (2013). *Five Steps to Happiness: Learning to explore and understand your emotional mind*. Dublin: Liberties Press.

Ng, M., Fleming, T., Robinson, M., Thomson, B., Graetz, N., Margono, C., . . .

Gakidou, E. (2014). 'Global, regional, and national prevalence of overweight and obesity in children and adults during 1980-2013: A systematic analysis for the Global Burden of Disease Study 2013'. *The Lancet*.

Nock, M. K., & Kessler, R. C. (2006). 'Prevalence of and risk factors for suicide attempts versus suicide gestures: Analysis of the National Comorbidity Survey'. *J Abnorm Psychol*, 115(3), 616-623.

O'Neill, B., & Dinh, T. (2014). 'Net children go mobile: Initial findings from Ireland'.

Owens, M., Herbert, J., Jones, P. B., Sahakian, B. J., Wilkinson, P. O., Dunn, V. J., . . . Goodyer, I. M. (2014). 'Elevated morning cortisol is a stratified population-level biomarker for major depression in boys only with high depressive symptoms'. *Proc Natl Acad Sci USA*, 111(9), 3638-3643.

Palmer, B. A., Pankratz, V. S., & Bostwick, J. M. (2005). 'The lifetime risk of suicide in schizophrenia: A reexamination'. *Arch Gen Psychiatry*, 62(3), 247-253.

Patton, G. C., Coffey, C., Sawyer, S. M., Viner, R. M., Haller, D. M., Bose, K., . . . Mathers, C. D. (2009). 'Global patterns of mortality in young people: a systematic analysis of population health data'. *The Lancet*, 374(9693), 881-892.

Pfeifer, J. H., & Allen, N. B. (2012). 'Arrested development? Reconsidering dual-systems models of brain function in adolescence and disorders'. *Trends Cogn Sci*, 16(6), 322-329.

Roberts, D. F., Foehr, U. G., & Rideout, V. (2011). 'Generation M: Media in the Lives of 8–18 Year-Olds'. California: Henry J. Kaiser Family Foundation.

Sawyer, S. M., Afifi, R. A., Bearinger, L. H., Blakemore, S. J., Dick, B., Ezeh, A. C., & Patton, G. C. (2012). 'Adolescence: A foundation for future health'. *The Lancet*, 379(9826), 1630-1640.

Scowcroft, E. (2014). 'Suicide statistics report 2014'. Samaritans.

Shneidman, E. S. (1969). *On the nature of suicide*. San Francisco: Jossey Bass.

Shneidman, E. S. (2008). *A Commonsense Book of Death: Reflections at ninety of a lifelong thanatologist*. Washington D.C: Rowman & Littlefield.

Singh, A., Uijtdewilligen, L., Twisk, J. W., van Mechelen, W., & Chinapaw, M. J. (2012). 'Physical activity and performance at school: A systematic review of the literature including a methodological quality assessment'. *Arch Pediatr Adolesc Med*, 166(1), 49-55.

Smith, M. J., Cobia, D. J., Wang, L., Alpert, K. I., Cronenwett, W. J., Goldman,

M. B., . . . Csernansky, J. G. (2014). 'Cannabis-related working memory deficits and associated subcortical morphological differences in healthy individuals and schizophrenia subjects'. *Schizophr Bull*, 40(2), 287-299.

Spear, L. P. (2000). 'Neurobehavioral changes in adolescence'. *Current directions in psychological science*, 9(4), 111-114.

Stallard, P., Sayal, K., Phillips, R., Taylor, J. A., Spears, M., Anderson, R., . . . Montgomery, A. A. (2012). 'Classroom-based cognitive behavioural therapy in reducing symptoms of depression in high-risk adolescents: Pragmatic cluster randomised controlled trial'. *BMJ*, 345, e6058.

Strauch, B. (2007). *The Primal Teen: What the new discoveries about the teenage brain tell us about our kids*. New York: Random House LLC.

Strenziok, M., Krueger, F., Pulaski, S. J., Openshaw, A. E., Zamboni, G., van der Meer, E., & Grafman, J. (2010). 'Lower lateral orbitofrontal cortex density associated with more frequent exposure to television and movie violence in male adolescents'. *J Adolesc Health*, 46(6), 607-609.

Sturman, D. A., & Moghaddam, B. (2011). 'The neurobiology of adolescence: Changes in brain architecture, functional dynamics, and behavioral tendencies'. *Neurosci Biobehav Rev*, 35(8), 1704-1712.

Swab, D. (2014). *We are our brains: From the womb to Alzheimers*. Allen Lane, an imprint of Penguin Books.

Teicher, M. H., Anderson, C. M., Ohashi, K., & Polcari, A. (2013). 'Childhood maltreatment: Altered network centrality of cingulate, precuneus, temporal pole and insula'. *Biol Psychiatry*.

Teicher, M. H., Anderson, C. M., & Polcari, A. (2012). 'Childhood maltreatment is associated with reduced volume in the hippocampal subfields CA3, dentate gyrus, and subiculum'. *Proc Natl Acad Sci USA*, 109(9), E563-572.

Teicher, M. H., Samson, J. A., Polcari, A., & McGreenery, C. E. (2006). 'Sticks, stones, and hurtful words: Relative effects of various forms of childhood maltreatment'. *Am J Psychiatry*, 163(6), 993-1000.

Thapar, A., Collishaw, S., Pine, D. S., & Thapar, A. K. (2012). 'Depression in adolescence'. *The Lancet*, 379(9820), 1056-1067.

Turecki, G., Ernst, C., Jollant, F., Labonte, B., & Mechawar, N. (2012). 'The neurodevelopmental origins of suicidal behavior'. *Trends Neurosci*, 35(1), 14-23.

Vijayakumar L, John S, Pirkis J, and Whiteford H. (2005) 'Suicide in developing countries (2) – risk factors'. Crisis; Vol. 26(3):112–119

Voss, M. W., Nagamatsu, L. S., Liu-Ambrose, T., & Kramer, A. F. (2011). 'Exercise, brain, and cognition across the life span'. *J Appl Physiol*, 111(5), 1505-1513.

Walsh, D. (2014). *Why Do They Act That Way? Revised and Updated: A survival guide to the adolescent brain for you and your teen*. London: Simon and Schuster.

Wasserman, D., Cheng, Q., & Jiang, G. X. (2005). 'Global suicide rates among young people aged 15-19'. *World Psychiatry*, 4(2), 114-120.

Weare, K. (2012). 'Evidence for the impact of mindfulness on children and young people. The Mindfulness in Schools Project in association with Mood Disorders Centre. Available at *http://mindfulnessinschools.org/*.

World Health Organisation. (2012). 'Depression fact-sheet No. 369'.

Yau, P. L., Castro, M. G., Tagani, A., Tsui, W. H., & Convit, A. (2012). 'Obesity and metabolic syndrome and functional and structural brain impairments in adolescence'. *Pediatrics*, 130(4), 856-864.

Yurgelun-Todd, D. A., Killgore, W. D., & Young, A. D. (2002). 'Sex differences in cerebral tissue volume and cognitive performance during adolescence'. *Psychol Rep*, 91(3), 743-757.

Help Groups and Contact Details

AWARE

Aware is a voluntary organisation established in 1985 to support those experiencing depression and their families. Aware endeavours to create a society where people with mood disorders and their families are understood and supported, and to obtain the resources to enable them to defeat depression. Weekly support group meetings at approximately fifty locations nationwide, including Northern Ireland, offer peer support and provide factual information, and enable people to gain the skills they need to help them cope with depression. Aware's 'Beat the Blues' educational programme is run in secondary schools.

Helpline: 1890 303 302
info@aware.ie | www.aware.ie | (01) 661 7211
72 Lower Leeson Street, Dublin 2

SAMARITANS

Samaritans was started in 1953 in London by a young vicar called Chad Varah; the first branch in the Republic of Ireland opened in Dublin in 1970. Samaritans provides a twenty-four-hour-a-day confidential service offering emotional support for people who are experiencing feelings of distress or despair, including those which may lead to suicide.

Helpline: 1850 60 90 90
jo@samaritans.org | www.samaritans.org
Texts: 0872 60 90 90

GROW

Established in Ireland in 1969, GROW is Ireland's largest mutual-help organisation in the area of mental health. It is anonymous, nondenominational,
confidential and free. No referrals are necessary. Grow aims to achieve self-
activation through mutual help. Its members are enabled, over time, to craft a
step-by-step recovery or personal-growth plan, and to develop leadership
skills that will help others.

Helpline: 1890 474 474
grownational@grow.ie | www.grow.ie | 056 61624
Barrack Street, Kilkenny

IRISH SUICIDOLOGY ASSOCIATION

The Irish Association of Suicidology aims to facilitate communication
between clinicians, volunteers, survivors and researchers in all matters relating to suicide and suicidal behaviour; to promote awareness of the problems
of suicide and suicidal behaviour in the general public by holding confer-
ences and workshops and through the communication of relevant materials
through the media; to ensure that the public is better informed about suicide
prevention; to support and encourage relevant research; and to encourage
and support the formation of groups to help those bereaved by suicide.

094 925 0858 | office@ias.ie | www.ias.ie
16 New Antrim Street, Castlebar, County Mayo

CONSOLE

Console is a registered charity supporting and helping people bereaved through suicide. They respect each individual's unique journey through the grieving process following their tragic loss. Console promotes positive mental health within the community in an effort to reduce the high number of attempted suicides and deaths through suicide.

Helpline: 1800 201 890
info@console.ie | www.console.ie | 01 857 4300
Console Dublin: All Hallows College,
Gracepark Rd, Drumcondra, Dublin 9

RAINBOWS IRELAND

Rainbows was founded in America by Suzy Yehl Marta to help children and adults who have been bereaved through parental death, separation or divorce to work through the grieving process which follows any significant loss. The charity provides a safe setting in which children can talk through their feelings with other children who are experiencing similar situations.

01 473 4175
Loreto Centre, Crumlin Road, Dublin 12

CHILDLINE

ChildLine, a service run by the ISPCC, seeks to empower and support children using the medium of telecommunications and information technology. The service is designed for all children and young people up to the age of eighteen in Ireland.

Helpline: 1890 66 66 66

CUAN MHUIRE

Cuan Mhuire is a charitable organisation founded by Sister Consilio Fitzgerald in 1965. It provides a comprehensive structured, abstinence-based residential programme dealing with alcohol, gambling and drug addiction in the north and south of Ireland, with centres in Athy, Athenry, Newry, Limerick and Cork.

063 00555 | cuanmhuire@gmail.com

GAMBLERS ANONYMOUS IRELAND AND GAM-ANON

Holds self-help meetings for gamblers and those close to them.

Dublin 01 872 1133
Cork 087 349 4450
Galway 087 349 4450
info@gamblersanonymous.ie

AL-ANON / ALATEEN

Self-help meetings for spouses and teenagers (aged twelve to seventeen) affected by those addicted to alcohol.

01 873 2699 | info@al-anon-ireland.org
5 Capel Street, Dublin 1
028 9068 2368
Peace House, 224 Lisburn Road, Belfast

NARCOTICS ANONYMOUS

Self-help groups for those addicted to drugs.

01 672 8000 | na@ireland.org
4–5 Eustace Street, Dublin 2

THE IRISH COUNCIL FOR PSYCHOTHERAPY

Produces a directory of psychotherapists working in Ireland.

01 272 2105 | info@icpty.ie
73 Quinns Road, Shankhill, County Dublin

SCHIZOPHRENIA IRELAND

Schizophrenia Ireland is the national organisation dedicated to upholding the rights and addressing the needs of all those affected by enduring mental illness, including schizophrenia, schizo-affective disorder and bipolar disorder, through the promotion and provision of high-quality services, and by working to ensure the continual enhancement of the quality of life of the people it serves.

01 860 1620 | info@sirl.ie
38 Blessington Street, Dublin 7

THE IRISH ASSOCIATION OF COGNITIVE BEHAVIOURAL THERAPY

This organisation was founded in 2003 by Enda Murphy and Brian Kelly. Its primary aim is the provision of low-intensity CBT/CBM training and support to health professionals and organisations for use in their clinical practice.

cbtireland@eircom.net

NO PANIC

No Panic is a charity which aims to faclitate the relief and rehabilitation of people suffering from panic attacks, phobias, obsessive compulsive disorders and other related anxiety disorders, including tranquillizer withdrawal, and to provide support to sufferers and their families and carers. Founded by Colin M. Hammond in the UK, this group has extended its activities to Ireland, where it is organised by therapist Caroline McGuigan.

Helpline Ireland: 01 272 1897
UK head office: TEL: +44 (0) 1952 590005
FAX: +44 (0) 1952 270962
Helpline (UK Free-Phone): 0808 808 0545
Non-UK: 0044 1 952 590545
Ireland office: 01 272 1872

HEADSTRONG

Headstrong is a new initiative spearheaded by psychologist Dr Tony Bates, working with communities in Ireland to ensure that young people aged twelve to twenty-five are better supported to achieve mental health and well-being. Headstrong was set up in response to an identified need to address the issue of youth mental health in Ireland. It is an independent, non-profit NGO. It acts as an expert partner to the Health Services Executive and other people and services concerned with providing mental health and well-being support to young people in Ireland. Headstrong views mental health as existing along a continuum spanning general well-being to distress to mental health disorders that require specialised care. Headstrong's Jigsaw Programme aims to change the way communities in Ireland think about mental health and support young people in the process.

www.headstrong.ie | info@headstrong.ie | 01 6607343

Flagging the Problem
Dr Harry Barry

Flagging the Problem presents a new way of identifying and dealing with mental health problems using colour coded flags by a medical doctor with extensive experience in the treatment of mental health issues.

Flagging The Problem: A New Approach to Mental Health is made up of five main sections. Each is marked with a coloured flag, represents a particular mental state or area of concern: Green Flag explains the normal mood system, the Red Flag deals with depression, the Yellow Flag addresses anxiety, the Purple Flag deals with addiction and the White Flag addresses the issue of suicide. There is a technical section, and extra appendices at the end of the book, including information on self-help groups and a list of commonly used medicines.

Flagging the Therapy
Dr Harry Barry

Flagging the Therapy: Pathways Out of Depression and Anxiety follows on from Dr Barry's best-selling book, *Flagging the Problem*.

Applying a system which uses colour-coded flags for various mental states and problems, Dr Barry explains the role our minds and brains play in the manifestation of depression and anxiety, and how these in turn can be shaped to lead us out of illness. The book takes a holistic view and examines the numerous medical, psychological and complimentary therapies that can all help in negotiating a pathway out of depression and anxiety.

His use of fictionalised case studies makes the book both accessible and easily manageable for all readers.

Flagging Stress
Dr Harry Barry

Flagging Stress is the third instalment in Dr Harry Barry's hugelysuccessful 'Flagging' series. It aims to provide readers with the necessary skills to indentify and manage stress in their lives. When stress builds up, it can overwhelm an individual and lead to potentially serious health problems like heart disease or obesity on the one hand and depression or suicide on the other.

Flagging Stress is an indispensable tool on coping with the stresses of modern life. By identifying the different kinds of stress - and in particular the dangers of 'toxic' stress, Dr Barry shows us how to identify where our stress is coming from and how we can effectively confront, manage and reduce it in our lives.

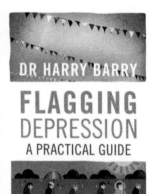

Flagging Depression
Dr Harry Barry

The fourth instalment of Dr Harry Barry's best-selling 'Flagging' series, *Flagging Depression* not only reaches out to those dealing with depression, but also their friends and family, offering vital assistance. With the current economic climate causing increased stress and depression in our day-to-day lives, mental health issues and higher suicide rates are a worrying trend. *Flagging Depression* lays out a practical four step approach with particular emphasis on how to feel better, get better and stay well.

Despite being so prevalent , there is still lingering reluctance to talk about depression and its effects. Dr Barry is determined to break the silence and provide practical advice to those suffering from depression as well as their families and friends.

Five Steps to Happiness
Enda Murphy

With over thirty years' experience in the field of mental health, Enda Murphy draws on case histories to inform readers about the five modes of behaviour that can cause mental health problems. Through a writing style that is free from psychobabble and jargon, readers are offered qualified advice on how to cope with and overcome panic attacks, anxiety and depression by changing just five ways of behaving. The book also sets out how to deal with our emotions, and how we can avoid the errors in our thinking that cause mental health problems. Readers are invited to change their ways of thinking to live happier and more emotionally healthy lives.

Although this book specifically targets those who suffer from mental health problems, it is also essential reading for anybody interested in why such conditions occur: family members and loved ones of those who suffer,as well as therapists and health professionals.